COMPETE

TER

PASSENGER SHIP   No. 111626

Douglas Pike

duly qualified to fulfil the duties of
Merchant Service, the Minister of Transport
the Merchant Shipping Acts and of all other
you this Certificate of Competency.

OF TRANSPORT and CIVIL AVIATION and

.... 19 58 .

A Deputy Secretary of the
Ministry of Transport and
Civil Aviation.

AR GENERAL OF SHIPPING AND SEAMEN.

Challenges

Dag Pike

Challenges

Bosun Publications

Published by Bosun Publications

First published in Great Britain in 2006

Tel: 01932 242436
Email: info@bosun-publications.demon.co.uk
www.bosun-publications.co.uk

ISBN: 0-9546932-7-2

A CIP catalogue record for this book is available
from the British Library.

Typeset in 12pt Minion
Printed in England by
The Cromwell Press Ltd

Book design and production by
FW Barter ARCA
Bosun Publications

CONTENTS

Dedication

This book is dedicated to Cath, my wife, my four children Ben, Cath, Jo and Jess and the collection of grandchildren, Emma, Joseph, Alice, Harry, Ruby, Sonny and ? (on the way but not delivered). Thanks for everything and for not laughing too much at my attempts to get things down on paper.

Thanks

Obviously my thanks to my family and also my publisher Fred and editor Peter who had faith in my ability and who contributed so much to getting this book into a shape fit for publishing.
Thanks to my parents for seeing me through the war and packing me off to sea afterwards.
Thanks to the RNLI for giving me the opportunity to go out in weather conditions when the prudent seaman stays in harbour.
Thanks to all those who had faith in my navigation capabilities and gave me the chance to race in offshore powerboats at the top level. In particular I should mention Carlo Bonomi and Fabio Buzzi. Fabio still remains a close friend despite thinking that he knows more about navigation than I do
Thanks to Richard Branson and Ted Toleman for getting the Virgin project off the ground and asking me to participate.
This book has been written relying heavily on my memory whilst I can still get access to it. There are bound to be people who come out of the woodwork to contradict what I remember, which is fine and my only excuse for any mistakes is accelerating old age brought on by pounding through a million or more waves in my lifetime.

FOREWORD

I t can't be by coincidence that Dag and I were born on the same day of the same month, though ten years apart. As an engineer of course, I don't subscribe to the signs of the zodiac or horoscopes at all. But I must confess in quieter moments I muse over our many similarities, sure that Dag must do the same!

Completely alike, we are both Aquarians and proud of it. We share the same genius and eccentric streak, acknowledging the same obstinacy and compulsion to keep working. And like me, because Aquarius is a water sign, I know Dag has been in his element most of the time, especially out on the water.

Dag grew up on the water, seasick from it often, but always delighted by it - winning many times with me and other friends, sinking occasionally (though never with me!), resurfacing with new strength and trying again - so doggedly determined, the Atlantic record had to be his!

All this is perfectly normal for Dag. He's done it his whole life!

What's not normal is that when most of us might ease off at the age of 73, he's ready to do it all over again. Given the chance, he'd jump immediately into any flotation toy I suggest to him, like the very fast hydroplane on his birthday. That's not just normal, that's WONDERFUL!

So Dag, many thanks for navigating for your Italian friend, for always pointing me in the right direction, such a difficult reflex for all Italians. Thanks too for your passion, your professionalism and your dedication.

Yes please... do it all again!

Fabio Buzzi, 24th June 2006

PROLOGUE

WELCOME TO CALM & STORM

The horizon seemed to be playing tricks. The heaving of the ship defied gravity. Every roll threatened to be the last, as the walls became decks. She was like a ship in her death throes, her equilibrium destroyed, unable to survive with that shifting cargo of grain. For all of us in her crew, it was like dying in slow motion. How much more, we wondered, could this fine ship take?

You desperately wanted to do something. But there were few options. So you clung to the rail on the high side of the ship, hoping the tiny effect of your extra weight would help the stability. You pulled on your lifejacket, so you might float a bit longer if the ship did go, although doing so would only prolong your agony in these icy waters. You held your breath with every roll, each one further and more extreme than the one before. It was the natural thing to do - you never knew, somehow it might help. And you were scared. So very scared that death might come to you at such a young age.

For twenty-four hours we lived on that knife-edge. Eventually the wind eased and the rolling became less. Almost, so very nearly almost, we became another statistic on the North Atlantic Ocean's long list of casualties.

But we lived to sail another day.

Accidents happen in all walks of life. A plane crash is almost certainly terminal. The world spins out of control in a car crash, and nothing you can do has any influence on the outcome. At sea, such things tend to happen in slow motion. You hopefully have some chance to negotiate, to change the odds before it's too late. The sea is not an adversary. Nothing you do will change the sea or its behaviour. Neither cursing nor swearing, both traditional outlets for seaman, are any help at all. At sea you need to use your wits, your experience, and maybe a bit of technology. Hopefully with these, you will find a way through. At least, that's how it works for me. And I have long familiarity of coping with the worst - and the best - that the sea can offer.

Most of my life has been spent on the sea, or working with it. I have experienced most of its moods. It can provide unbelievable excitement, even pure bliss. Nearly every way you turn, it captures your emotion. The sea's majesty is awe-inspiring. Its moods are sullen, dark and mysterious. I love the sea. It has created many of the best and most exciting moments in my life. It has also taken me near to death. Though always, it is the technology of ships and boats, not the sea itself - that has let me down.

This therefore is a book about a love affair. My personal love affair with the sea. About going down to the sea in ships. About business in fast waters. About surviving in rough waters. About this wonderful mistress who completely rules my life.

CHAPTER 1

THE PASSION AWAKES

Just eight years old
And already I wanted
to go to sea.

I was just eight years old when I started my love affair. It was in war-torn England and living just south of London, we were in the thick of the bombing. It was a violent change from a childhood of summers full of sunshine and winters cleansed with snow. Certainly from where I am now, it makes me think. Instead of TV, we would go outside and watch the real-life Battle of Britain in the skies right over our heads. Real planes would crash in real flames, and if one was a German, we all cheered. There were bullets too, flying about everywhere. But as kids there was no sense of danger, it was all too wonderfully exciting.

The scenario changed at night. Then we were under the bombs raining down from the fleets of German bombers overhead. Once the air-raid sirens went, you waited for the drone of engines, then for the loud explosions. The worst was when they crept closer and closer, coming for you. Luckily, apart from an incendiary bomb in our garden, we escaped anything direct. My father had built an air-raid shelter in the garden for us to take cover when a raid was on. The trouble was, he never finished the roof, so the best shelter we had was the cupboard under the stairs. Afterwards, if you weren't bombed or injured, you carried on as normal - except of course, for the rationing. I don't remember going hungry, but we all missed our sweets. Whenever each month's new allocation came up, we would blow it all in a couple of hours, gorging our whole sweet ration in one go.

Modern war is very remote to how it was then. It happens somewhere far away and all we know of it is what's on TV. Living in the Home Counties during World War Two put us right in the front line.

Though most of the action was with troops fighting in France and the terrible shipping losses, we were also right in the thick of it back home. As kids we listened to the propaganda, not really taking it in. All I remembered was the excitement and the buzz. On the way to school we always looked, searching heads down for souvenirs from the action of the night before - tail-fins from incendiary bombs, shrapnel - whatever we could find. More sobering were the empty seats in class - friends who had been killed or injured the night before. It must have been horrific for our parents. To this day, I don't know how they coped.

It took two years of bombing before it was decided to evacuate children to safer places out of London. The day came when we found ourselves saying a tearful farewell to our parents at Paddington Station and taking the train west. Carrying our cheap suitcases, with cardboard boxes holding our gas masks around our necks, we were a pathetic sight. It must have been heart-rending for our parents, not really knowing if they would ever see us again.

For us of course, it was the start of a big adventure. By evening we were in the playground of the local school in Ruan Minor, a tiny village in remote Cornwall. As I remember it, we all had to line up, then prospective "hosts" would pick out the kids they liked the look of. Two of my brothers went to a farm. We other two were boarded with this retired couple who must have wondered what hit them. The excitement and adventure of being evacuated was not without sadness. I was dreadfully homesick for the first week and cried myself to sleep every night. The elderly couple we were staying with must have been equally devastated. Their home was invaded by two unruly kids who looked as though they would never adjust. I am not sure if we ever really did.

We were based in the fishing village of Cadgwith, which I now know as one of the prettiest villages on the South Coast of Cornwall. When I hear tales from other people who were evacuated during the war, I can't believe how lucky we were to end up in such a wonderful place. It was just heaven, boats in the harbour, beaches to play on, the sea to swim in, fields to roam, and pretty much total freedom except for going to school. The problem was, it gave unlimited scope for mischief in this

The Cornish magic of Cadgwith
No wonder I loved the place. Unchanged for hundreds of years, Cadgwith is
at the end of England, on the eastern side of the Lizard Peninsula in Cornwall.
Fishing boats still go out every day, not for pilchards any more but for crab
(several tons a week), lobster, mackerel, shark and mullet. The lifeboat house
I used to prowl is still there too, though it closed down in 1963. The weather is
superb - winters are mild, frost is rare and snow is almost unknown. Spring is
always early. Daffodils bloom so easily they are grown commercially. It really is
a picture postcard village.

new, exciting and largely unregulated world. Which got me into serious
trouble when I set light to a haystack. A million miles from London with
so many opportunities, I guess we missed the battleground and the
nightly houses on fire, which possibly explains why I started my own.
Certainly I had no argument with this life by the seaside. And it was
where I fell in love, starting the affair of a lifetime.

The sea and the boats in the harbour totally fascinated me. London
went to the back of my mind. Cadgwith had a very active fleet of small
fishing boats that went out on day trips, launching and recovering from
the sheltered beach. The lifeboat was even more active, retrieving dead
bodies from crashed aircraft or ships that had sunk. That was the only
war we saw in deepest Cornwall. Whenever the lifeboat maroons went
off, we rushed to the harbour along with most of the village to watch the
launch. There were long hours of waiting before the return. Sometimes

The family on ice
London was less fun than Cornwall, though it brought the family back together again.

we were allowed to help with the fishing boats, but never anything to do with the lifeboat. That was for trained men who were very professional about their job.

The harbour was alive and I spent every possible moment down there. I would stare for hours at the horizon, wondering what lay beyond. It was my introduction to the sea and I fell in love with it. And everything about it too. I can't say that was when I decided to work with the sea for the rest of my life. You didn't make that kind of decision at eight years old. I do know that my fascination was total. Summer's calm or winter's storm, this was my new world.

The war was a crazy time. Especially as we were in Cornwall when things had gone quiet in London. The Battle of Britain was over and the rain of "Doodlebugs" and V2 rockets had yet to start. So my parents brought us back, which I can fully understand because it must have been hell for them. I was sorry to leave the sea - and London was not the same. Here we were, back in the suburbs, cycling the four-mile ride to school every day. It was on one of these rides that I saw my first Doodlebug come down.

They were scary, coming over at night when you were in bed, a lazy, distinctive drone. When the engine stopped, you knew it was coming down and going to explode. The engine told you it had to be somewhere close, but you never knew where. It all depended on when it ran out of fuel and which way the wind was blowing. With practice you got quite expert at judging how far away it was when the engine stopped. And if it would hit the ground nearby.

The first one I saw landed about half a mile away as I cycled home from school. On another day there was a plane crash even closer. Being inquisitive, I went across to have a look. There was only a hole where the German fighter had nose-dived straight in. Bizarre though they were, events like these were every day occurrences. It was war and the world you knew was far behind. Bizarre was routine.

Then one night, lying in bed, the engine of this Doodlebug stopped. It seemed to be just overhead, so I knew it would be close. The next moment there was this "whooshing" noise, then an almighty explosion. All the ceilings came down and heavy stuff landed on my bed. When the dust settled, our parents rushed in to see if we were OK. The house was still standing but a bit the worse for wear. That Doodlebug had landed barely 50 yards away, a little too close for comfort. It was the first of quite a few narrow escapes in my life. War was reality and we had just missed becoming another casualty statistic.

How much of my later attitude towards risk was triggered by those wartime experiences, I wonder? These days, "risk" is an unacceptable word. You are not even allowed to blow your nose without thinking of the consequences.

At last the war was over and life became more stable. It was also more boring. Now I had to concentrate on my studies. There were no excuses like air raid sirens to offer a break. I had never been good at routine and the war certainly gave us every excuse to break it. But the end of hostilities brought the biggest break of all. Up came the chance to go boating, and my fascination for the sea returned.

I did this by joining the Sea Scouts, like the Boy Scouts, except we played in boats. There were lots of boats around too, wartime craft that had been decommissioned. Our Scout group was based on the River Thames, in an old motor torpedo boat with the engines removed. It was a mess inside, but slowly we knocked it into shape, spending weekends on board. This was real messing about in boats, and at our River Thames base, we also had access to a couple of sailing dinghies. By the time I was twelve, I had learnt to sail the hard way, by my mistakes. I made lots of these because there was no one around with any experience of sailing.

At grammar school, academic subjects were not my favourite. I had a passion for woodwork, and once I had learnt the rudiments of using the tools, I was allowed to build a kayak. This was pretty amateurish stuff, but I managed to build the wooden framework all right. My problems came when I wanted to cover it. So soon after the war, everything was still in short supply, so it was near impossible to get the right materials for the job. I had to make do with heavy war surplus stuff that was very difficult to seal. I made a little trailer from pram wheels, so that I could tow my creation behind my bike down to the river. I was proud of it, so the blow to my pride when water poured in through the seams was hard to bear. I had to take it all the way home again for another go at sealing the seams. Much effort and heartache later it eventually worked. And I had learned the quick lesson that water has to stay outside the boat if you want to survive. In some of my later exploits, I was not always so good at keeping it out.

After experience with the kayak, and the sailing dinghies, and occasionally rowing on the river, there came a chance for my first trip to sea. This was in another wartime surplus boat, one which had an engine that actually worked. Ex-Navy, it was a 20-foot open boat that thankfully propelled itself without physical exertion. I don't know where the fuel for our planned trip came from. Fuel was in very short supply and rationed like everything else in those days, even long after the war had ended. Anyway, our Scout Master was in charge and seemed to have a knack for scrounging things like boats and fuel, so we set off on a day trip all the way down the Thames to Ramsgate. Apart from Cadgwith, this was my first experience in tidal waters, the magic of being out on the open sea. I still remember the excitement of seeing the big ships on the river and all the other traffic. My new world was opening, and I wanted to be part of it.

All went well until after we rounded the North Foreland and were close to Ramsgate. The euphoria came to an abrupt halt as we ran hard aground. No amount of pushing and pulling with the engine would shift the boat. Stuck fast, we were in no danger of sinking, and as far as we could tell there was no damage. It was fortunate too, that our plight was seen from the shore. In those days we had no radio or safety gear.

After several hours, the lifeboat from Ramsgate came out, pulled us off the sand and towed us into harbour. It transpired that the charts we had on board were pre-war because we could not get anything more up-to-date. That sandbank had developed during the war years, so it was not entirely our fault. The lifeboat towed us in with no damage done except to our pride, and we made it safely back up the Thames without further drama.

I guess with hindsight that grounding on my first trip to sea was an omen, a foretaste of what was to come over the next 50 years. Being rescued on my first trip to sea was not a deterrent either. It was an adventure. After the excitement of the war years, I probably needed some sort spice in my life.

In those days too, there was none of that dreaded safety-first attitude that gets in the way of sailing today. You lived by your wits and sorted out your problems as they came along. In our sophisticated Twenty-First Century, there are so many "do this's" and "don't do that's" that half the pleasure of going to sea has been lost. Whatever happened to common sense, or should I say, seaman-like sense? How can you really learn seamanship if you don't make mistakes on the way? That was how I grew up in boats: so you developed a natural instinct about what would work and what wouldn't.

That trip to Ramsgate was just the prelude to greater things. Next summer at the age of fourteen, I was off to do more serious things at sea. That was the year that the Olympic Games came to Britain, and the sailing events took place in Torquay. As a Sea Scout, I was lucky enough to be asked to help with the proceedings, mainly by

Tor Bay, Devon, 10 August 1948 during the 1948 Olympics. Round the buoys in the Six Metre sailing event. My job was to row the contestants out to their yachts.

rowing the crews out to their yachts. They were all Six Metre and Dragon's Classes in those days, with everything very casual, in a very British way. Nor were the Olympics all posh and professional as they are now. It was my big chance to meet many of my sailing heroes, actually on the water in the same boat as me. Up close, I could see what top-flight competition was all about. It was an exciting week, another part of my learning curve. Increasingly, the sea was becoming a part of my life.

After the Games there was an offer from the Rear Commodore of the Royal Naval Sailing Association to take one of us on a trip up-Channel in his yacht. This was a thank-you gesture for the work we had done. Everybody wanted to go, but I was the lucky one with the draw for the place. That was another trend, for I have always been lucky in raffles and draws. So here was my chance for my first sail in a proper ocean racing yacht. And as it turned out, my first gale at sea. It was to be a simple sail across Lyme Bay, then on to Poole. But we had to negotiate the dreaded Portland Race on the way, and as the wind freshened to a gale, what should have been a nice day's sail turned into a nightmare of howling winds and huge breaking waves. This in turn meant that we had to go outside the Portland Race, and it was the middle of the night before we finally found shelter inside Portland Harbour. Already, at the age of fourteen, I was building up a fund of experience in rough seas and exciting sailing.

Going aground and meeting a gale might have been good reasons for ending my sea-going career. But when the owner of the yacht EVARNE suggested that I might like to sail in the North Sea Race, I jumped at the chance. Captain Baraclough, the owner, was a very experienced sailor and EVARNE was a Bermudan cutter some 40-feet long. I think that my parents must have been a bit worried about all this adventurous boating. But they were very good and did nothing but encourage me, probably glad to get rid of me for a few days. I was excited by the prospect of another trip to sea. That too was a trend. All my life I could

Sailing on EVARNE
My first ocean sailing race at the age of fifteen. Note the trendy sailing gear.

never said "no" to anything that might be exciting or dangerous. So I completed my first ocean sailing race at the age of fifteen, something that I reminded Ted Heath about when he had a party to celebrate his 30 years of ocean racing. Just for perspective, I told him it was 55 years earlier that I had started my first ocean sailing race. I don't remember his comment!

I realised by now that I was firmly into boats and my love of the sea was not going to go away. These were serious times at school, with exams looming that would decide my future. Back then, you also had to squeeze two years of conscription into the armed forces at some point in your education. I had scraped through Matriculation by the skin of my teeth and was going on to take my Higher Schools Certificate, the entry exam to university. Somehow I had to fit in two years of National Service, usually done between school and university, and not something with any appeal at all. I can't say that school had much appeal either. Whilst I could shine in the maths and physics that I enjoyed, the rest of the subjects did not interest me much. And without interest, it was not easy to learn.

I think it was the careers teacher at school who first pointed me down the route I was to take. 'Why not make a career out of going to sea in the Merchant Navy, instead of wasting two years on National Service?'

The more I thought about it, the more it made sense. My parents seemed to agree, probably because they wanted to see the back of me. I think I was a pretty rebellious teenager, not going off the rails, but definitely wanting to do what I wanted to do instead of what other people wanted me to do. That I was good at maths and physics pointed me in the direction of the sea because they were the skills you needed for navigation. So Mother ended up pulling strings, and I was signed up for four years as an apprentice with a shipping company.

During the war, Mother had worked in the Ministry of Labour, allocating staff to shipping offices. You can imagine the influence she had amongst the top brass of the shipping world. A couple of meetings with company officials, a visit to the Shipping Federation office in London, and I signed away four years of my life as an apprentice on a tramp ship that would be roaming the world. My sea-going education now started in earnest, though it was difficult to know just what I was getting into.

The step from going to school, to going to sea on a ship, was just too big to imagine. But it looked exciting and there was no turning back now.

CHAPTER 2

FIRE, COLLISION, STORM AND GROUNDING

At 16 and ready for sea
I was so proud in my apprentice's uniform, but there were very few chances to wear it.

It was an exciting time, making all the preparations for going off to sea. I felt very grown-up at school, leaving to go off on a life of adventure, and leaving behind those others with years of study and the possibility of conscription. There were all the fittings for uniforms and buying tin trunks to pack my clothes in. I could not wait for Christmas to be over and to go off on New Year's Day to join "my" ship in London Docks. Whilst I loved the idea of all my brand spanking new uniforms, I felt really annoyed about the list of uniform requirements that the owners sent to my parents. In reality the ship I was going to join was a dirty old tramp. Yet with delusions of grandeur, James Nourse Limited insisted on smart tropical whites and all the trimmings. My parents were never well off and it must have been a considerable struggle for them to buy this tin trunk full of gear, much of which I would never wear, or only rarely, on board the ship. It was only a few years ago that I finally got rid of the last of the white trousers and tunics, still virtually brand new. James Nourse Ltd was one of the oldest British shipping lines and whilst they might have been something special in their heyday, by the time I joined they were reduced to a fleet of seven ships, a shadow of their former glory.

Joining the MARJATA on New Year's Day 1950, at the Royal Albert Dock in London, was quite an experience. Talk about walking into a new world! This was the heyday of the London Docks, crowded with ships at virtually every berth. From London, cargoes went to all corners of the globe, from barges that came down the river, from the warehouses on the quays - loaded by cranes, by trucks and by dockers everywhere. I was experiencing London's Docks at their peak, when the unions ruled and there were five men to do every job. There were moments in life when you discovered things you never knew before. Well, this was a new world, a new experience, a new everything.

There I was in my smart new uniform, thinking I was important and trying to carry my tin trunk. In reality, I was out of place amongst all this work and chaos, straight out of school and very wet behind the ears. Being thrust into this grown-up world was a culture shock that I had not experienced before, not even during the war. Nor have I experienced

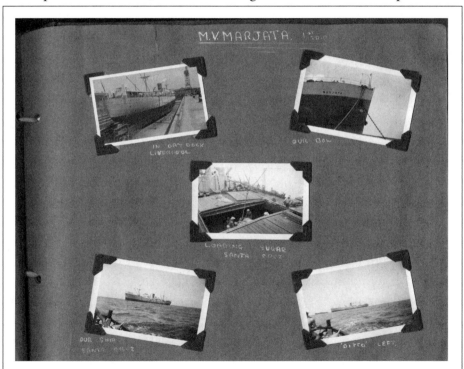

The good ship MARJATA
Like any crewman I was proud of my ship, as these pictures from my album show. Clockwise from top left: in dry dock at Liverpool; our proud bow; at anchor in Santa Cruz; aboard the shore tender coming home to the ship; centre - the hard work of loading sugar.

it since. From big shot at school, I was back to the beginning, on the very bottom rung of the ladder.

It did not take long to realise that as an apprentice you were the lowest of the low. And as a newly-joined one you were even lower. The 6,000-ton MARJATA had British officers and an Indian crew - and in those days, Indian seaman were not very high on the social ladder either. Well, we young apprentices slotted in several miles below them. That smart uniform was soon stowed away, hardly to be seen again during the voyage. Then it was on with the working clothes and down into the holds, in a token attempt to ensure that the London dockers did not broach any of the cargo. Talk about sending a boy to do a man's job. I just did not have the courage to see anything out of place, down in those darkened holds. Anyway, you didn't argue with a London docker wielding a steel cargo hook.

Those two days before we sailed passed in a daze as I tried to acclimatise myself to this new world; sharing a tiny cabin with three other apprentices, sleeping in a bunk, feeling the noise and bustle of shipboard life, and trying to understand a routine that was a million miles from school life. If I had to go through the same experience again today, I am sure I would run away. But you couldn't run with a tin trunk in tow, so I stayed. I was thrust into an adult world, totally alien, because nothing I had done or experienced at school had prepared me for it. In those two days in port, I grew up. But it was a near thing. And I could so easily have decided that going to sea was not for me. My main thought, I suppose, was that it could only get better as I learnt the ropes. But I was far from convinced. Even now, I can feel the pain and trauma of those first days. It could have been homesickness of course. It was all so different from what I had expected.

I have to say that things did turn for the better once we put to sea - the old sailor's yearning as I know it now, of longing to get away from the evils of port, out to the fresh, clean sea. Aboard MARJATA though, that took a while. Leaving the Royal Albert Dock meant passing through locks, then tugs to take us out into the river, where everything was muddy and dirty. But at least the ship belonged to the crew once more, and our first job was cleaning her down, to get rid of the harbour grime.

Here I was, going down the river that we had negotiated only three years before in that small open boat. How proud I felt, going to sea, out through the Port of London, a-jostle with shipping of all sorts. I still get a thrill travelling the Thames, this river that has so much history, and has been so much part of my life. What a difference 30 years later, coming back triumphant in our record-breaking VIRGIN ATLANTIC CHALLENGER II, so utterly unlike this first trip, creeping down river in a tramp ship. The pilot station for London was off Dungeness, out in the English Channel. It was a long journey through the buoys, inching down the twisting channels to where we finally dropped the pilot. Now we were in open waters, properly at sea. But there was nothing to confirm it. A thick fog had come down and covered everything.

Fog was hated in those days, because we navigated literally with a compass and a watch. There was no radar or electronics, except for a radio direction finder, and there was no chance of using a sextant or getting your bearings in those conditions. Outward bound was not so bad because you were heading out into wider waters. But the Channel was just as busy then as it is now, and there was no "one-way" system to separate ships travelling in opposite directions. There was only the mournful sound of the ship's siren every minute to warn other shipping.

I suppose it was no surprise that we collided with another ship, I just had no experience to warn me it was not normal. The bang when it came, was heavy enough to make the ship lurch. We all rushed outside to see what had happened. There, passing down the ship's side just a few feet away, was this other ship with a rather bent bow. We got away with a few mangled railings and some bent plates, no serious damage. I was only sixteen. Already I had experienced a gale, a grounding and a collision. There were worse disasters to come.

As the voyage went on, I realised that life at sea was going to be an adventure - and in the years to follow, the good ship MARJATA showed me virtually everything that life at sea could throw at her. She had a charmed life, and not even fire, collision, groundings or storms could destroy her. I had no experience to put this first collision into proper perspective. As the fog cleared and the wind freshened into a westerly gale, my more immediate concern was being seasick. The MARJATA rolled her way across the Bay of Biscay, making me miserable for three days and nights. Once more I contemplated abandoning life at sea, but as always when the sick feeling goes, I soon forgot it and life went on. It was exciting going through the Straits of Gibraltar, seeing the Rock in reality instead of in a geography book. Then it was on to Genoa in Italy, which by chance the Queen, as Princess Elizabeth, was visiting. Years later when I met Prince Phillip, I reminded him of this occasion - and how our experiences of Genoa were in very contrasting circumstances.

The excitement continued with a sand storm during our transit of the Suez Canal, and onward to the newly partitioned and independent India, though at that stage British influence was still very strong. Coming from a relatively sheltered life of England and school, nothing quite prepared you for India, not even with an Indian crew on board to encourage your taste for the "strange" food. Our first port in India was Bombay, then Madras and Cochin before reaching Calcutta. Calcutta was our main destination in India, virtually a "home" port where the crew were changed and the ship went into dry dock for a quick refit. Once painted and back in business, the MARJATA moored out in the river, made fast to heavy buoys by big chains, a precaution against the very strong current. During spring tides, the Hoogly River had a very

Up the creek with a vengeance
In Calcutta (now Kolkata), we were a hundred miles from the sea, up the tricky Hoogly River.

Heavy buoys secure our river moorings
The Hugli (Hoogly) river is a tributary of the Ganges that flows through the middle of Calcutta. It has a seven foot bore that moves at up river to seven miles an hour, frequently over-turning small boats and drowning their crews.

violent bore, requiring us on full engine stand-by as its breaking wave rushed up the river. All the smaller boats headed out into mid-stream to ride the wave, blowing their whistles as it came and generating tremendous excitement. When the wave struck, the ship surged forward, stretching the mooring chains bar-tight with their three-ton buoys spinning. Inevitably when this happened small boats would capsize and sometimes people drowned. On one occasion a body even turned up amongst the barges moored alongside the ship. Life tended to be cheap in those days in India, so it was not easy to get the authorities to sort out the situation.

Not far along the coast in Burma it was much the same, another interesting place to visit, with both Rangoon and Bassein on our list of ports. Like Calcutta these places were both up a winding river, around 100 miles from the sea. On the Bassein River there were acres and acres of floating hyacinths, so thick it seemed we were moving over land.

There must have been a civil war going on because the ship was raked with bursts of machine-gun fire and it paid to stay inside. The local riverboats all had sandbags around the bridge! Tied up at Bassein, we were warned that thieving was rampant. I was given the job of patrolling the ship at night, armed with a heavy metal torch. What a job for a seventeen-year old - but I was growing up quickly by then. One night I saw movement under one of the lifeboat covers. I dragged out this local lad with all our lifeboat stores in his hands. When he tried to run, I hit him over the head with the torch, then we locked him up in a toilet. Next day I had to appear in court, where I gave my statement to a magistrate who typed it out on an ancient typewriter. The accused watched from the dock, with a ball and chain around his ankle. There were only three Europeans in Bassein at that time, two river pilots and the harbour master. Local justice was rough, quick and quite probably severe.

Our regular route with Nourse Line was in general cargo to India, with anything from railway carriages to bottles of ink. In Calcutta we might load a full cargo of "gunny bags", the empty sacks used for transporting sugar. These gunny bags would be delivered to around twenty ports in the Caribbean, with sometimes a call at Mauritius and Cape Town on the way. Once we had got rid of the bags, we then might load a full cargo of bulk sugar or grain to take back to UK. But of course, being a tramp ship there was no regular pattern and we tended to go wherever the cargoes took us. On one trip we went out to New Zealand via the Panama Canal, calling at lonely Pitcairn Island in the middle of the Pacific on the way, their first ship for six months. On another voyage, we took a military cargo from Australia to Korea for the war that was taking place there. It was a way to see the world, but we were way off the tourist routes, and so often it was the seamier side of places that we saw. Docksides never seemed to have quite the attraction of tourist beaches.

Talking about the seamier side of life, I came close to getting mugged in Guyana, or British Guiana, as it was called in those days. Walking along some of the back streets in Georgetown, the capital, this big, black man came up to me and demanded money, threatening with a knife. He was misguided thinking that a young apprentice was going to have any money anyway, but he had also chosen the wrong guy. I could run faster than he could, and I made it back to the safety of the main street. Guyana had its good points though, and I had enough money saved up to take the seaplane trip up-country to the Kaieteur Falls. This spectacular waterfall was nearly 800 feet high and the plane landed at the top. When it was time to leave, we took off right over the edge of the falls. Wow!

There was excitement of a different kind shortly after we left the Panama Canal, on our way across the Pacific. A hurricane forced us to heave-to for more than two days as it raged about. The seas in hurricane force winds were hard to describe, because you could hardly see them. There was no place where the water ended and the air began, no horizon, nothing but that incredible wet wind. Everything just seemed to be solid water and it was difficult to breathe. So difficult that if you had the courage to go outside, it almost felt like drowning. If you got a glimpse of a wave through the murk, it seemed to tower over the ship, its breaking crest threatening to engulf you. The ship reeled under the hammer blows of the waves and it was quite awesome seeing the incredible power of nature in the raw. Thankfully, the good ship MARJATA battled its way through and after the storm the damage was substantial. The two lifeboats on the weather side were flattened hard against their davits, leaving just the wooden thwarts sticking out like broken bones from the squashed metal side. Solid steel plating had sheered through, and on the foredeck, the steel guard over the windlass gears was shaped to the teeth underneath it from the tremendous pounding of water. After surviving a storm like that you blessed the Clyde shipyard workers who built the ship and thanked God the engine kept going, grateful to be unscathed and able to continue the voyage.

Another hurricane found us in the harbour at Cienfuegus in Cuba

The MARJATA was a lucky ship

At least for me she was. But her luck changed when she was sold and renamed DENNY ROSE. Any sailor will tell you that changing a ship's name brings disaster. On 31st August 1964 she departed Toledo under her new name with a cargo of iron ore bound for Chiba. She was last heard from on 13th September at a position of 25° 15' N, 134° 23' E. She ran into a typhoon never to be seen again.

Morro Castle, Havana, Cuba
The original castle at the entrance to Havana harbour, after which the famous cruise ship was named before she caught fire off New Jersey. The original fort was built by the Spanish in 1589 to protect the city from buccaneers. The British captured it in 1762.

with nowhere to run. The old wooden jetty we tied up to had little hope of withstanding hurricane force winds, so the captain filled all the ballast tanks with water and sat the ship on the seabed to relieve the strain on the mooring ropes. Not a procedure you would find in the textbooks and one we were lucky to survive. Especially as going outside while it happened was not an option. Sheets of corrugated iron were slicing through the air and debris of all sorts was whirling about. Battened down in our cabin felt like being in a war zone, surrounded by the incredible noise of storm-rubble being hurled against the ship. If there was any choice with a hurricane, my preference was always to head out to the open sea before the storm arrived. Though these days with the kind of warning systems we have, it should be possible to avoid one altogether.

Waterspouts were another natural hazard we had to face out at sea. On one occasion, steaming through the Doldrums, this long dark cloud loomed ahead, stretching from horizon to horizon. From its black underside twisted as many as twenty waterspouts. Now waterspouts are like tornadoes, with vicious winds in a very localised area - something to be avoided. But trying to find a way through that maze of waterspouts up ahead was difficult because we could not easily anticipate the direction in which they were heading.

We got very close to one, and the noise and turmoil were tremendous. We dashed inside for cover before it marched right across the ship. A lot of the wooden awnings and other fittings were smashed, but we came out relatively unharmed, another short but terrifying experience of the forces of nature.

One passage in that ship that sticks in my mind was the long run across the Southern Ocean from Cape Town to Melbourne. This was something like 6,000 miles non-stop, and the seas ran pretty wild down in those southern latitudes. We passed by remote St Paul's Island on the way, with the weather pretty fair to that point, only blowing around Force 8 at times. Then it really started as the westerly gales caught up with us, Force 9 or 10 becoming quite regular happenings. In one storm, the lashings holding the deck cargo stowed on the hatches carried away, and it was only the booms of the stowed derricks that stopped the lot sweeping overboard. The derricks ended up a bit battered and bent, but we only lost a small proportion of the cargo as we finally made our weary way into Melbourne - after a long passage lasting nearly 30 days.

Disaster always seemed to be a close companion of the MARJATA. In Karachi for instance, the forward tug-line parted when we were being towed between berths. This allowed the bow to swing into the quay, where it struck one of the tall dockside cranes with a mighty crash. The crane tipped, then seemed to hover forever, as if trying to decide which way to fall. Finally it crashed over onto the warehouse roof alongside, half-destroying it in a great mess of falling steel and bricks. The ship came away unscathed, but watching that crane crash was a spectacular sight, a picture that will always live in my memory.

I sometimes think that harbours can be more dangerous for ships than the open sea. When something goes wrong in harbour the consequences can be immediate, like that tug-line parting. We had a similar situation in Houston, Texas, when the steering gear failed as we were heading up the main channel into harbour. We dropped the anchor to hold her, but 6,000 tons of ship takes a bit of stopping, and she ran hard aground. With the stern blocking the main channel, we were not at all popular in such a busy port. Again, our luck held and we were towed off without damage. Give me the open sea any time, you have longer to sort out problems before they get serious.

Cuba was a great place in those pre-Castro days, rum of course being one of the main attractions. Our first port of call in Cuba was always Santiago, where the ship had to be fumigated. This meant being sent ashore for the day, with the princely sum of five dollars to get by on. On a pay packet of only sixty-five pounds a year, that seemed like a fortune.

Especially when the word amongst the apprentices was that you could drink and eat all day for free at the Bacardi rum distillery in town, and still come back with your five dollars intact. Years later, when I caught up with George Bacardi of the rum family in the Bahamas, he had no idea what a life-saver his distillery had been.

Havana, the capital of Cuba was a much more degenerate place in those days, catering for every vice of the American tourists who flocked across by ferry from Key West. Here you could find every sort of sexual deviation you could imagine, but we young apprentices with only a few coins to rattle usually got no further than the Dos Hermanos Bar just outside the dock gates. Only a few years back, I returned to Havana when they were staging an offshore power boat race, and walking through town it started to look familiar. Wandering some more, I found the dock gates, and there was the Dos Hermanos Bar, exactly the same fifty years later. Of course I dropped by that evening and passed the time drinking with a Russian ship's captain. Only the girls had changed, probably the grandchildren of the ones I had met all those years ago.

In the austerity days of Britain just after the war things were pretty bleak in terms of luxury goods. So my first visit to the US gave me a taste of how little that country had been affected by the war. Here there were sweets galore in the shops and everything else you might possibly want.

That was the upside. The downside was that our visit coincided with the McCarthy era, when Americans were scared of Communists hiding under their beds. All our crew were lined up on deck as we arrived in Galveston, the Immigration officials questioning every one of us, 'Are you a communist?' Of course we all answered 'No.' Unfortunately our Chinese carpenter had a passport issued by the communist government in China. He was not allowed ashore and an armed guard was stationed at the foot of the gangway to make sure he stayed on board. That carpenter allowed me to use all his tools and he was a brilliant craftsman.

I felt so sorry for him to be treated in this way. Unfair yes, but that was one of the things about going to sea, you were not immune to the influence of politics.

MARJATA's engine did not always keep going at sea, and one time we drifted for three days whilst the engineers stripped and rebuilt the main engine after a serious mechanical failure. We carried spares on board for nearly all of the engine except the main block and the crankshaft, so the engineers really had to be capable of fixing anything. Another time the engine caught fire, very scary with dense smoke billowing out of the engine room skylight, hundreds of miles from help. It took a day to extinguish the fire before repairing the damage, but ships were designed to be self-sufficient in those days, and we always made it to harbour.

That early experience taught me a lot, and ever since I've always liked to be able to fix things at sea - but what can you do with modern engine electronics? Boats, and ships for that matter, are just not designed to be fixed at sea any more.

Material failures were one thing, but sailing with a Captain who seemed perpetually drunk multiplied the risks. I was with Captain Reynolds for fourteen months and they were not pleasant. He would storm out of his cabin, hurling empty bottles into the sea, so we made it our business never to get in his way, because it could only be trouble. He nearly met his end one time, going into Singapore at night. The plan was to anchor and wait for our berth to be clear the next morning. But in his drunken state, the Captain waved away the offer of a pilot when the cutter came alongside. Getting into the anchorage was pretty straightforward, or it should have been. The captain however, got his bearings all wrong, and the next thing was a terrible grinding sound as we hit the bottom, slowing almost to a stop. There must have been just enough depth, because the ship bounced across the bottom, then out into deep water again. Immediately the anchor was dropped, and the tanks sounded to see if there was any water coming in. The hull seemed to be intact, but we did not know if any damage had been done, so divers went down the next morning for an inspection. They found that the hull plating had been bent, in and out around the frames as they scraped across the rocks. There was no actual hole, and as we were only going into Singapore to discharge the last of our cargo before a routine dry-docking in Calcutta, we were given permission to sail to where the damage could be permanently repaired.

By that time I had gained some seniority as an apprentice, and was moved up to watch-keeping on the bridge, away from all the painting and maintenance. On that run to Calcutta I was on watch with the Mate when the engine-room rang to say there was something knocking on the outside of the hull! Now in theory, nothing could be knocking on the outside of the hull, because there was nothing there to do it. But as the day wore on, you could hear the knocking right throughout the ship. When we stopped, the knocking stopped, which was more than a little bit scary. Then quite suddenly, it stopped altogether! We did not find out what it was until the ship was in dry dock, when it was found that a whole section of the bilge keel was missing. From this we assumed it had been partly torn off in the grounding, and was swinging against the hull until it broke away altogether. In olden times, our experience might well have been imagined as sea monsters or the like. It was certainly one of my most eerie experiences at sea.

I have often tried to work out whether strange happenings at sea only seemed strange because I was still a novice. On land, you could always find someone with experience of something strange, but at sea you were ensconced in your own little world most of the time. On MARJATA there were just thirty or so people on board, most of them Indians with a different approach to life, so getting things in perspective was not always easy. Often away for weeks or more at sea, you could see why sailors needed some adjusting to shore-life, and how strange happenings could take on a life of their own, totally out of proportion.

Most of the time, life at sea was purely routine. As apprentices, most of our time was spent cleaning, painting and polishing brass, all the dirty chores. Four of us were crammed into one small cabin, with no air-conditioning against the heat of the tropics, only small portholes. It was my apprentice shipmates who gave me my nickname "Dag" after the comic-strip character Dagwood Bumstead, because my hair stuck up on end at the back. I suppose these days it could be quite fashionable. But back then, like most nicknames, it was not meant to be complimentary. Still, anything was better than my other nickname at the time. "Wog" was short for my Christian name, Roderick.

In between these bouts of hard manual labour, we got time off for studying. Apprentices were supposed to learn how to be navigators, as well as deckhands and dogsbodies. After a couple of years, we were to start keeping watches on the bridge, learning how to navigate with sextant and compass. This was my first real taste of navigation, and I loved the way you measured angles from the sun and stars to work out where you were. To me, the whole mechanics of navigating was a challenge, often calculating where you were with the minimum of information. I guess it was a bit like the marine detective work that I got involved with later in life as a consultant. In those days, fixing your position was what counted, and in good conditions you could plot where the ship was to within a mile or so, most of the time. But when clouds obscured the sun, or bad visibility prevented you from taking bearings, the ship's position might not be fixed for several days. That was when you relied on dead-reckoning, supposedly working out where you were by estimating your speed and course, then allowing for the effect of winds, currents and tides. Though there was a sound basis for this, it often became like intelligent guesswork, so that making a landfall was a nervous experience. Thankfully, we made it safely most of the time. I never thought that I would end up writing a book about using sextants and navigation from those early experiences.

We carried every sort of cargo you could imagine on that ship. General cargoes might be anything from cars and trucks to machinery and currency notes. Most of it was in big wooden boxes that had to be stowed in the right sequence to be unloaded correctly at the various ports of call. This required a lot of coordination and preparation, so tackling cargo plans was one of our regular jobs. It was particularly difficult if there was a cargo like the gunny bags, where all the bales looked the same. We had to ensure careful marking and division of the bales to make sure that the right cargo went to the right port. And with the ship calling at twenty-five ports around the Caribbean, this meant plenty of head-work. We had a new port virtually every day and we steamed between ports overnight.

Bulk cargoes were a lot easier. They came aboard at one port and left at the next. They also brought their own problems. Once, a full cargo of salt was loaded in the bottom of the ship at Karachi, where it lay solid and heavy, making MARJATA'S roll swing like a pendulum. From Karachi we headed south down the coast of India, with the South West Monsoon blowing a steady Force 6, the ship rolling us and our guts out for three days. Each roll was so sudden and severe, it was nearly impossible to eat or drink. As for sleeping, it became a forgotten reflex because staying in your bunk was nearly impossible. There was a huge sigh of relief as we rounded the bottom of Sri Lanka, Ceylon in those days, into the relative shelter of the East Coast where our destination lay.

Sugar was another bulk cargo that was not very welcome on board. This was thick, gooey, brown sugar, making the whole ship a sticky mess that took months to get rid of. With a lot of bulk cargoes such as coal, the dust or bits of whatever stuff it was seemed to permeate everywhere around the ship, I guess one of the penalties for living so close to the job. There was nowhere on board to hide or escape, and if the cargo was being worked at night, you had to live with the noise too. Out of this experience I developed the technique of being able to sleep pretty well anywhere.

Occasionally we would carry livestock, and that made life even more interesting. Needless to say, it was our job as apprentices to feed and clean the animals, though anything was a good break from routine. One time, on a voyage from India to Cape Town, we had six thoroughbred horses and a number of smaller animals which we carried in stalls on the after deck. Now this deck was only twelve feet above the waterline when the ship was loaded, so when we hit the inevitable storm, the poor horses got more than their share of waves and spray crashing over them. They were not very happy about this, and one was so scared it broke out of its stall and ran loose over the deck. Nothing in your training taught you how to round up a scared horse on a heaving deck in a howling gale, but it was our job as apprentices to handle it. Since we always got whatever dirty work was going, it was reckoned to be part of our training. In all fairness, a great deal of how we were treated depended on whoever the Mate was at the time. Some were brilliant, remembering their own days as apprentices. Others seemed to enjoy giving us the worst jobs, like cleaning the bilges, or crawling through the double bottom tanks. A more exciting job was to replace the bulb of the masthead navigation light, at night, in a howling gale. Climbing the mast was never easy. With the ship rolling, it was a nightmare. The mast swung out over the sea with each roll, so that you clung on by the skin of your teeth. It was a small taste of what it must have been like in a sailing ship, and I wonder what the Health and Safety people would have to say about that these days.

On one of the breaks between voyages when the MARJATA was back in the UK, I was transferred to make a short trip on her near-sister ship, TAPTI. She was making a short voyage with no cargo from Liverpool around the north of Scotland to the North-East Coast, where she was due to start loading cargo. We sailed from Liverpool during the day with a weather forecast that promised very little except pain. By that night we were heading up to the Minches into the teeth of a northerly gale, in blizzard conditions that reduced visibility to nil. With the ship empty of cargo and riding high, we were probably making a lot of leeway. Since we had no means of fixing our position, we relied on dead reckoning, helped by a strong dose of prayer.

It was not good enough, and we knew something was wrong when the seas suddenly died down. That could only mean one thing. That we were under the lee of the land somewhere. But according to our dead-reckoning, land should have been at least ten miles away, definitely not ahead. It seemed like a good idea to head back out to sea, as we were probably close in to the shore, definitely not where we wanted to be. It was too late. With a terrible grinding noise that we felt rather than heard, even above the screaming wind, the ship ran up onto the rocks.

In the very limited visibility, we could barely see the shore. As we were not where we should have been, we had no clue where we were. It turned out later that we had hit a group of rocks between the islands of Tiree and Coll. Tracking our likely route across the chart years afterwards, we must have passed very close to the Skerryvore Lighthouse on our way, but we saw nothing. We felt pretty safe on board, sitting

TAPTI on Eileen Soa Rocks

During a north-westerly gale on the night of 17th January 1953, TAPTI ran aground on the Eileen Soa rocks in the Gunna Sound, Outer Hebrides. The sound of her hitting them was one of the worst I've ever heard. All 62 of our crew were rescued by the Mallaig lifeboat, SIR ARTHUR ROSE, whose coxswain, Bruce Watt, and seven crew received special RNLI awards. TAPTI rolled off the rocks and sank three days later.

there perched on the rocks, so it was not until daylight that we lowered the ship's boats and held them alongside. This gave us a safe stepping-stone into the Mallaig lifeboat that found us in the storm and came alongside to take us ashore. It must have been quite a serious rescue as the lifeboat crew got awards for it.

That was my first serious shipwreck. But my last voyage as an apprentice on the MARJATA was very nearly my last voyage ever. We had loaded a full cargo of grain in Galveston, Texas, and were heading across the Atlantic, homeward bound.

Now grain is a very difficult cargo to carry, because in bulk it behaves like a liquid. If the ship rolls, the cargo rolls with it, causing her to list alarmingly. To stop this, temporary bulkheads called shifting boards are rigged longitudinally in each hold, so that when the ship rolls, the grain's movement is limited and things stay reasonably safe.

So there we were, with the grain supposedly safely stowed, excited to be heading home after many months away. It was winter in the North Atlantic, an ocean not noted for being calm at that time of the year. It is in fact so wild, ships are marked with a special Winter North Atlantic load line, lower on the hull than usual to give them extra freeboard, an extra margin of safety in the severe conditions so often experienced.

We were following a relatively southerly route across the Atlantic from the Gulf of Mexico, but sure enough we picked up this big storm as we approached the Bay of Biscay. This was no more than your average winter North Atlantic storm, with the wind at a steady Force 10. We were steaming at moderate speed, as usual making slow rough-weather progress, with the ship rolling and pitching in heavy following seas.

Nothing to worry about, we had been through much worse, and we knew that MARJATA could cope with everything that came along. Then the wind shifted round onto the beam. The rolling got worse, though the ship was still coping well. But on one particularly heavy lurch, one of the shifting boards carried away with a loud cracking noise. Immediately the cargo moved, and the ship developed a big list over to starboard. This caused the shifting boards in two more of the holds to break away, and now we were in serious trouble. The ship was listing to thirty degrees - rolling further to twice that - with nothing we could do about it. Now ships can only roll so far before they loose their stability and roll right over, a disaster we were not a million miles away from.

It really was scary, because the ship would roll as a wave passed underneath, and you would be walking on the bulkheads instead of on the deck. As it rolled to say sixty degrees, it seemed to hang there and hover, as if deciding whether to come back or keep going over. Everything seemed to happen in slow motion and on each roll we all held our breath. Nobody spoke because there was nothing we could do.

We just had to find a speed and heading where the rolling was minimised. We couldn't even try filling the ballast tanks for more stability. If we did, the water would slosh around with a "free surface" like the "liquid" grain shifting in the holds, making the situation worse. All we could do was pray and wait for the storm to ease, hoping we would be still there when it did. This desperate situation was not helped by the knowledge that a near-sister ship had capsized in the Irish Sea in a very similar situation with the loss of all hands.

Of course we sent out a distress message, but not really in the hope that anyone could help. With the ship listing at that angle, it was not possible to launch the lifeboats. The tension on board was tremendous, none of us knowing if we would live from one moment to the next. Slowly, as the hours passed and the ship did not capsize, the tension eased and some sense of normality returned. Nobody could live at that level of tension for long, so there were glimmers of hope that we might survive. If the ship had not gone in the first couple of hours, maybe she would not go at all. And that taught me something. Time and time again I was surprised at how quickly you could adapt to a situation that seemed to have gone totally out of control. It happened to me during the war and I have seen it in several near-disasters since. Suddenly you felt hungry and thirsty. Conversation returned, a bit tense maybe, because you were still trying to keep below panic level. Going below was a unthinkable because you felt you might be trapped, forgetting that in icy water like that, you were not going to survive for long anyway. And that was how it was. The storm eased after thirty-six hours and we made our way up the Irish Sea to Liverpool, still with our thirty-degree list. It was with considerable relief that we stepped ashore and could actually stand upright again.

The good ship MARJATA was a survivor. She went through nearly every type of disaster that could happen at sea and she saw safely me through for the four years of my apprenticeship. It was an interesting time, making the transition from schoolboy to ship's officer. Though when I came ashore to study for my Second Mate's Certificate, I found that I had lost touch with many friends. Most of them were probably away doing National Service.

CHAPTER 3

GUARDIANS OF THE COAST

Trinity House was established by Royal Charter from Henry VIII in 1514. It was originally a fraternity of mariners known as the Guild of the Holy Trinity. It got teeth in 1604, when James I conferred rights of compulsory pilotage on shipping in and around England, together with the exclusive right to license pilots on the Thames. Until 1987, Trinity House was the Pilotage Authority for London and over 40 other Districts, including Southampton and Harwich. Today the Corporation is a fraternity of 300 Brethren drawn from the Royal and Merchant Navies and leading figures in the shipping industry.

Trinity House was a strange organisation. On one level it had a lot of authority as befitted an establishment that was even older than the Royal Navy. However, its very age meant that it tended to live off tradition and pomp. When I joined their lighthouse tender fleet, Trinity was going through the painful process of bringing the organisation and its finances up to date to meet the requirements of modern government. It was in 1955 that I joined and Trinity still lived largely in the past. That was great as far as the freedom it gave, particularly as you did not always need a logical reason for doing what you thought best. The important thing was to get the job done and keep the lights burning. It was like serving in a miniature navy, with the whole organisation living on past glories. Change was resisted and modern technology struggled to make impact.

I knew very little about what I was getting into when I signed up as Second Mate on one of their lighthouse tenders. My sole reason for joining was so that I could get home at nights for at least half the

Aboard the Trinity House ship READY
READY was a full-sized 2,000-ton ship. And with my Second Mate's ticket I was fully qualified to take her to sea.

week. During my stay ashore, sitting my exams in London, I had met a girl. It was not long before we got married, and for me, like nearly all sailors, home life beckoned. By joining Trinity House, I could still pursue a life at sea, and combine it with some sort of home life.

With hindsight, I have long had a tendency to jump into things without really knowing much about them. I have always preferred something that felt right to any deep analysis of a situation. Sailor's wisdom, you see. I am convinced that thinking about something too much, or going into too great a depth over it, will always give you a reason for not doing it. But when you make an emotional decision, jumping in before your thoughts get in the way, you are more likely to be proved right. On balance, I don't think that I have ever made a bad decision, or one that I regret from following this conviction. I certainly have some exciting and life-changing decisions to show for it out of a long career.

This decision was certainly an emotional one - I wanted to spend more time at home. The business of work and earning money had to fit in with that, and the Trinity House offer seemed just right for this combination. In any case, life on the Trinity ships promised some interesting sea-going experiences.

Being at sea for Trinity was very rarely dull. Though there was none of the excitement of visiting foreign ports, or the occasional near-disaster in mid-ocean, there was none of the boredom either: no long weeks of steaming from port to port, none of the dull routine of ocean watch-keeping. With Trinity I entered a new world of small-ship operations, grabbing at the chance to develop new skills. For instance in my deep-sea days, the captain was always on the bridge within twenty miles of land to take charge of the navigation. Imagine my surprise when we left Harwich on my first Trinity House ship. No sooner were we outside the harbour than the captain said, 'Take her down to Sea Reach,' and handed over the watch to me. Here we were in the Thames estuary, one of the busiest shipping lanes around Britain, and I was in charge of a 1,000-ton ship. In fact I had never even seen her until the night before. At twenty-three years old it seemed a big step forward - a far cry from my first voyages down the river.

It was a steep learning curve, but I loved the responsibility. There I was, rushing around on that bridge, trying to look at the chart, learn how the Decca Navigator worked, and watching out for other ships and buoys. There were sandbanks and shallows close by, so I was both scared and elated. They were intense days, and I have never worked so hard at navigation. Which made it all the more amazing that after a few weeks I was confident enough to take the ship all the way back up the Thames, not worrying if there were others all round us, I knew it would work out. I have to give full marks to the quartermasters who took the wheel on those Trinity ships, and who probably knew more about navigation in those waters than most of the officers. They were very helpful and diplomatic, and got me out of trouble more than once.

Navigation at close quarters was not the only thing I learnt at Trinity. As big ships got bigger, with less "feel" of the sea, it became obvious that seamanship was a dying art. Trinity lighthouse tenders were one of the few places left where seamanship counted, and once again the learning curve was steep - you didn't get a second chance taking a small boat into a lighthouse just feet off the rocks, then transferring personnel and stores in difficult sea conditions. It called for fine judgement, which these days I doubt whether health and safety rules, or other regulations would allow to happen.

And why? Life does not seem any more secure. In fact, just observing all these regulations makes the job more difficult. So where's the gain? Or is it simply having a scapegoat to blame if things do go wrong?

Back then, when people asked what my job was, I used to say "picking up boys", which raised a few eyebrows. Well, I never was much good at spelling. In reality, picking up buoys to service them was another of those jobs with high hazards and small safety margins - but like everything else, we got the job done. In the nine years that I worked with Trinity I do not recall a serious accident, which showed what you could do with good seamanship and an experienced crew. On one memorable occasion, a buoy light in the Needles Channel had gone out, so we were despatched to relight it. Normally we would have lifted the buoy and done the work in relative safety on deck, not possible this time because of the sea and tide conditions. We had to do it the hard way, lowering the boat and then jumping right onto the buoy. As luck would have it, water had got into the works so we had to change the whole thing, no easy job when it weighed over a hundred pounds. To make life more difficult, the buoy itself was rising and falling ten feet in the waves, with a vicious corkscrew motion. We took it in turns, working on the light, then moving around the buoy to leeward to be seasick. Well, the motion of any buoy in a seaway was sure to make the most hardened seaman feel queasy. The only thing to beat it for discomfort and unpleasantness was sitting in a life-raft. To make things worse, jumping up onto that buoy was relatively easy, but jumping back into the boat was a nightmare. It took nearly two hours before we had the job done.

In those days, Trinity House acted as a sort of clearing house for all the jobs at sea that did not come into some other jurisdiction. We would do surveys, blow up wrecks that were a danger to shipping, collect floating debris and even recover dead bodies. Once in the Thames Estuary we had a report of a small submarine drifting in the Barrow Deep. It turned out to be a floating steel pile, some 80 feet long and 3 feet in diameter. It was a slow time-consuming job lifting that out of the water, but it was a potential danger to shipping so it was our job to sort it out. At least we got the proceeds when it was sold for scrap.

Another time a buoy had broken from its moorings and drifted ashore. Here was another bit of seamanship to improvise: the plan being that the ship would anchor off, and I would go in with the boat to fire a rocket line ashore. This would be used to haul a bigger line that could attach to the buoy and return to the ship, so the buoy could be hauled off and recovered.

You planned these things, but Sod's Law always dictated that something would not go according to plan. In this case it was the boat taking a heavy roll just as I pulled the trigger on the line gun. The plan had been to fire the rocket into the low cliffs behind the beach, but with the momentary change in elevation the rocket took off over the cliff and disappeared into some trees behind. A thin orange line trailed after it, running up the cliff and over the trees, then out of sight. By the time our shore party had tracked it down, the rocket had landed in the road running behind the trees, right in the path of a car. It must have seemed like World War Three to the driver, but fortunately no damage was done. The police were not too happy about our rocket attack, determined not to understand it was a new way to pick up buoys.

Then there was the buoy that broke adrift in a big storm and ended up a mile or more inland on some marshes on the North Norfolk Coast. This area was part of a bombing range, hostile territory in which to carry out a search. Anyway we landed on the beach, first making sure that the range was not in use that day. After wading a river and trudging through the marshes we found the buoy, but there was no way we were going to shift four tons of metal. So we left it where it was and headed back to the beach. Next thing there were these low-flying jets screaming overhead and the bombing range was very much in use! We made it back to the ship in record time.

The usual ship routine was to leave harbour with a load of replacement buoys on deck, then lift and service those that were due for their six month check. The weather was critical to the lifting operation because you didn't want a four-ton buoy swinging from the derrick head if the ship was rolling. We had to plan for gaps in the weather at the more exposed buoy stations, working inshore in more sheltered waters if the elements turned nasty. Each night we would hole up at an anchorage close by. Working at night was too risky, even though we all wanted to get the job done and be off home. However, one ship I worked on had a captain who preferred to be at sea because he did not enjoy his home life. It made for a fairly mutinous crew and was not a happy ship.

When a ship sank in the shipping lanes, which they seemed to do with some frequency, it was our job to survey the wreck to see if it was safe for shipping. We did not have sophisticated echo sounders for survey work in those days, so we used fairly basic methods. This entailed a lot of drifting over the wreck with ropes at a preset depth. If they caught up in the wreck, then we could measure the depth of water over it. Primitive, but effective.

If a wreck was deemed dangerous to shipping, we first marked its position with buoys, then tried to break it up with explosives. I can't imagine that Health and Safety would allow us to do that these days, certainly not in the way we went about it. As I recall, it was potentially lethal - talk about hit or miss. We would put the detonator onto the explosive, which was in long metal canisters of 50 pounds each, choosing enough for a big bang. Then we would lower the lot to the sea bed and let the ship drift with the tide until the charge caught up in the wreck. Paying out the firing line, we would retire to a safe distance and fire the charge, hoping for spectacular results. A good blast would send up a large plume of water, and if we were lucky, bits of debris. We always had a second boat standing by, not to pick up our pieces if the explosion was premature, but to collect all the fish that had been stunned by the blast.

Some of the explosive we were using was past its sell-by date and liable to misfire. If a charge failed to go off, we would wait a few minutes, then slide another one down the line in the hope it would set off the first. Most of the time it worked, but on one unbelievable occasion we ended up with five charges down the same line, all duds. Time to buoy off the line, retire for the night, and ponder what to do next. Eventually, and very gingerly, we hauled up the charges to see if anything had happened. The detonators had fired all right, and they had blown the explosive right out of the canister without setting it off! When we checked the date of the stuff, it was some twenty years old, almost prehistoric.

You can imagine we were quite angry about being supplied with such potentially dangerous explosive. So when we arrived back in port, I took the empty canisters up to the Superintendent's office to show him. I was ordered out with the comment, 'Don't bring that dangerous stuff in here'. He was quite happy for us to go to sea with it and risk being blown up, but he didn't want it anywhere near his office.

Trinity House had a motley collection of ships at that time, only two of them post-war vessels. The rest were of various vintages that had managed to survive the war. The one I was assigned to on a permanent basis was the BEACON, a coal-burning steamship built in 1923. She was magnificent, with a tall upright funnel and beautiful mahogany panelling in the officers' cabins. But she was really much too small to handle the heavy modern buoys.

We were actually lifting ten-tonners with a wooden derrick and six-fold rope falls. And the ship was so small, we had to take down half the rigging to create enough space just to land the buoy on the deck. She came from a different era, when there ratlines to climb the mast, not a steel ladder.

Being a coal-burner at least ensured that we were in port every week to avoid running out of fuel. We needed around 85 tons of coal a time, brought to the ship in trucks, then loaded by men heaving wicker baskets on their shoulders to dump it into the bunkers. See what I meant about Trinity being in the past?

The BEACON was based at Cowes, on the Isle of Wight, and the area she served included the Channel Islands. This was a real bonus, as every time we crossed the Channel, we qualified for duty-free cigarettes and booze. A week servicing buoys and lighthouses in the Channel Islands would mean coming back with sore throats and pounding heads, but it was a nice break in the routine. With their big rise and fall, the Channel Islands' strong tides were a real challenge, forcing most of our buoy servicing to be done around slack water.

The BEACON had a Decca Navigator system, but no radar. Which meant in fog that we were always feeling our way around. On one of our trips in dense fog across the Channel, we could hear this deep-throated siren of another ship on our port bow. We knew there was something big out there, so we were down to dead slow. The rumbling siren came closer and closer, to the point where it became really scary. It was so close in the fog, you could feel the siren's vibrations going right through the ship. We peered ahead, trying to pick up some lights or some other indication of where it was. Then it appeared, a wall of lights that seemed to rise up in front of us, little more than 100 yards away. We went full astern, gaping at the ocean liner QUEEN MARY, at that time the biggest ship in the world. It seemed to take ages before she finally passed clear, and she was so big that there were no lights at the waterline where we had been looking. They were above our heads, deck after deck of portholes, saloon windows, and her enclosed promenade, ghostly in the grey nothing. Near misses like that were part of navigating in those days, when you were really blind in fog. Today, ships are so confident of what is around them in fog, they no longer bother to sound their sirens - a serious hazard for small craft without radar.

A few months later, I was on the Trinity House Yacht PATRICIA, in fog as we entered Plymouth Harbour. This time we had radar, and just inside the breakwater there was what looked like measles on the display, targets everywhere ahead. We slowed right down to see what was going on, to be surrounded by a fleet of sailing dinghies that were racing in the fog! The Captain seethed, but there was nothing to do except wait until they were out of our way before starting the engines again. Suddenly, one last dinghy came from right under our bow, its forlorn helmsman in glasses staring up at us. Though we had nearly run him down, the Captain responded by shouting over the bridge rail, 'You bespectacled c—t'. Sailors could be so polite sometimes.

On Trinity House duties, we had to deal with all sorts of weather conditions around the Britain. This called for serious small boat handling, particularly reaching the isolated rock lighthouses. One of the most difficult was Bishop Rock Lighthouse, wide open to the Atlantic and one I was to see in very different circumstances years later. Virtually everything we did was weather-dependant in some way, so we grew adept at interpreting weather forecasts, another skill that would prove useful in the years ahead. Though picking up buoys in rough weather was decidedly risky, there was more latitude in getting relief crews out to their lightships and lighthouses. Of course there were more than a couple of times when the normally placid British weather became extreme, and as "keepers of the lights" we had to scramble.

It was in the winter of 1968 that a huge cold spell descended over

Britain. Normal winter snows were easy enough to deal with, but this was extreme cold, and it went on for a long time. It was so cold that the sea started to freeze over, and I had a mental picture of ploughing into large ice flows that were floating down the Thames Estuary. These were not too much of a problem, though they did slow our progress. The real headache was the buoys, so top-heavy with frozen spray that they rolled over and capsized. Of course that put their lights out, though the buoys themselves was still intact, they just happened to be upside down.

There was not lot we could do with the deep freeze making everything solid. Our job began when the thaw started and we had to get all the buoys up into running order again. It was a real challenge how much the ice on the water affected our normal boating and ship-board operations. Just trying to moor in harbour and run the boat ashore became near impossible tasks. Working on deck, out in the open, some of the crew risked hypothermia as we did not have the right clothing for such extreme cold.

Strong winds brought another near-disaster. We were quite used to the regular winter gales that swept the coasts, but this day the winds screamed up to hurricane force, with steady blows of 110 mph recorded. That was not the sort of wind you wanted to be at sea in, but we felt snug in harbour. I was at home, getting ready for bed and listening to the note of the wind in the wires rising and rising. That was when the phone rang, calling me down to the ship immediately.

The westerly wind was whistling straight down Harwich Harbour, and it was all we could do to crawl out onto the jetty on our hands and knees. One ship, the TRITON was moored on the windward side of the jetty. The seas were crashing over her, banging her heavily against the jetty. She was a tough, converted trawler, but she never went to sea again after that - except to the breakers yard. Her side was smashed in against the concrete jetty. Our ship, the READY was on the leeward side of the jetty, and already the mooring ropes were straining to pull apart with the severe pressure of the wind pushing at her. Something had to give, but we could not hang around to find out what. The engines were fired up, and on the order, we cut all the ropes with an axe and put her engines full ahead to drive her out into deeper water. We spent that night riding out the storm and trying to find what shelter we could. And I can tell you, those conditions in Harwich Harbour felt a lot worse than all the hurricanes I had been through in the Caribbean.

Towing lightships was another of our jobs, and we would have a lightship following behind on the end of a long tow wire, which was fine when the weather was good. But on one passage from the Tyne down to the Thames with a refitted lightship, we were 75 miles out in the North Sea when we were caught by a gale. With the lightship in tow, all we could do was dodge very slowly, seeking the best course to relieve the strain on the tow wire.

Towing jobs like these were quite rare, so imagine my surprise one night on watch when I saw red and green navigation lights coming up close astern. 'It's a sailing ship,' I thought, forgetting we were under power, so how could she be catching up with us? 'It's a sailing ship bearing down on us'. I was about to alter course to get out of the way, when I realised that it was the lightship we were towing, swung out on our quarter.

Another unusual job was changing over the anchor chains on a lightship. As you might imagine, they had massive anchors and chains to hold them in position. Every so often a chain would have to be renewed when it got worn. This meant slipping the chain onto a buoy and temporarily anchoring the lightship while we picked up the chain, did the business with a new one, then reversed the procedure. It was a full day's job and one for which settled weather was very necessary.

These sorts of event provided a break from the normal routine - if ever there was "normal" in Trinity House. Probably the biggest change I had was when I transferred to the PATRICIA, the flagship of the fleet. During the winter, PATRICIA would work like a normal buoy tender, but once summer came she was tarted up with a full paint-job to serve as the Trinity House Yacht. Her summer function was to accommodate a party of the Elder Brethren - the bosses of Trinity House - on their annual inspection of the buoys and lights. During this cruise, the ship was run more or less on Navy lines but without the guns. We would have to do all the saluting and standing to attention that went with the role, which worked well most of the time. However, when we took these somewhat elderly gentlemen, mainly ex-ship's captains, across the heaving sea to a slippery rock lighthouse, they had to scramble for their lives just like the rest of us.

When I joined her, PATRICIA was getting a bit long in the tooth. She was built in 1936 and at that time she had been a very modern ship with diesel electric propulsion. Electric installations in those days did not have the efficient insulating materials of modern systems and there were continuing problems with reliability. One day we were picking up a buoy which was hanging from the top of the derrick, when all the deck machinery winches and capstans packed up from an electrical fire. So there we were, moored to the seabed by the buoy hanging from the top of the derrick, with a strong tide about to start flowing. With electrically powered winches there was no way to lower the buoy, a situation that was starting to look serious. Somehow we managed to secure the buoy chain alongside, restoring a degree of stability. We stayed like that for two days while the electrics were repaired, and thank goodness the weather stayed calm.

The PATRICIA was part of the long tradition of Trinity House, which granted her the right to be the only vessel allowed to precede the Royal Yacht when the Queen was on board, coming into home waters. This "privilege", conferred by Royal Charter from Henry VIII in 1513, symbolized the long importance to navigation of Trinity House. It meant that in theory, we were acting as pilots, showing the Royal Yacht the way into harbour. Normally a procession of ships like this would all keep station on the leading vessel - but for some royal or historic reason, we were expected to keep station on the Royal Yacht following behind us. Another tradition that made navigation tricky.

As the navigating officer, it was my job to organise and plan these events, and we were supposed to hold station just 400 yards in front of BRITANNIA. It was on one unforgettable occasion, leading the Royal yacht out of the River Humber, that another electrical problem stopped one of our engines. This meant we slowed rapidly, forcing BRITANNIA to take pretty rapid avoiding action.

These royal escort duties were always tense moments because your navigating skills were being put to the test under very public scrutiny. It was one thing to navigate privately when all that was important was to arrive safely. It added a lot of tension to the situation when every move you made was watched closely, so I always planned these royal occasions carefully.

One time we were doing an escort into Harwich Harbour, which was our home port. Here we decided to put on a bit of a show and do a full-speed turn around the Cork Lightship at the entrance to the harbour before taking up our position at the required two cables in front of BRITANNIA (one cable is 120 fathoms, or 720 feet), which would be steaming at a steady speed. We did some practice runs to make sure that the timing was right and everything looked set for the big day.

What I had not planned for was thick fog on the morning that BRITANNIA arrived. However we were committed, and using the radar had been part of my plans anyway, so I convinced the Captain that it would all work. Some of the Elder Brethren were up on the monkey island above the bridge, all dressed up in their smart uniforms and swords whilst the captain and I were in the wheelhouse, focusing on the controls and navigation. All went well and there was the BRITANNIA on the radar just where I expected her to be, and there was the Cork Lightship. Everything looked set, even though we could not see BRITANNIA, except on the radar. Full-speed, which was a modest 14 knots anyway, was ordered and the helm was put over to start the high-speed 180-degree turn around the lightship. Everything looked fine and BRITANNIA was now so close that she seemed to take up half of the radar picture. I had my head down in the radar concentrating like mad, then I heard this huge gasp go up. I looked out through the wheelhouse windows. There, coming out of the fog, was the broad dark blue expanse of BRITANNIA, getting longer and longer as we headed full tilt for her midships!

It was one of those "Oh shit" situations where the only solution was to write out your resignation there and then. It was too late to slow down, there seemed to be no way around either end of her, and we were now so close that we could see the Queen on deck waving. I think everybody on board froze, which was probably a good thing because with that first glimpse of BRITANNIA we had not realised that our helm was still hard over and we were actually turning out of harm's way, just as planned. That aside, I am still haunted by that deep blue vision coming out of the fog, a moment frozen in time forever. Everything worked out in the end and we headed into harbour where we anchored precisely at 10.00 hours just as planned. The captain turned to me and said, 'I don't know about you, but I need a drink after that.' That morning gin helped to steady my shattered nerves.

The Royal Yacht BRITANNIA was launched in 1953, serving Queen and country for forty-four years with 968 official voyages and sailing over a million miles. Now permanently moored in Leith, BRITANNIA is the city of Edinburgh's living monument to the world's most famous family.

One of the good things about working with Trinity House was the absence of rigid routine. During my time there, I had achieved my Master's qualification and had risen to chief officer, which meant that I was in charge of the fore-deck when we were lifting buoys. I also had to organise the general running of the ship. One day we were due to sail at around 07.00 hours when we realised there was no sign of the Captain. It turned out that he was sick, so after phoning the Superintendent, I was detailed to take the ship to sea. My first command! Nothing quite prepared you for the responsibility in which it was you that drove the ship, and you that made all the decisions with nobody there to ask. It was probably just as well it happened suddenly like that, you didn't have time to think about it, you just did it.

This was where my years of training and experience come in. I was only 28 years old and had been at sea for little more than 12 years, but thankfully it all worked out. Later, I was to act as relief captain on several of the Trinity ships - brilliant experience because there were few places where I could get such hands-on experience of ship handling. With working ships like these, I had to cope with all sorts of situations, not just taking them in and out of harbour.

Trinity House was going through big changes at this time. New ships were being built and the organisation was being tightened up. Ship operation was controlled more closely from the shore, so that instead of planning your own programme, adapting as you went along to the weather and tides, you had to ask for permission for any deviation. It was supposed to be more efficient, but I was not convinced. I was pretty settled in what I was doing and it was a pretty interesting life, I could also expect steady promotion as the older generations retired. It did entail moving house and family at intervals though, because it was necessary to live near wherever my ship was based, not an easy thing with children at school.

Then I saw the newspaper advertisement that took my life in a whole new direction.

CHAPTER 4

ROUGH SEAS AND RESCUES

That advertisement was placed by the Royal National Lifeboat Institution, who wanted an Inspector of Lifeboats. I was not really looking for another job, as I was pretty happy with my life in Trinity House, particularly as I had moved up to be one of the youngest Captains they had ever had. OK, promotion was rather like stepping into a dead man's shoes, but I had just hit lucky and found a quick path upwards - except that carrying on another thirty years before pension day was not the most exciting prospect. So really, I was more intrigued by the advert than seriously wanting the job. What was an Inspector of Lifeboats, and what did he do? So I put pen to paper and applied, more out of curiosity than as a serious job application. 356 other people did the same, narrowing down to a list of 20 who were requested to attend an interview in London - and I was one of the chosen few! That made me sit up a bit, wondering what the job was all about. I thought lifeboats were just lifeboats, which hopefully worked when you needed them.

At the interview I found out more, and quite liked what I saw. Basically an Inspector was allocated to a sector of coastline and expected to make sure all lifeboats in that sector were working effectively. It was very much a shore-based job, though with the opportunity to take the lifeboats to sea on regular inspections. So yes, I was attracted by the combination of sea-going experience and shore life.

It sounded like a doddle with my small boat experience, and thanks to my intimate knowledge of the coastline gained from Trinity House, I had all the right qualifications. The was only one snag. I was not a serving Royal Navy officer, not even a Reservist. But then, just being called for that interview suggested Navy rank was not critical. Anyway

Trinity House ran a close second to the Royal Navy in terms of status, a definite rung up the poshness ladder from the Merchant Navy. That first interview was pretty informal, a sort of 'getting to know you' exercise which I sailed through to a short-list of six. After that, the interviews became more serious, and were conducted by an impressive panel of distinguished gentlemen. The RNLI were making sure only the right sort of people got into their organisation.

Anyway I passed that test as well, though it was not the end of the saga. I have to say I was now seriously interested in the job, which was now down to two candidates, both to be interviewed by the whole Management Committee of the RNLI. I think there were twenty-six of them at that time, all people who had made their mark in life; admirals, bishops and people from the financial world. Most of the questions I was asked were about playing rugby, which I think was the thing that confirmed the job for me. So there I was, handing in my notice to Trinity House and putting on my lifeboat hat. I still found it hard to believe. I had been chosen out of 356 people, but it was playing rugby on top of my by now extensive small boat experience that did the trick. I got the feeling that they had never had anyone with small boat experience apply for the job before. So rugby was the clincher. Phew!

Now I was truly shore-based, an inspector who could set up office in my own house, plan my own trips to the various lifeboat stations in my area, even take out two of three craft each week, to be sure they were up to the job when the call came. There was also the responsibility of bedding-in new crew, and liaising through the local committees and Honorary Secretaries who carried out day-to-day running of the lifeboat stations. At first it seemed I would be driving a car more than a ship, but the prospects were good, especially in those days, when the arrival of the Inspector at a lifeboat station could be quite an event. You can imagine the stir in some of the smaller ports and harbours.

I started with ten days training alongside one of the established inspectors, my initiation into the drinking habits of lifeboat crews. After that I was on my own, the intention being that I would remain an Assistant Inspector for my first year, getting to know the ropes. But with the luck that always seemed to follow me around - or maybe I was just in the right place at the right time - the Inspector I was going to work with was involved in a serious car crash. So there I was, thrown in at the deep end, with all the lifeboat stations from the Wash to the Isle of Wight, including the Channel Islands, as my patch. Of course, this was the coast I knew intimately from my Trinity days, and I spoke the same language as the lifeboat crews. Not as terrifying as it might have been.

Since I now had a shore job, I persuaded myself I should not use the title "Captain" any more, preferring to be ordinary "Mister". I was happy to be called "Captain" on board a ship, then it was my job. But not being Royal Navy, it seemed pretentious to use the title on shore. This preference caused some consternation amongst the local people. All their previous inspectors had been Captains or Commanders with some kind of naval rank. But contrariwise, when I told them I wanted to be plain old Mister, the comment was; 'You're not called Captain, oh thank goodness we have someone we can talk to'.

When I joined, I was very surprised at the traditional attitudes that prevailed in the RNLI, rather like when I started with Trinity. The lifeboats were slow and designed only to cope with the worst sea conditions. There was little regard for the changing pattern of casualties, or any kind of emphasis on speed. Part of my learning curve with lifeboats was to take out some of the new designs and see how they handled. One of these was the self-righting 37-foot Oakley. It looked very much the part of a traditional lifeboat, solid and seaworthy. After taking it out on a sea trial, I even complained to the designer that the boat would not steer properly. The response was: 'They are all like that'.

Now in my mind, if there is one thing you really need in a lifeboat, it is good manoeuvrability. But when you put the helm over in this one, you sat for ever, waiting for something to happen. Not only that, it was a twin-screw boat you could not turn short-round on the engines! How could you possibly work safely alongside a casualty with that level of manoeuvrability?

The need for change was very evident to me. But tradition ruled and lifeboats had always been designed that way. So why change? Speed was

A handful in heavy seas Though the Oakley 37 was built to take rough punishment, she was slow and difficult to handle. Her helm response was so slow you could count to ten before she reacted to putting the wheel over.

another factor that was absolutely vital. And I very quickly discovered that 8 knots was just not fast enough to get to many modern types of casualty in time.

Finally the RNLI took the plunge and imported a 44-foot steel lifeboat that had been developed by the US Coast Guard. It would do 15 knots. This was a major step forward, and whilst 15 knots was still not very fast, it was close to double the current speed. What a difference.

Here was a boat with a lot of power that you could really drive into the waves, a huge advance from the old boats that just let the sea take charge. And it was so manoeuvrable, you could make sit up and beg. I did several evaluation trips in it, and what a revelation. On one run, I took the boat to Holland for the Dutch lifeboat people have a look at.

We made the trip up-Channel in a freshening wind what was blowing Force 9 by the time we went into Dover for breakfast and refuelling. It freshened still more while we were eating, and by the time we left harbour, the cross-Channel ferries had stopped running the wind was so fierce. It was really wild out in the Dover Straits, but of course in a lifeboat there was not the option of saying it was too rough. When an emergency called, the boat had to go out, no matter what. Putting back was out of the question with lives at stake. Anyway the boat was under

US Coast Guard 44-foot lifeboat
Acquired on loan for special tests in 1964, this US Coast Guard 44-foot MLB was the RNLI's first fast-boat, though her 15-knot speed would be slow by today's standards. The RNLI built 21 of them under licence, naming them the "Waveney" class after the river where they were built.

test, and here were the perfect conditions.

The seas were chaotic out in mid-Channel, with the wind against the tide and the waves building up, towering over the boat in big, breaking crests. I tried to nurse the boat through the waves, but one went right over the top and carried away the radar scanner. With visibility close to nil, navigation became something of a challenge. We came across a buoy in mid-Channel, but its whole topside had been washed away, so it gave no clue as to where we were. Finally we sighted the French coast, and some eight hours after leaving Dover we crawled into Dunkirk, very battered and bruised. The harbour master there took us through the lock into the dock and said, first, that we were crazy, and second, he would not let us out again until the conditions moderated considerably.

Well we had no argument with that, we were too impressed that we had averaged over 6 knots in such extreme sea conditions. But that was

Designed to go where the prudent seaman fears to tread
The RNLI's 44-foot American lifeboats were built for rough seas, able to take this kind of treatment and more. They worked hard too. On station at Yaquina Bay, the US Coast Guard's hero USCG-44300 was involved in 500-600 rescue missions a year.

the thing about a lifeboat. Not only did it have to survive extreme conditions, it had to have the extra to go out and help others. After that trip we were pretty convinced this new design met the job-spec.

This was an exciting time to be involved in life-boating because this new 44-footer coincided with the introduction of small, fast, inshore craft, the RNLI's main response to the new requirement for speed.

Tradition went out of the window, but not without a struggle. It was quite a challenge convincing traditional lifeboat crews that these small inflatables were viable for rescues. So it became my job to introduce them to the stations and train the crews. I was training myself at the same time, a foretaste of the future. It was my first experience with boats capable of around 30 knots, my first taste of high performance. My strategy was to show crews the basics of driving and operating, then let them get on with it, promising I would be back in a couple of weeks to take the boats away. Of course they were so hooked, they would not let me take them away. I had no intention of doing so anyway, letting them find out for themselves just how good these new inflatable boats were. Small, fast-boats brought a lot of new young blood into the RNLI, and that had to be a good thing.

After a year of working on the coast, I was given the job of managing this expanding inshore lifeboat fleet, looking after the maintenance and development of something like 120 of these boats. Maintenance was a real problem, because the crews gave them such a hard ride. It was a tribute to what these small boats could do, but keeping the fleet in good order was a considerable challenge. A lot of these inflatables were working off open beaches which involved dragging them across sand and shingle, quickly wearing out the fabric bottom. To reduce this wear and tear, we replaced the aft part of the fabric with a piece of plywood. You would be right in thinking of this as the first rigid inflatable boat (RIB), even though we only rigidised half the bottom. It did not work anyway, merely moving the wear problem further forward.

The next step was to replace the whole of the bottom of the boat with a plywood section that resembled the fabric shape. This did not work either. We were putting a rigid section into a flexible boat, and it was just not strong enough. It was an idea worth following though, because in calm water that early prototype performed better than the fabric-floored boats. Development work was moved down to Atlantic College in South Wales - a perfect project for students already operating an inshore boat as a fully-fledged lifeboat station. It was a tough testing ground, with a rocky open beach, and it took something like ten prototypes before coming up with what was later to become the Atlantic 21 inshore lifeboat. Twin outboards and a deep vee hull made it a very successful concept, from which the modern RIB was developed for commercial and leisure use. The real key was the deep-vee hull that gave enough depth for the very heavy stresses these boats took operating in the waves. It was exciting to be involved in this type of development, with the terrific impact it had on the small boat market down the years. I look at RIBs today and think how far they have developed since those

The first RIB, or rigid inflatable boat
Inflatables were perfect for the RNLI's inshore work, fast and highly manoeuvrable. But rough treatment during launch and recovery over rocks or sand caused a lot of damage. Flat plywood bottoms were better, as long as the weather was calm. After much testing, it took the addition of a deep vee hull to perfect the breed. That's me at the helm.

early days, over forty years ago, from such very small beginnings.

My experience with small, fast-boats was growing rapidly. To put one of them through a prolonged test, I planned a trip from London to the Channel Islands. It was the kind of distance that should show up any problems with crew comfort or durability of the boat. Accordingly, two of us set off in this little 15-foot inflatable. Running down the Thames was fine, but once we rounded the corner into the English Channel, the weather took a turn for the worse.

A RIB in the rough
The deep vee hull was well-suited to rough weather, giving a more comfortable and safer ride.

One of the prototype early RIBS being tested at Atlantic college.

Now that we headed right into the waves, the virtually flat bottom on the boat gave us a very rough ride. We soon realised that we were not going to make it all the way to the Channel Islands and called a halt at Littlehampton. On a trip like that it was very easy to switch off into a sort of trance to cope with the pain and discomfort. Despite that, I will always be grateful to the RNLI for giving me the reflexes of how to evaluate what is happening to a boat and crew, even when conditions are extremely uncomfortable. Yes, of course, you wanted to get back to harbour and out of the rough seas. But the job was to analyse what was happening to the boat and how it reacted to the waves. It was a unique experience, going out in severe conditions when more prudent seamen would normally stay in harbour. My experience of rough seas was growing too.

I made the Channel Islands in a small boat a couple of years later, when the International Lifeboat Conference was being held in St Malo. Every four years, these conferences attracted lifeboat people from around the world, to discuss techniques and problems - and bring with them their latest designs of lifeboat. I was given the job of taking a prototype 17-footer with a hard hull across the Channel to the conference, in the company of a fleet of larger lifeboats. We stopped off in Jersey the night before our arrival in St Malo, where I had a lot of friends from both lifeboat and Trinity days. Over a beer or two, we plotted how to make an impact with our St Malo arrival, settling for a bagpiper on the bow of the leading boat. That would stir up the French. I was impressed too. Not only could the local people of Jersey find a bagpiper in the middle of the night, they found one prepared to leave with us early the next morning.

So there we were, at the lock entrance to the St Malo dock, our bagpiper playing his heart out as we prided ourselves on the great show were we putting on. What we failed to realise was that a square-rigged sail training ship was going into harbour at the same time, a much bigger attraction than our tiny lifeboats. Worse, she had an all-girl crew, which for the French spectators, was far more significant. Bagpipes were no contest for pretty girls decorating the yard-arms of a sailing ship, even if the piper wore a kilt!

Graduating from inshore lifeboats, I moved on to a spell at testing new designs for full-sized lifeboats. There was more time with a developed version of that American 44-footer, and I did a lot of trials

The Inspector of Lifeboats at work
Aboard the Walmer lifeboat Charles Dibden in 1960, one of 19 lifeboats that evacuated our troops from Dunkirk in World War II. Walmer got their first D-class RIB four years later.

The RNLI's first GRP hull
Built of glass reinforced polymer or GRP, this Nelson hulled craft was a test-bed for
comparing against more expensive wood and steel construction. She proved herself when
I took her out into Portland Race with breaking seas at 20 knots.

with a 40-foot Nelson hull that was fitted with all sorts of strain gauges.
This was the first GRP hull to be used in the RNLI, and the first 'lifeboat'
capable of over 20 knots. The idea was to take the boat out into rough
seas, and see what stresses a fast-boat hull could take. The Nelson hull
might not have made for the best lifeboat, but it gave valuable
experience of a fast-boat in rough seas.

Finding rough seas was never easy, because it never blew when you
wanted it to. Eventually I got the boat out into the Portland Race when a
westerly gale was blowing. Now the Portland Race, off the end of Portland
Bill, is a notorious place for wild, confused seas, particularly when the
wind is against the tide. We ran into these breaking seas at about 20 knots,
and the boat lifted to the first wave. Just as we got to the crest, what seemed
like a huge great hole appeared on the other side. I was convinced I could
see the seabed in that hole, it looked so deep. The boat flew out of the
water, then dropped like an express lift before hitting bottom, sending all
the strain gauges off the scale. The boat survived though, and I realised
that there was a lot more to driving fast-boats in rough seas than I first
thought. That steep learning curve still applies to this day.

Another very rough trip was down the Irish Sea in a prototype 48-foot traditional lifeboat, a voyage that proved to me the performance and reliability of traditional design in surviving a wild, Force 10 sea. This new lifeboat had been running trials out on the west coast of Ireland and had yet to encounter real rough seas in those Atlantic waters.

I travelled out to Rosslare to take over the boat for its run back to Littlehampton, enjoying a good night in the pub before sailing the next day. Up until about 11.00 pm it was just a quiet drink with the crew, who were from Cromer, out on the east coast of England. Then the place started to fill up, everyone carrying some sort of musical instrument, and the evening really got going. There was singing and music, and everybody in the room had to do a turn. When the Cromer boys got onto the table with their traditional clog dancing, it brought the house down.

Overnight, the wind had been freshening, and the plan was to leave later in the day, making an overnight run down to Land's End, then head up-Channel. As we left Rosslare, there was a nasty, confused sea generated by a very strong north-westerly wind and the strong tides. It was only as we moved out clear of the land that we got a full measure of the scale of seas running. The further out we went, the worse it got. Then we hit the full force of the wind roaring down the Irish Sea. Virtually the whole crew were seasick, and I spent that night on the wheel, for once in my life just somehow not succumbing.

It was a wild ride in those huge seas, so big I suddenly realised why they put windows in the roof of the wheelhouse. When the boat was on the back of a wave, I could look up and see the next looming crest breaking astern in the pale moonlight. It was scary and exciting at the same time, the boat giving a lot of confidence. Most of that night I was on a complete high, singing out loud as I steered the boat down the waves.

Still today, with long experience of rough seas, that trip stands out as one of the most exciting. But that's what confidence in the boat does, turn really rough seas into a tremendous experience. In most boats you are just too scared to appreciate the conditions.

Next morning we made our landfall off Land's End for the icing on the cake. Despite running hard across the tides from Rosslare, our course was absolutely spot-on. That was a real feat in those days, for we were navigating on just a compass and a watch. There were none of the sophisticated electronics that lifeboats have today.

I could never understand why the RNLI did not fit their boats with electronics. Even back in Trinity House we had used the Decca Navigator, and radar was now commonplace in smaller craft. But there seemed a great reluctance in the RNLI to move forward. The argument was always that in extreme conditions, tried and tested methods were the only way to go. It was not appreciated that modern navigation systems could actually make operations safer. Or that it could help locate casualties out on the open ocean. Local knowledge was deemed the key to lifeboat navigation, and that is how it stayed for a very long time.

Voyages like that Irish Sea trip kindled a renewed interest in small boat navigation techniques, and I became quite skilled at them. As the Inspector it was always my job to take a new lifeboat around the coast to its designated station, which made for further interesting voyages.

When we left Cowes with the new lifeboat for Newquay in Wales it was thick fog. But of course, in the RNLI tradition of sailing whatever the weather, we headed off. It was tricky in the fog, navigating down the Solent and out through the Needles Channel, but with planning before-hand and making sure that the crew steered an accurate course, we made it without mishap. Although this was slow speed running, it was to be an experience that stood me in good stead in navigating racing powerboats. It had a similar approach to the use, or should I say non-use, of electronic systems.

The Newquay trip was memorable for another reason. It was blowing hard from the northwest when we rounded Land's End, heading up to Padstow for a refuelling stop before the final run to Newquay. As we were off the other Newquay, the one in Cornwall, the Coastguard called us up to say a fisherman had been washed off the rocks, and requested we carry out a search. Newquay was a wide curving bay, with huge breakers crashing into its shallow waters. If the casualty was sighted in the breakers, we would have attempted a rescue.

My plan was to stay just outside the breakers, prowling up and down keeping a sharp lookout, in parallel with search teams on the shore. The whole crew were on deck, staring shorewards, when I suddenly became aware it was dark. I glanced round to seaward, and there was a towering wall of water, virtually alongside us, with the sun shining weakly through it. You knew when you saw the sun shining through a wave that you were likely to be in serious trouble. But there was not a lot I could do. Back then, traditional lifeboats still had a poor steering response, so we just had to watch this wall of water coming towards us. It must have been at least 25 feet high and the top was starting to break. I had visions of this wave picking us up and rolling the boat into the shore, turning us into another casualty statistic. Sure enough, we rose on the wave like a jet lifting off, passed through the crest and watched it crash down just to leeward of us. It was a very narrow escape, and a salutary lesson that there were always waves out there that were bigger, sometimes much bigger than the average, and that you needed to allow good safety margins for them. I guess it would have been called a "rogue wave", a term I disliked because I should have expected one in those conditions. I knew there would be others lurking out there. You just hoped that most of the time you would not meet up with one.

The excitement of that trip did not finish with the big wave experience. We had to make Padstow for fuel, and the Doom Bar at the Padstow entrance has an evil reputation that reflects its name. We ran in over the bar with big breaking seas and close to a gale of wind behind us. I think it was the only time I have used a drogue to help steady the course as the boat ran in. All traditional lifeboats carried drogues to compensate for their poor steering control in following seas, and it did have a remarkable effect. It was as though some external force had taken over the steering and was taking us safely into harbour. With experiences like that, you can imagine why seamen get hooked on religion. I certainly have to say that crossing the Doom Bar on that wild evening was just like a religious experience.

The worst sea conditions I ever encountered were off the north coast of Scotland in the winter. At that time I was based in the RNLI's London office, bogged down in administration, not something that excited me a great deal. One morning the phone rang. It was the Chief Inspector with, 'How soon can you be in the Shetland Islands?'

I had to think for a minute, responding that it might take 24 hours to get there. 'Well,' said the great man, 'you're on your way'. It was a more exciting break from paperwork than I ever realised.

At that time, the RNLI was experimenting with two new 70-foot lifeboats with full-time crews as roving lifeboat cruisers. The idea was to provide quicker response in areas where coverage was weak or dictated by tidal conditions. One was to be based in the Bristol Channel, the other in the North of Scotland. The Scottish skipper was ill and they

Faster boats, quicker recovery
Introduced in 1971, the Arun was the RNLI's first UK-designed 'fast' lifeboat. Capable of 18 knots, she had a prominent wheelhouse, upper steering position and carried a Y boat on top of her deckhouse. This one was based at Portrush, on Northern Ireland's Causeway Coast and named RICHARD EVANS after the RNLI's greatest living hero, Richard Evans of Moelfre, who twice won the Institution's Gold Medal.

wanted me to take his place. I could not think of a bigger contrast than sitting at a desk one day, to being lifeboat skipper in some of the wildest seas in the world, the next.

This 70-foot lifeboat had living accommodation on board and was mainly based at Lerwick in the Shetlands, with a cruising area that extended throughout the Orkney and Shetland Islands. That put it right in the path of regular gales that swept in from the Atlantic, where tides ran strongly from the North Sea into the Atlantic and back again. It was wild country and I thought of "cruising" these waters with a degree of apprehension. They had a fearsome reputation.

But first I had to get through the Uphelya celebrations that take place in Lerwick every winter. This involved a procession through the town and burning the replica of a Viking longboat. Accompanied by copious quantities of whisky, the whole thing lasted for three or four days. Quite a challenge, keeping the lifeboat active and the crew sober! With Uphelya safely out of the way, we set out to patrol around the Orkney Islands and back again so that I could get familiar with the area. Storms were forecast, but of course part of my job was to evaluate the new design in extreme conditions. The seas were bad enough as we headed south through the Sumburgh Race that lies to the south of Shetland. The plan was then to make the rounds down the west side of Orkney, past the Old Man of Hoy and into the Pentland Firth.

Pentland Firth is the two-mile channel that separates Orkney from the Scottish mainland, renowned for perhaps the strongest tides in the world. Some can run up to 10 knots at spring tide, so strong that if you fly over the area, it looks as though islands in the channel have bow waves. The seas are pretty wild even when there is not much wind, with strong eddies and breaking seas. The Admiralty pilot book is very definite about its advice: *This channel should not be attempted by small craft except at slack water.* Add to that a westerly gale blowing in from the Atlantic against the tide, and you might perhaps have some idea of the maelstrom you can encounter.

We turned into the Firth, and I had never seen anything quite like it. There was no pattern or sense to the waves. They came at us from all directions, first from one side and then the other. Like that giant wave off Newquay, huge breaking crests reared intermittently alongside, disappearing as quickly as they came. In minutes, we were punch drunk from the violent motion of the boat. Thank God it was strongly-built, because surviving in those conditions was difficult enough, and turning round to go back was not an option. At one time I drove the boat from the small open-helm station above the main bridge, thinking that if I was higher, I might be able to anticipate the seas better. Then a huge wave curled up out of nowhere, and the whole boat was underwater except the small area where I stood. I was very alone and very frightened, knowing it was time to get out of there. Even with one of the best and most reliable boats in the world, we were not going to survive if we hung around much longer. I headed into shore and relative shelter.

If I had not seen it, I would not have believed that such sea conditions could exist. It looked like the end of the world, and even though we went through it at probably the worst time, I really had not expected it to be so bad. The strange thing is that the Pentland Firth can also be very nice. Years later, we went through in a fast powerboat doing the Round Scotland Race, and it was close to calm the whole way through. It was much the same when we passed through there on our Round Britain record-attempt. With memories of that lifeboat trip, I briefed the driver, Fabio Buzzi, to expect the worst. It turned out to be a nice easy ride. To this day though, I would not take anything for granted in the Pentland Firth. Our lifeboat trip was not just a bad day, it was a very bad day.

From these adventures testing lifeboats and playing in rough seas, I was moved to Bristol, where I looked after lifeboats in the Bristol Channel and Wales. This was back to the routine of an inspector's job and I loved travelling through the mountains of Wales to some of the more remote parts of the coast. It might sound idyllic working with lifeboats, but it was really hard work. Arriving at a lifeboat station to take the boat out on exercise tended to be a big day for the crews. After going to sea and the serious part of the job, there was perhaps a meeting with the local committee people before partying with the crew, which of course, it was part of my job to join in. It was how I learnt the real truth about the politics of lifeboat stations. And believe me, dealing with pretty well all volunteers all of the time, there was always plenty of politics to deal with.

My favourite example was when I set up a new inshore lifeboat at Cardigan. After two weeks of training and learning to cope with the difficult seas at the river entrance, it was time to put the lifeboat officially on call. In typical lifeboat fashion, that was also the time for a party. As you might expect, Cardigan was also a focus of Welsh nationalism, so not unexpectedly it was around midnight that a deputation came up to see me saying, 'You have the name of the lifeboat station in English on the lifeboat shed, why can't we have it in Welsh as well?'

I did not see that as a major problem so I said, 'Let me have a translation and I will see what I can do'

Half an hour later they came back, saying that they could not translate the name into Welsh because back in those days they did not have the words to say "Inshore Lifeboat". So of course, we left just the English version on the shed. But at least honour was satisfied. (Nowadays, with all the science-fiction technology we have around, I could just punch it into my computer and see what it says. *Draeth Bywydfad* looks very convincing.)

It was a tiring job, but I became frustrated with the way it was changing. At first I had been exasperated by the traditional approach, and the slow speed of the boats. Now I was vexed by the way the job was controlled. When I started, if I found a problem at a lifeboat station, I worked out a solution and got it sorted, letting head office in London know. I was free to make changes and get on with the job. But now I had to ask head office for permission before I did virtually anything, and began to feel I was little more than a messenger boy.

I suppose I could have carried on, accepting this situation until I picked up my pension. But it was not what I wanted out of the job, and it was certainly not my style. That, and the lack of progress bringing lifeboat designs into line with modern technology, was making me increasingly frustrated.

It was time to move on. But where to? Life-boating did not really qualify me for much else. I thought and thought. Then I realised I had already found a route forward.

CHAPTER 5

WORKING WITH WORDS

The catalyst for making a move came from people I knew through the Mumbles Lifeboat in South Wales. They were in the fish business, buying and selling fish wholesale, mainly the more expensive types: lobsters, prawns, crabs and oysters. They wanted me involved because through my lifeboat work I had contacts with lots of inshore fishermen around the coasts of Wales. My job would be to go around and negotiate buying catches as they came ashore.

I can't say that the fish business had immediate appeal. But it was an interesting move into the commercial world. Their offer looked good, so I decided to make the move, a decision reinforced by a couple of sidelines I had worked on whilst I was with the RNLI. One was writing, the other was doing survey work on small boats. I knew I could not afford to jump into either of these careers full-time, but combined with interesting earnings from the fish business, it seemed a good way to soften the break from the security of the RNLI. With children at school and a home to support, I needed money, and I was not convinced that writing and survey work were a reliable enough source of income. The fish business was a good way to bridge the gap. Maybe it was the "life begins at forty" syndrome, but I was not sure that I wanted to be working for other people all my life. It was a step towards being my own master.

The writing started by accident. I think we all want to write a book, and I was keen because my father had written a couple. As a failed English student though, writing was not one of my best skills. Up until this point, the most I had written were reports on board ship, or for the RNLI. Writing a book seemed like a distant possibility. Then I saw a letter in *Motor Boat & Yachting* magazine from someone who was writing a book about handling powerboats in rough seas and wanted anyone with experience of them to make contact. Well, I probably had unique experience of driving boats in rough seas, so I got in touch. We arranged to meet and discuss the possibilities, where I quickly recognised he only wanted to pick my brains, then use my experience in his book. I was not inclined to give away my hard-won experience just like that, and I recognised that he actually knew very little. I proposed that we should collaborate on the book and share the proceeds. He went away to think about it, and I thought that was the last of him.

A few weeks later, a letter arrived from Adlard Coles, the book publishers. It explained that after meeting with me, the other guy had backed out of writing it. They invited me to take it over, and a contract was even included with the letter. So there I was with a contract to write a book, without having written anything of any length before. It was a dream start to a writing career, scary and exciting because I still had to do the writing. As I was land-based in the RNLI's London office at the time, I had the evenings to myself to get my head down and write. Besides, when you knew a subject from personal experience it really was quite easy, just something you had to keep on at. It took about six months for the book to come together. I don't think the RNLI were too happy, but as it was in my own time there was not a lot they could say.

The book was published over a year later and got pretty good reviews. The one I remember in particular was by the doyen of yachting editors, Bernard Hayman, editor of *Yachting World*. He started his review by saying 'I hate this book... '. Well, that seemed like the end of a promising career in writing. Then I read on and he said, '... because it kept me awake all night'. I think the book did reasonably well, simply because no one had had the experience to write about the subject before.

Powerboats in Rough Seas was exciting to write, and hard work. Whilst you may have had the experience, you still had to translate your book into words. Then when the work was done and the parcel arrived in the post, suddenly you realised it was actually your book, real and alive, in print. You put so much emotional energy into it and you really laid yourself on the line. So yes, there was enormous satisfaction when it finally hit the bookstalls.

The publishing of that book came towards the end of my time with the RNLI, and it gave me the confidence to think that I could possibly make some money out of writing. I started contributing articles for magazines as requests came in, and my embryo career was up and running. Once I left the RNLI and started working in the fish business, I shopped around drumming up further work, and my writing career really took off.

Since then I have written 29 books, so I think I can say I am reasonably well-established. It still means every book is a new beginning and a challenge, but I think that is the exciting part. It holds the same thrill as going out in rough seas, because you start from scratch every time. Writing is a very lonely life, sitting at your desk and getting the words together. Then suddenly you are in the spotlight when the book is published.

The survey work was much more bread-and-butter stuff, but I knew that I could not just rely on writing to make a living. I quite enjoyed crawling around in the bottom of boats, and the work took me to a lot of interesting places where I met a lot of interesting people. It also got me into a bit of trouble, flying back from Dublin after a survey there. When I got off in Bristol, a gentlemen in a brown raincoat accosted me, wanting to know why I had been to Dublin. He showed me his Special Branch badge and I explained about the survey. He appeared again as I collected my luggage, which when it was opened for inspection had a pair of muddy boots and a hammer on top. Though they were the genuine tools of my trade, that took a bit of explaining away. So six months later, when the same guy was there as I flew out of Bristol to Amsterdam, I began to feel like a marked man.

On another survey of a fishing boat, I said that the craft was dangerous in its present condition because the bottom rudder bracket had been cut away, leaving the rudder unsupported. In my report, I was very categoric that this boat should not go to sea until modifications had been made, and that was that. Months later I went back to the same port and asked if they knew what had happened to that boat.

'Oh they went to sea and the rudder fell off after 50 miles.'

It's nice to know that you get things right sometimes.

When I left the RNLI and started out in the fishing business, I took the writing and survey work to a more serious level. It was just as well, because the fishing business did not work out too well. We were buying a lot of fish and moving it on to customers at a reasonable profit, but fishing was very much a cash business. You paid the fisherman in cash when you bought the fish, and hoped to be paid quickly when you sold it. We used air transport a lot to ship the lobsters abroad, and as high-value cargoes we insured them to be on the safe side. The lobsters were dispatched alive, packed in ice - until British Airways managed to leave two loads parked on a hot runway in Madrid. They were well and truly dead when they were unpacked, totally useless. Of course we claimed on the insurance, but it took a long time to settle up. Meanwhile that was our working capital sitting out there on that runway. Without cash, there was no more fish, and so the business folded.

This was a pretty difficult time in my life. My job evaporated just as I was getting separated and divorced. The writing and the survey work was building up, though I was not convinced either would bring in money at the level I needed. I moved into a small flat in Bristol, but one way or another life seemed to be going downhill fast. A new love in my life helped, except it still wasn't time to sit down and moan. So I set to, determined to build up my new businesses.

The survey work brought in a small but regular income. The writing, on the other hand showed more promise, so I did the rounds of the magazines trying to build up a demand for my work. I also went out looking for stories to report on, one of which turned out to be a voyage covering the Cod War for a fishing magazine. I didn't expect it would generate a lot of income, but at least it was a chance to get back to sea for a while. I had never been north of Iceland in winter, so the trip offered excitement as well.

The assignment took me to Greenock, where I joined the LLOYDSMAN, the biggest tug in the UK fleet. She was going up to the waters off Iceland to act as an escort for the trawler fleet that was being

When push comes to shove

The Cod War was very real and I was right in it. No guns were fired, but it was dangerous just the same. British and Icelandic ships played with each other, feinting, trying to cut each other off, eventually ramming each other. All this in fierce Atlantic storms in the middle of winter! In this remarkable picture, the British trawler ARCTIC CORSAIR has rammed and hit the stern of the Icelandic gunboat ODINN. THE ARCTIC CORSAIR'S bows were so badly damaged that seawater filled her fo'c'sle and chain locker. The ODINN was out of action for two weeks.

attacked by the Icelandic gunboats. The Icelanders disputed the right of British trawlers to fish within their 200-mile limits. LLOYDSMAN was not armed, but she was very strongly built, and the aim was to ward off the gunboats rather than actually fight them. This was a "gentlemen's war" and the gunboats used the tactic of trying to cut the trawl wires as their way of attacking the fishing boats.

There were a couple of TV crews on board, but I was the only journalist, so I found myself in demand from national newspapers wanting first-hand reports of what was going on. As it turned out, this "quiet trip" became very busy and I sent back several reports every day by radio. The fishing battles were one thing, the severe weather was quite another. On the way up to Iceland we spent some time in a Force 12 storm, standing by a French trawler that was on fire and drifting.

Force 12, on fire and drifting
In seas like this there was little we could do except stand by this French trawler we met on our way to "The Cod Wars". They got home safely.

They sorted themselves out, so we continued on our way. Up off the north coast of Iceland in the depths of winter is a wild place, where it would be a good day if it was only blowing Force 8. It was not just the wind, but the cold. And when the wind went round to the north, the ships iced up, forcing us to run south for warmer waters and safety.

It really was a crazy place to be "fighting", but that was what the politicians wanted. Some of the manoeuvres, like both sides trying to ram each other, were extremely dangerous. We would probably have been safer firing guns at each other. It was the gunboats that really had the difficult job. They were not built for this rough-and-tumble role, so their thin plating suffered severely when there was a collision. It might have been the "Second Cod War", but it was the weather that really won the battle. Needless to say, Iceland got away with it in the end, which marked the downturn of the British deep-water fishing fleet.

Another interesting job that turned up was to deliver a British-built 80-foot patrol boat out to Greece. That meant a journey of close to 3,000 miles, quite an epic. The boat itself was particularly interesting because it was the first big deep-vee hull that had ever been built. I had been in a lot of smaller deep-vees and was always impressed by the way they handled in rough seas. Nobody quite knew how this larger version would behave, but all went well on the early trials in the Solent. The Bay of Biscay crossing was uneventful this time, so it was in the Mediterranean that the boat had its first real test. We were heading to make a landfall in Palma in Majorca. Some 50 miles out the wind started freshening, the waves began building, and soon we were running in close to a gale. I kept slowing the boat down all the way to make the ride easier, then I remembered that with a deep-vee hull there was often a better ride to be had by going faster. The extra speed allowed the boat to span the waves and partially cut through them, rather than contouring over them. It was worth a try, as I wanted to get into Palma before dark. I opened the throttles. There were a few big bangs as the speed picked up, then we were running level and true on top of the waves. What a ride. 30 knots in a gale of wind was pretty exciting in a big boat, and we made Palma in just over an hour. I had learnt a lot more about the performance of big deep-vee hulls.

That boat was painted dark-grey and the interior was a big bare box, waiting to be fitted out in Greece when their navy took her over. She was flying the Panamanian flag for the trip, and had three Brits and three Greeks as crew. She looked pretty suspicious at the best of times, and when we went into Messina in Sicily, they definitely did not like us. An armed guard was placed over the boat while they searched it from top to bottom, and we were allowed ashore to spend the night in a hotel. They were convinced that we were smugglers or worse, so I think they were glad to see the back of us when we were escorted out of harbour the next day.

That boat, with her 2,000 hp MTU engines, ran so reliably that we made Greece in good time, passing through the Corinth Canal for delivery near Athens. I was paid off and decided that I would travel back on the Orient Express to London. The guy in the ticket office at Athens did not blink an eyelid when I asked for a single to London. That night I dined in the traditional mahogany-panelled dining car and on returning to my compartment found I was sharing it with a ship's engineer and his wife. We consumed a bottle of brandy or two that night and they left in the morning whilst I continued up into what was then Yugoslavia. After a stop-over in Belgrade, I found I was sharing my compartment with a Red Army colonel. Then it was on into Italy, where I was joined by five chatting Italian ladies. The whole three-day trip was quite an adventure, and I had achieved another of my life's ambitions, travelling on the Orient Express.

I did a similar delivery a few months later in another of those Don Shead-designed large deep-vees, this one a fully-fitted yacht destined for Gibraltar. The memorable thing about that voyage was when the propeller shaft parted company with the gearbox. The link coupling had the shaft on a taper secured by a nut that pulled it securely into the taper. When going ahead, the shaft was pushed into the taper by the propeller so it was securely locked. We had safely crossed the Bay of Biscay, but it was at La Coruña in Spain, giving the engines a touch astern to come alongside, that the shaft came out of the taper. We were only saved from sinking because the propeller hit the rudder on its way, which the stopped the shaft from coming right out. When we stripped the coupling, we found that there was no locking washer on the nut. It had simply unscrewed itself on the long run across the Bay.

Later on that same trip, we were hoping to have enough fuel to make Gibraltar after a refuelling stop in Lisbon. The gauge was getting dangerously low some distance before Gibraltar, so I decided to divert into Cadiz to be safe. At the time relations between Spain and Britain were at a low ebb over ownership of Gibraltar. Which meant a yacht registered in Gibraltar was not the most welcome of customers. Whilst we were refuelling, an angry crowd gathered on the quay shouting *'Bastardo Inglese'*. I was quite glad to get the fuel and run before anything worse happened.

A problem of a different sort was on the delivery of a pre-war Danish icebreaker. Once more the destination was Greece, where the ship would be converted into a yacht. It had not been to sea for a couple of years, and the problems showed up as soon as we got out to sea from Milford Haven. The engine choked and we found that there was a huge amount of dirt coming through from the fuel tanks. All that time lying idle, the tanks had corroded. Out in the open sea, the movement of the ship had stirred up the years of sludge and the filters could not cope. We made it back to port using up the last of the filters we had on board. It took a few weeks before the tanks were cleaned out and we could set off again.

I enjoyed these delivery trips, as they were always a learning curve to add to my experience. Years later, I delivered a 30-metre, 50-knot yacht out to Spain, at the same time acting as trials skipper for the shipyard. On the first trial trip to sea, I quickly found that the gearbox controls had been installed back-to-front, so "Ahead" was "Astern" and vice-versa. The engineer said it would only take a minute or so to fix, so I stopped the yacht in the middle of the dock. Five minutes later they were still tweaking, and without power we drifted into a supply ship that was alongside the dock, putting the first dent into the bright, shiny topsides of the yacht. I have no doubt that engineers have different time clocks to the rest of us. The delivery trip went well after that, except the short range of this fuel-hungry 4,000 hp yacht meant we had to go round the edge of the Bay of Biscay, refuelling in hops, instead of straight across.

Another delivery trip was for the landlord of my Bristol flat, who had bought a steel Dutch-built motor yacht and wanted it taken from Bristol to Le Havre, where he would take over and make the trip down to the Mediterranean through the French canals. Any trip down the Bristol Channel was a nervous one because there were so very few places where you could run for shelter at low tide. You felt a lot happier once you rounded Land's End and headed up-Channel. This was at also night, and our plan was to call in at Plymouth for fuel in the early morning, before heading across the Channel. We had just rounded the Lizard at about 3.00 in the morning when we could smell burning. Quickly the whole of the wheelhouse filled with smoke and we were fighting a fire we could not see. Where the very acrid smoke was coming from we had no idea, though we guessed it was an electrical fault. But turning off the electrics did not stop the burning. We ripped down the deckhead panels, trying to find the seat of the fire. It turned out to be in the foam lining of the superstructure, initially started by an electrical short-circuit. At last we got it sorted and the fire was put out, then we had time to look around to see where we were. Drifting down with the tide, we were only a few hundred yards off the end of the Lizard lifeboat slipway! If they had launched the lifeboat to come to our rescue, they would have run slap into us on the way down.

Back on dry land, I always rushed to get the mail when it came through the door of my flat. Mail bought the cheques, and balancing the books in those days was quite a struggle. I was making the classic switch to working for myself at the age of forty, and it was never going to be easy. I got quite skilled at identifying letters before I opened them, particularly the ones with cheques in them. Then one day there was a very smart envelope with a gold coat of arms embossed on the back that I did not recognise.

I opened up the envelope and there was a letter headed 'Buckingham Palace'! It was an invitation to a drinks party with Prince Phillip. Well that brought a bit of joy into my life, so of course I

My invitation to Buckingham Palace
In my capacity as a member of the Yachting Journalists' Association, the Duke of Edinburgh wanted to meet me!

accepted. At that time there was a newly-formed Yachting Journalists' Association which I had joined. In its honour, Prince Phillip was doing his PR job, making contact with all the yachting journalists. Money was still tight and I had a clapped out old Renault-4 with a big dent in the bonnet where a cow had sat on it. The invitation asked that if I was coming by car could I please let them know so they could send me a parking sticker. So there I was outside Buckingham Palace, in my best and only suit, when I got cold feet. You couldn't just drive into Buckingham Palace in a clapped out old Renault-4. I went round the Victoria Memorial outside the palace several times, plucking up courage to drive in. It was a great party - and just as exciting to drive out into the London traffic again.

Towards the end of this period, things started to pick up. I got married again, acquired two more children, and started my third book. A steady flow of writing work kept me busy and I had found a new interest - offshore powerboat racing. My excitement for driving boats in rough seas was replaced by the thrill of very high speeds. Not only had I found a new love in my life, I was building a new career. And I had a new sport, combining my love for the sea and navigation with the thrill of competition.

CHAPTER 6

THE HOT FIRE OF COMPETITION

It was just a casual comment. But it got me involved in a sport that was to dominate my life for the next twenty-five years. I was talking to Peter Trowel, who was with University Marine at the time, the company that was supplying the RNLI with its outboard motors. The conversation got around to offshore powerboat racing.

'Most of the racers that I read about don't seem to have a clue where they are going when they get out to sea,' I said. 'They just follow the boat in front, and when the leading boat gets it wrong, they all get it wrong. It can't be so difficult to navigate a fast-boat.'

Of course I was talking from my point of view as a professional navigator. To my untrained eye, all you had to do was to speed everything up a bit to cope with the faster pace.

Peter came right back and said, 'Well if you think it's so easy, why don't you come and navigate the boat we're entering in the Round Britain Race?'

Here was my chance, and in true form I was not going to turn it down. Peter was part of a team that boat-builder Dick Read had got together to take part in this new epic race - to be like no offshore race had ever been before. Most offshore racing back then in 1967 was probably not more than 120 miles in length, with courses close inshore. The only formidable challenge to boats and crews was the classic Cowes-Torquay Race. This new Round Britain Race was going to last for 10 days, with a race each day. It would cover some

My first ride in a racer
With its twin 350 hp Evinrudes running through stern drives, this Dick Read 32-footer did 40 knots in the 1967 Round Britain race.

of the most difficult sea conditions around Britain. Talk about starting at the top.

Well the boat was built, a 32-footer designed around the then new "ragged chine" lines that were supposed to be the latest word in sea-going fast-boats. The power came from a couple of 350 hp Evinrude petrol engines coupled to stern drives, so the top speed was a modest 40 knots. This was hoped to get more competitive when the really fast-boats had to slow down in rough seas, and we would all be more evenly matched. On a race of this length, reliability was going to be much more important than out-and-out speed. Fail to finish one leg of the race and there was no chance of winning overall, you were classed as a second-class finisher. Dick Read built the boat at Topsham near Exeter and before the big race, we decided that a trial run across the Channel to Guernsey would be a good idea to bed down both boat and crew. Plus it would give us some idea of what we were in for.

It was a fine day when we set out, and in three hours we made our destination for the night, right according to plan. So far so good. The return trip was next morning. But when we got up, there was thick fog. Well, we might have to cope with fog in the race, so this was to be make or break for me, my first and possibly last chance to navigate at high speed in a race boat. We decided to head for Alderney, then have a second look at things before heading out into the Channel. Our navigation equipment was a compass, a watch and a depth sounder. I made my plans accordingly. We sighted a few rocks on the way into Alderney, with the fog as thick as ever. Visibility was down to 300 yards. I was concerned about making the landfall on the other side of the Channel because I did not know the coastline too well around Exmouth. To reassure me, the local guys said that if I could find the coast, they would recognise where we were, then we could head in accordingly.

So we set out across the Channel, blowing the horn because we were crossing the busy shipping lanes, hoping naïvely that anything ahead might hear it. We did not sight a single thing on the way. Then, when my dead reckoning said we should be getting into shallower water, we eased back on the speed, switched on the echo sounder and crept in to make our landfall. It was a pretty safe coastline on which to adopt this tactic, there were no off-lying rocks or shoals. As the water shallowed, it suddenly went dark. There, just 300 yards away in front of us, dark cliffs loomed out of the fog. That was when the argument started. All the cliffs around Exmouth were a shade of red. These were red cliffs too, but the locals could not agree which side of the entrance we were. To resolve the situation, I said we should head out again, motor along the coast, then make another landfall hoping for a more positive identification.

By now it was getting properly dark. As we closed the shore, there were lights ahead and a beach. But still nothing positive that our two locals could identify. Without a clue where we were, with this beach and lights in sight, we decided to anchor and put the dinghy overboard. The lights suggested there were people. All we had to do was go ashore and ask - a simple navigation tactic, and this was no time to have pride. The beach was deserted. Finally we found a man in a car, parked up in the road. We banged on the window to ask him where we were. He rolled it down.

'I don't know. I've been driving for hours in this fog and haven't got a clue where I am.'

So much for local knowledge. We eventually found a pub. Feeling a bit stupid, we went in to ask where we were.

'In such and such road.'

'No, I mean which town are we in?'

That bought some strange looks. It turned out we were in Budleigh Salterton. After that, it was not too difficult to find our way home by boat, not the best start to my career as a navigator in offshore powerboat racing. The fog experience was valuable though. One leg of the race had dense fog all the way. Once again, make or break for me.

When the race started, about twenty boats made it all the way up the West Coast of Britain, to transit the Caledonian Canal for the trip across Scotland. The next leg was to leave Inverness for the long run down the East Coast and on to the finish at Portsmouth. This leg was due to overnight at Dundee. But there was thick fog at the start, and fog forecast for the whole leg of the race. It became a real challenge just to find the start line. Somehow we got there when the flag went down. After that of course, the easy thing would have been to do what most of the other boats did, follow the only two boats that were fitted with radar. But they were relatively slow boats. So on the principle that if you followed you didn't win, we opted to go it alone, trusting to my navigation skills. We ran out of Inverness Firth into open water, planning to head east for 65 miles until we could round Kinnaird Head and turn south towards Dundee. But there was a problem along this North Coast - patches of rocks lying far offshore, which meant we had to set a course well clear. We would not see anything until we closed Kinnaird Head, where the chart showed clear water for making our landfall.

After something like an hour-and-a-half of not seeing a thing, I decided it was time to turn in towards land. My landfall point was some three miles inside the headland. That would give me a bit of latitude for any error in calculation, where I knew I could make a safe landfall at a steep-to beach. Once land was sighted, it would simply be a matter of turning left to find the headland. The rest of the crew seemed to have faith in what I was doing, but you can imagine how nervous I was about this landfall. Of course I tried not to show it, but as time went on I was stretched out, almost right over the windscreen, willing the land to show. Imagine my surprise when out of the fog came, not the beach I was expecting, but Kinnaird Head itself, with the lighthouse perched on top! The crew looked at me in amazement. It was the perfect landfall as far as they were concerned. And magic to see it come out of the fog after running blind for 65 miles. It was time to keep my mouth shut. With my navigator's career under scrutiny, I was not going to admit I was actually three miles out in my landfall. It was a close thing too. If we had been out by just another half-mile to seaward, we would have missed the headland altogether, heading out into the North Sea where we would probably have run out of fuel. As it was we carried on, now easy going, running from headland to headland with just a few miles between.

Our gamble had paid off and we came in first on that leg, my reputation as a very competent navigator climbing rapidly. I realised how lucky I had been, but when luck was on your side you grabbed it with both hands. As a navigator you were only as good as your last landfall, and people tended to remember the ones you got wrong more than the ones you got right. In the greater scheme of things we did not do particularly well in that race, coming in tenth overall. In our defence, we were in a slower boat than many of our competitors. At least we finished, despite having to replace a stern drive leg at sea five times. That on its own was quite an achievement, as anyone who has tried to change a stern drive at sea will know. With so much practice we could do it in just over half an hour, which must have been some sort of record.

Winners of the Cowes - Torquay - Cowes Powerboat race. Carlo Bonomi, Dag Pike and Richie Powers

Now that I was on the map as a navigator of fast-boats, I was next asked to navigate in a little Class 3 boat, a bit of a come-down, but it was racing, and I intended to take every chance that was offered. By now I was firmly hooked on offshore racing as a sport. This little Avenger 21 was fitted with a Volvo stern drive engine, not as powerful as its outboard-powered competitors. We still made an impact that season, finishing with several second and third places. During one race in the Solent, the driver managed to nose-dive the boat. Solid water came over the deck at speed, which shattered the windscreen. The metal frame of the windscreen wrapped itself around my crash helmet and I was bleeding from one eye.

For a while I could not see out of

Get it right,and racing pays
Advertisers pay good money to put their name on boats and racing gear. Even more if the boat is in the first three. Then of course, there's the prize money...

that eye, but we kept racing and came in to finish second. It was only when we stopped that the driver could see I was bleeding from my eye. Realising it was damaged, I got straight into my car and drove to the Bristol Eye Hospital. The surgeon who examined me said he had never seen an eye in such a condition that the victim could still see out of it. It was worrying at the time, but after ten days with an eye patch, I was fully back in business.

From that small boat I graduated up to a Class 1 boat, and the fun really started. HOT BOVRIL was a Don Shead design, built in cold-moulded plywood. It was a good hull, but let down by its machinery. This comprised two 500 hp turbo-charged Daytona petrol engines coupled to a single shaft. The idea of the single shaft was to keep the propeller as low as possible in the water. Unfortunately the torque from that single propeller meant that the boat was always leaning over to one

side. We had some success in HOT BOVRIL with one notable win, again in thick fog when we were the only boat to find the finish line. "Hot Bovril on a Foggy Day" was the headline in the Daily Telegraph next day, a great boost for the sponsors.

HOT BOVRIL was fast
Two big Daytona engines should have given her enough power. But the drive was through a single propeller, and except once in thick fog, the results were disappointing.

After HOT BOVRIL, I raced in a new gas turbine powered Class I boat. This was the first attempt to put a turbine in a race boat. It was certainly fast, but reliability was not its strong point. I don't think we finished one race that season because the engine would always let us down. On one occasion we were in a race that went up-Channel from Portsmouth, once again in thick fog. Yes, in those glory days' boats still raced in fog. We were running in the lead with the turbine really on song. We had located and rounded Beachy Head and were heading to the turning mark off Eastbourne. Then there was this almighty bang from the back of the boat as a 10-foot flame shot out of the turbine exhaust. That was our race run. We lay in the fog,

Don Shead designs make all the difference
Something of a legend in high-performance craft design, Don Shead grew up around boats. After racing an impressive array of offshore powerboats, Shead's own designs soon swept Europe and America, winning trophies across the board, including eight World Championships. His fame grew when he stepped outside the racing world into a commission from Tom Sopwith (of the English aviation family) for a 92-footer. This led to an order from King Juan Carlos of Spain to create FORTUNA, with a Lycoming turbine, the fastest 90-footer in the world - followed by a 56-foot runabout yacht for the Aga Khan. Since then, his designs have consistently put the Poole firm of Sunseeker on the international performance boat map. Mega-yachts, race boats, production cruisers, gas turbines, surface drives, water-jets — they do them all. This one is the Predator 95.

listening the tinkle of hot metal from the ruined turbine and the clatter of trains running along the shore. It was a long time before the next boat passed us in the fog. If only that turbine had kept going, we might well have been in front at the finish. As always with racing, if you didn't finish, you didn't win.

Class 1 put me in with the big boys of the sport, particularly the Italians and the Americans. In those days, all the serious racers came to Britain for the two big races that were part of the World Championship circuit. People had heard of my navigation skills and I was in demand. One day the phone rang. It was the then reigning World Champion, Carlo Bonomi from Italy.

'Dag will you be my navigator for the two British races, the Cowes-Torquay and the Needles Trophy?'

Carlo Bonomi
Carlo was my first encounter with the Italians and already World Champion when he invited me to be his navigator. In his Aeromarine-engined Cigarette DRY MARTINI he won 22 races and the 1973, 1974 World titles including the Cowes-Torquay-Cowes Race. "Cigarette" was the famous powerboat marque of American racing legend Don Aronow - named after the boat of a rum-running Prohibition-era gangster. The pedigree was certainly appropriate. Popular with the elite, cocaine runners also chose Cigarettes. "The King of Thunderboat Row", Aronow was gunned down in his car, creating a mystique for himself and the Cigarette stable that was recognised in TV's *Miami Vice* series. The high-profile murder generated a "bad boy" and "outlaw" image for powerboats across America, hyping the "Cigarette" name still further. The Shah of Iran and President George Bush Senior both owned Cigarettes.

Silly question. I had no hesitation in saying yes. This was the big time. But privately I was scared, wondering if I could perform at that level of competition. And at the high speeds at which these boats operated. When you raced with Carlo the world was watching, so any mistake you made became very obvious.

We started the first race off Bournemouth Pier, heading out to the Christchurch Ledge Buoy. At that early stage of the race we were lying fifth, the leading contenders sorting themselves out while we rounded a couple of the early buoys. Then all the boats in front of us headed off in what I knew to be the wrong direction, following each other like sheep. It would have been easy to follow. But I was positive they were wrong, telling Carlo to head in what I knew to be the right direction - towards the Christchurch Ledge Buoy. I could see Carlo's dilemma. Should he believe this new and untried navigator, or should he follow the crowd? Carlo, bless him went my way. We went into the lead and we won the race.

After that, my reputation was made. Some magazines called me "the best fast-boat navigator in the world." Who was I to argue? Ever since I was a boy, I had made a vow to be the best at something in the world. I did not know at the time what that something would be. Now I did.

But there was a downside. When you were the navigator you were only as good as your last landfall. And if you were at the top, there was only one way and that was down. I became really nervous about my navigation. But two weeks later, I was able to repeat the process. In the very next race, we jumped into the lead because the leading boats again took the wrong turn. I learnt my lesson. That you had to have faith in your ability. If you followed others, you were never going to win.

And that still holds today. I don't have any real magic about being a fast-boat navigator. Sure, you have a lot less time to make decisions and you are working in seconds rather than minutes. I just know that the two keys to success lie in preparation and concentration. On a fast-boat, there is very little you can do with your hands. You need them to hold on. Even reading a chart can be difficult. The boat bounces up and down violently in the waves, and the wind threatens to tear the chart out of your hands. All of which means that you have to work out everything beforehand, tailoring the chart so that the important details such as the race marks are clearly visible.

I used to spend hours before a race, poring over the chart and working out all the options. I possibly used only around thirty percent of my preparation work in a race. The trouble was trying to recognise which thirty percent was important. Since I never knew, I had to consider everything.

Then there was concentration. In the early days of racing there would be time to look around and even wave to the boats you were passing. At 60 or 70 mph, progress was quite leisurely. But as speeds rose towards the 100 mph mark, I realised that I had to be totally focused on the navigation.

If I found myself with nothing to do at a particular moment, then I knew I was missing something. When you were navigating with a compass and a watch there were plenty of clues out there to help. You just needed to be aware of everything that was going on around you, constantly checking what you saw against what was on the chart.

With modern electronic aids it is so much easier. The screen tells you virtually everything you need to know, which is why modern race boats only have a two-man crew. Of course the courses tend to be shorter as well, so these days the navigation is not the challenge it used to be.

Carlo asked me to race with him out in Key West after that. It was the final race in the World Championship and we had to win that race to clinch the title. Key West was a tough course for navigators because everything was low-lying. You didn't see things until the last moment and the course took the boats way out over open water to the Dry Tortugas.

That race day produced very lively seas. Up against us were six boats with the same hull and the same engines as ours. It was a hefty challenge and we were the only foreign entry. Carlo drove like a man possessed in those rough seas and it was pure poetry to watch him. Running for home, we were 10 miles in front of the next boat, though we did not know that at the time.

We were running so hard we were right on the limits of common sense. On top of that, as the boat used up fuel the ride became even more lively. A crack appeared in the side of the hull, and I could feel water entering every time we hit a wave. We kept going. Suddenly one engine faltered and stopped, just 20 miles short of the finish. A fuel line had broken under the strain and our race was run. The boat was swimming in petrol and I think we all passed out with the fumes. One of the first things I remember was the Coast Guard helicopter hovering overhead as they air-lifted Carlo and the Italian mechanic ashore, one with broken ribs, the other with a broken ankle. I stayed with the boat as it was towed in. With all the petrol fumes in the engine compartment it was just as well that we did not try to start her up again.

That race made me wonder whether this was a sport that I wanted to continue with. I had risen to the top and we had enjoyed a lot of success. The only way forward might be down, and Carlo himself was about to give up offshore racing anyway. I did a few more races with various Italian drivers, but the boats were getting faster and the sport

LADY ARRAN Fiona Bryde Colquhoun, Countess of Arran and wife of the 8th Earl of Arran was a top class powerboat pilot. In 1980 she was the first person to average 100 mph in an offshore boat and in 1981 was awarded the Segrave Trophy. Together with Lady Aitken she also won the Cowes-Torquay Ladies Award. But she is most famous for her electric boat achievements. On Wednesday 22nd November 1989, at the age of 71, Lady Arran set a new World Record of 50.825 mph (81.793 kph) in an electric boat named AN STRADAG, a name which in Gaelic means "the spark." This beat the previous record set by Miss Nickel Eagle in 1978, by a clear 5 mph. It was seven years before the Americans took this record back - with a speed of 70.6 mph in 1996.

was starting to get very dangerous. Boats were operating beyond the point of reason, with more powerful engines in what were relatively small hulls. One of the more interesting boats that I race-navigated at that time was an innovative three-pointer design driven by Lady Arran.

There was a lot of power in this small boat and it had tremendous potential. It was also the wettest boat I have ever sat in. At speed there was a constant flow of very heavy spray straight over the cockpit, making it almost impossible to see where we were going. I look at the pictures of that boat now and realise it was the two forward sponsons that caused the trouble. At the time all we knew was that something was seriously wrong with the design. As often happens with new ideas, the full implications of such a layout were not obvious on the drawing board.

There was a welcome change of pace when I was asked to navigate with a crew from the Argentine. Juan Taylor had a Hunt-designed 29-footer that was racing in Class II as a cabin boat. That seemed like a more gentle way of life and I did several races with the team in Europe. One of them turned out to be one of the toughest I have ever experienced. This was on Lake Geneva in Switzerland, not exactly an

Against fog and gale
Racing with Argentine Juan Taylor on Lake Geneva was more challenging than being at sea. One end of the lake was in fog, and at the other it was blowing a gale!

"offshore" race, but conditions on that lake could be worse than the open sea. On race day, one end of the 50-mile lake was covered in thick fog. At the other, it was blowing a gale, with very short, vicious seas! Well, we started at the rough end, but after 10 minutes of racing the boat came to an abrupt halt with a broken fuel line. The break was at the tank connection, and the two Argentine guys wanted to stop there and go home. I persuaded them that since they had come all the way from Argentina to race, they should not just give up after ten minutes. We managed to fix the fuel pipe and got the engines going again, working our way round the course in the thick fog and rough seas. We did not see a single thing on the way, apart from the turning marks of the course. No other boats, nothing. It was as though the world had stopped and we were left out there to circuit the lake endlessly. When we finally crossed the finish line, everybody was amazed. It turned out that only two boats had finished the course, which made us second overall and earned us virtually every other class prize. It just goes to show that it pays to keep going, even when everything seems a lost cause.

By 1975 I had almost given up offshore racing to focus on my writing career. I was still involved in racing - as a race official and in scrutineering. It wasn't the same of course. Then I met Fabio Buzzi.

Fabio was a rare breed. An offshore racer who not only designed and built his own boats, but raced them hard himself. Among builders there is a strong incentive to race hard because winning sells more boats.

Designer-drivers such as Don Shead and Don Aronow have been some of the stars of the offshore racing scene. Later on, Fabio even produced all the machinery and most of the fittings for his race boats.

Fabio Buzzi

A mechanical engineer with his own 'FB' design company, Fabio Buzzi began to compete in offshore racing in 1978, winning the Italian and European Class 3 Championships. The following year he set the world speed record for diesel boats at 191.58 km/h. With his own-designed Seatek engine he went on to win the Open class of the 1988 Italian, European and World Championships. He also won the APBA World Championship in Key West and came first in the Miami/Nassau/Miami event. Unrivalled, he holds 42 World Offshore Championships, 22 European Offshore Championships, 27 Italian Offshore Championships, 56 World Speed Records, the Harmsworth Trophy for 1993, 1994 and 1995, and all the main endurance records. His company, FB Design is the only one in the world whose craft have set world endurance and speed records in every existing class.

He could not get what he wanted from others, so he made them himself. I had certainly heard of Fabio's racing reputation, though mainly in Mediterranean races. I was introduced to him at the Genoa Boat Show and we hit it off immediately. We shared a similar and very professional approach to racing.

It turned out that Fabio needed a navigator for the second Round Britain Race to be held in 1984. Luckily for me, I was the chosen one. I loved these long distance races because you really had to work at them. They were the equivalent of ten normal races in ten days, extremely demanding, both physically and mentally. Best of all, navigating skills

WHITE IVECO
Another of Fabio's breakthrough designs, WHITE IVECO had four 500 hp Iveco diesels and was the first deep-vee hull in history to be fitted with steps.

counted for a lot, as I had found in that first Round Britain Race. It was also reliability rather than top speed that was going to win it, so the boats were relatively safe. My only worry was my advancing years. I was now over 50, and wondered if I could cope physically.

We were a truly international crew, three Italians, one Swede and me. The boat, WHITE IVECO, was like nothing we had ever seen before. She was a big, beamy 45-footer, fitted with four 500 hp Iveco diesels, each one with an individual shaft. That engine layout was right for long distance reliability. But it would not trim level with all that weight aft, and Fabio struggled to get it up and running. Never one to shirk from something new, Fabio cut the hull and fitted two steps under the engines, looking to generate more lift in the aft area of the deep-vee hull. She was a big, powerful wide-beamed boat, the first deep-vee hull

Ted Toleman Ted Toleman's 40-foot Cougar cat PETER STUYVESANT broke the elusive 100 mph barrier with a record 110.4 mph. A millionaire, Ted almost single-handedly kept the big boat class alive in British offshore racing in the early 80's. With Fabio Buzzi's team, I was racing against him when his red four-engined catamaran sank during the second Round Britain race. It was also with Ted Toleman, Richard Branson and Chay Blyth that I participated in an attempt on the Blue Riband for the fastest crossing of the Atlantic in 1984. Ted Toleman also had his Formula One Grand Prix Team.

in history fitted with steps. Today virtually all performance deep-vee hulls have steps like this. As I was to discover, Fabio had always been ahead of his time.

So we assembled at Portsmouth with 1,400 miles of racing in front of us. There was some pretty potent machinery lined up against us. Ted Toleman had a four-engined catamaran, there was a deep-vee monohull fitted with a pair of tuned Jaguar engines, and a couple of top Italian boats. For pure out-and-out speed we could not match any of them, particularly Toleman's cat. Our hope lay in consistency and the reliability of our diesel engines. We had to finish every leg of the race to qualify as finishers, and only then could we hope to win. We managed a third place on the first leg to Falmouth, in pretty good conditions. But rounding Land's End on the next leg, the weather looked much more threatening. Rough seas were churned up by the strong north-westerly wind promised in the forecast. This was our chance with our big heavy boat, though round Land's End the seas were so bad it was not a question of serious racing, more one of survival on the way across to Fishguard. Our tactic was to head up the Bristol Channel on the English side, then turn to get shelter under the lee of the Welsh Coast as we turned west again. At least with this tactic we would not be heading straight into the waves, as we would have been on the direct route. It would take longer, but we hoped for a better time.

Everything went according to plan and we picked up speed along the sheltered South Wales coast. Then it was north, through the very narrow Jack Sound, inside the off-lying islands. I was in familiar territory here, having made the passage several times in lifeboats. Poor Fabio did not know what to expect. The Sound was a welter of white foam, which Fabio interpreted as shallow water. In typical Fabio style, instead of slowing down, he increased speed and we went through like a cork out of a bottle. When we finally arrived in Fishguard, tired, exhausted and 40 minutes ahead of anyone else, Fabio announced that he had the best navigator in the world. He called me *Navigone,* which translated from Italian, means "big navigator". I reciprocated by calling him *Capitone* which I thought would mean "Big Captain". The Italian back-up crew fell about laughing. *Capitone* in Italian means "big eel".

I asked Fabio why he had increased speed going through Jack Sound and he replied, 'I thought it was shallow, so if I went faster we would draw less water!'

It was a new approach to navigating. After that Fabio and I had a brilliant working relationship, exactly the sort of teamwork a fast-boat needed to win races. There had to be trust between the members of the crew.

As we headed north on that Round Britain, the racing became routine, except in Scottish waters where the scenery was spectacular. By now we were winning nearly every leg. Toleman's boat had sunk in the rough seas on the Fishguard leg, while the Jaguar and Italian boats were showing dubious reliability. The Scottish waters were also familiar - from my earlier Round Britain race, but without the fog on leaving Inverness. As we headed south down the East Coast, we were well ahead on elapsed time. All we had to do was finish each leg in good time to take the prize. We listened to every beat of the engines, willing them to keep going and concentrating hard. There was big money at stake. Then the night before the last leg from Ramsgate back to Portsmouth, disaster struck.

At every stop, our boat would be lifted out of the water to check the propellers and rudders. We were by far the heaviest boat in the race, and as the crane lifted the boat from the water in Ramsgate Harbour, the weight became too much and started to pull it over. Everything seemed to happen in slow motion. I was still in the boat as the crane began to tip, crunching the boat with a sickening impact onto the dock wall. As it fell, it hooked on a big iron bollard at the dock edge, which stopped the boat from falling all the way back into the water. It punched through the bottom of the boat in the worst possible place.

The fall damaged one of the steps in the hull, the bulkhead above, and distorted the engine beds. It looked like our race was run. The other competitors, bless them, told the organisers that they wanted the race to finish in Ramsgate so that we could be declared the winners. But that of course, was not Fabio's style. Determined, he set to, and with a lot of help, managed to repair the boat so it could race by the morning. Incredibly, he had made up an aluminium sub-frame and was able to laminate over the damage to get the boat running just an hour before the start. Everybody thought we would just finish that last leg at modest speed, that was all we had to do to win. Again, that was not

CESA and MIURA
The brilliance of Fabio against the might of Lamborghini. With its distinctive wing for stability and four 1000 hp Seatek engines designed and built by Fabio, CESA was just unbeatable.

Fabio's style. And so we came in first to clinch a memorable overall victory.

I achieved another of my ambitions that day in Portsmouth at the end of the race. I had always wanted to step ashore from a voyage and have a band playing for me. So here was the band of the Royal Marines, and they were playing "Congratulations". It was a great moment and the party went on long into the night. Before the race Fabio had promised a night of Dom Peringnon champagne. Sadly, the Holiday Inn where we were staying had only two bottles of the stuff.

That victory got me hooked on offshore racing again and I became Fabio's regular navigator. He was developing the concept of four-engined diesel race boats to challenge the petrol boats. The high torque of the diesels created a new problem with gearbox reliability. In one race, gearboxes packed up one after another, leaving us drifting and waiting for a tow. Then there was the development of the Seatek diesel, with its promise of huge power from a compact and lightweight engine. When reliable gearboxes and these new powerful engines came together, they created one of the most successful and dominating race boats in the history of the sport.

CESA was such an exciting boat to ride in. She stood out from the crowd with her raised wing at the stern, another first from Fabio. The wing was put there to aid stability at very high speeds. Going fast, a monohull had very little contact with the water, which made it unstable. CESA was not only very fast, she was very reliable as well. That boat started nineteen races in one season and finished them all, winning sixteen and coming second when she did not win. With over 4,000 hp in a 46-footer, her top speed was around 125 mph. I never knew monohulls could go so fast.

We went on to win the prestigious Cowes-Torquay-Cowes race in CESA in 1986, the second time I had been in the winning boat for that event. It was a very tough race. At the start we leapt into the lead, only to stop after ten minutes as all the engines faltered. It looked like the end and we had thoughts of being back in Cowes in time for a nice lunch. Then Fabio remembered he had forgotten to turn on one of the fuel tanks. That remedied, we were off in pursuit with 15 minutes to catch up. By the time we arrived at the halfway refuelling stop in Torquay, we were in sixth place. A TV crew asked me what we would do on the way back.

'We'll just pick them off, one by one, and come in first', I replied.

Which is exactly what we did, overtaking the leader as we raced up the Solent to the finish. It was a breath-taking ride. Out in the open water we were running at 110 mph in a Force 4 wind, and running in waves over a metre high. Fabio had that boat trimmed so perfectly we hardly pitched at all, just riding level and true. I never imagined that a boat could run so fast in those conditions. It was pure fast-boat magic.

That race was soon after the successful Virgin Atlantic Challenge record and that day Richard Branson was riding in one of the other race boats. On the morning of the race, Richard bet me that his boat would come in ahead of ours, with a bottle of champagne riding on the result. Well we won the race, so there was no argument over the winner of the bet. At the prize-giving he presented me with a Shalnazar of champagne (equivalent to 12 normal bottles) in settlement of the debt. There I was, walking down Cowes High Street clutching this huge bottle of champagne. Crowds fell in behind me, thinking I was going to a party. I felt like the Pied Piper. There was all-round disappointment when I turned into a restaurant for a meal.

We went on that season to race in Guernsey where the World Championships were being held. By now, the format of the championships had changed, to be decided over three races at the same location in the same week. Races in Guernsey were always tough, partly because the strong tides stirred up some nasty seas, partly because navigation could be quite difficult - finding isolated buoys with little or no clue when you were getting close.

Venice-Monte Carlo
For the second year of this event, Fabio entered a very fast 4,000 hp gas turbine powered boat. Though it was quick, it was not successful, and our Japanese sponsor attacked the boat with a chain saw in disgust, after the race.

CESA was running on top form and we won the first race after a very close battle in the early stages. CESA was a heavy boat with a lot of power and that was the perfect combination for rough weather work. In that first race, just one boat kept up with us. Then, as we hit some lively seas around the distant turn mark, she flew into the air alongside us at maybe 20 feet above the water, landing very heavily. We stopped to check that the crew were OK and then went on to win without a serious challenge. One down, two to go. We won the second race in the same convincing fashion. So after just two out of three races, the championship was ours. Nobody could catch us, but we did the third race anyway, winning that too, to prove we were the most convincing champions ever.

It was another good time to stop racing as I was not getting any younger. At 53, I was beginning to feel the punishment. However there were more long-distance races being planned and I could not turn them down. One of these was the first Venice-to-Monte Carlo Race, two places which by themselves were a strong incentive to take part. There were few restrictions on engine size and power, so we had an even more powerful version of CESA, starting the race as favourites.

However this was one time when CESA was not reliable. On the first leg, one of the propeller shafts did not want to handle the extra power of the up-rated engines and promptly broke. That in itself was not too serious, we still had three more engines. But the broken end of the shaft went through the sump of one of the other engines. Speed dropped dramatically, and on our two remaining engines we crawled into harbour. When the back-up service van arrived, it took six hours to change engines and shafts. We just made the finish line before the allocated time expired. Now we had a mountain to climb, catching up. We won every other leg of the race, but still could not make up the lost time, arriving in Monte Carlo in third place overall. CESA had really been flying in that race. On one of the legs we covered 200 nautical miles in well under 2 hours.

The following year there was another Venice-Monte Carlo race for which Fabio entered a 60-foot gas turbine powered boat. With 4,000 hp from the lightweight turbine, the boat was fast. Uncharacteristically, Fabio forgot one little thing. The turbine only had a 40-amp alternator for charging the batteries. With the steering motor alone taking 50 amps, we ran out of battery power on every leg of the race, with my navigation electronics the first devices to go down. It was a good job that I had cut my teeth on basic navigation. And that I still did all my preparation on paper - just in case. Our driver in that boat was a short Japanese guy who put the money up. He did not speak English, so we had to use sign language. It was not a successful race and later he took a chain saw to the boat, in disgust at his relationship with Fabio. Never the world's most diplomatic person, Fabio definitely reacted on that occasion.

I did one more race before finally deciding I'd had enough - a 1,000-mile dash from Rimini on the East Coast of Italy to Viareggio on the West Coast. There

LA GRAN ARGENTINA -
Launched in 1994, LA GRAN ARGENTINA was universally acknowledged to be the fastest monohull in the world. Her crew of two sat in an enclosed cockpit modelled on an F-16 fighter jet - a totally independent survival capsule should things go wrong at high speed.

were fixed refuelling stops, three of them if I remember correctly, and I was running in a 38-footer, built by Fabio but not driven by him on this occasion. We made very good time until we encountered mile after mile of fishing lines laid out on the water at night. They were marked by lights which were very dim and at those speeds we did not see them until it was too late. Even so we did the 1,000 miles in under 24 hours, so we were not exactly hanging about.

Now the racing started to wind down, as old age took its toll. This was difficult to come to terms with, as by now I was well-established in the record-breaking world of fast-boats, which had taken over my life. There was however one run I did in a racing boat that showed me just how fast they were advancing in design and speed. This was Fabio's superboat, LA GRAN ARGENTINA, which he raced with considerable success in the American series with Daniel Scioli. I was in Miami when the local race was on and Fabio said, 'Come out for a run in the boat.' Well I could not resist the offer, so there we were, heading down Government Cut in Miami Harbour in this 50-footer with something like 5,000 hp behind us. It was certainly a recipe for high speed.

In the harbour we cruised at a leisurely 100 mph with me on the wheel and Fabio behind on the throttles. His voice came over the intercom, 'OK, now I am going to switch in the second turbo-chargers'. With diesel engines that meant a considerable boost in power, and the speed leapt up to 120 mph. We were getting into the really exciting speed bracket when the voice came through again, 'OK, now I am going to open the throttles.' At 120 mph he was going to open the throttles! It had to be one of the world's best throw-away lines. All I could say in reply was, 'What the f—k have you been doing up to now?' It made me realise just how much fast-boat design had progressed, that you could run a 50-footer at 135 mph in waves over a metre high. I did not think that monohulls could go that fast without losing stability and you certainly felt the boat was riding on a knife-edge from the jelly-like feel of the steering. That was really life on the limit.

CHAPTER 7

CHALLENGING THE ATLANTIC

Ted Toleman

It started with a mysterious phone call. 'Dag can you come and have lunch with me?'

It was Ted Toleman on the line and he lived in Essex. I was in Stroud in Gloucestershire, a long way to go for lunch, especially when I did not know what it was about. But never one to say no outright, I said to Ted, 'Give us a clue what it's about.'

Ted loves his mysteries and said he could not talk about it on the phone. Could not, or would not. 'I'll tell you what,' he said, 'I'll send my helicopter to pick you up.'

Well that was an offer I couldn't refuse. So there I was, travelling by helicopter to a lunch date I knew nothing about. The helicopter suggested that it had to be something important. I also knew Ted was heavily involved in both offshore racing and Formula One car racing with his Toleman Team. The helicopter landed in the grounds of a hotel. I walked in, sat down and waited for lunch.

Ted wasted no time.

'Dag I'm planning an attempt on the Atlantic record, will you join the team as navigator?'

Bob Magoon

It was another offer I could not refuse. The Atlantic record? I jumped at the chance. And it was a new kind of challenge to get my teeth into. I knew there had been talk about a new attempt on this record, capturing the prestigious Blue Riband for the fastest crossing that had been contested by luxury Atlantic liners over the past 150 years.

The Hales Trophy
Awarded for the fastest Transatlantic Crossing Eastbound

The Blue Riband of the North Atlantic Eastbound

Date	Ship	Line	Journey Time	Speed
1900	DEUTSCHLAND	Hamburg – America	5 days 15 hrs	22.84
1907	LUSITANIA	Cunard	4 days 22 hrs 53min	23.61
1907	MAURETANIA	Cunard	4 days 22hrs 33min	23.69
1929	BREMEN	Norddeutscher Lloyd	4 days 14 hrs	27.91
1935	NORMANDIE	CGT	4 days 3 hrs	30.31
1936	QUEEN MARY	Cunard White Star	3 days 23 hrs	30.63
1952	UNITED STATES	United States Lines	3 days 10 hrs	35.59
1990	HOVERSPEED GB	Sea Containers	3 days 7 hrs	36.65
1998	CATALONIA	Buquebus	3 days 9 hrs	38.88
1998	CAT-LINK V	Scandilines Cat-Link	2 days 20 hrs	41.28

More than one hundred and fifty years ago, the Blue Riband was a mystical honour, a streaming pennant trailed from the masthead of the fastest ship across the Atlantic. Fifty ships have claimed it since, especially the formal trophy commissioned in 1934 by British MP Harold Hales, "for the ship which shall for the time being have crossed the Atlantic Ocean at the highest average speed". Great liners such as REX, NORMANDIE, QUEEN MARY and UNITED STATES have all held the Hales Trophy since its inception. The UNITED STATES won the Blue Riband Trophy on its maiden voyage in 1952, averaging 35.59 knots. But high-speed liners were pushed aside by jet travel in the 60's and now other kinds of craft have beaten the record. We did it ourselves aboard VIRGIN ATLANTIC CHALLENGER II in 1988. But did not qualify for the Hales trophy. That record was broken in 1990 by the catamaran car ferry HOVERSPEED GREAT BRITAIN, at an average speed of 36.65 knots. In June 1998, another catamaran, the CATALONIA raised the speed to 38.85 knots and in July, the CAT-LINK V set a new record speed of 39.897 knots.

American Bob Magoon had tried it a few years earlier. He started from Portugal on a fast East–West run, but had to give up at the Azores. Only a few motor boats had ever crossed the Atlantic, tiny things alongside record-breaking full-size ships. Since they were only invented around the turn of the century, none of these were robust enough or had come anywhere near setting a record for the crossing. Now here was Ted Toleman, out to prove it could be done using modern technology, and *he already had the boat under construction.*

VIRGIN ATLANTIC CHALLENGER as she was to become known, was tiny by modern standards. She was a 65-foot long catamaran powered by two 1,000 hp MTU diesels. It seemed almost impudent to think that a boat of that size could cross the Atlantic, let alone in record time.

However the calculations showed that it could be done, though it would mean refuelling three times on the way across. Ted said that he had chosen me for the navigator role because he had seen what I had done in the Round Britain Race earlier that year. He also knew that I had open ocean navigating experience. A rare combination of qualifications, and I now had to work out how I could combine my navigation skills in both these areas to fast-boat navigation across the Atlantic.

On the way back in the helicopter, I thought about the problems involved. So far as I knew, there were very few people out there who had experience of driving a fast-boat at night. I had done it once or twice, for short distances, but never out in the open sea. It was one of those things that was not done. As for the navigating, well satellite navigation was still in its infancy in those days. The best available electronic systems were Loran C on the US side and Decca Navigator on the British side of the Atlantic, but they petered out in the middle. I could forget about sextants and chronometers, there would be no chance of using them in a small fast-boat unless we stopped. And stopping was the one luxury we could not even consider. Yet somehow we would have to find those elusive refuelling ships in mid-ocean - so precise, pin-point navigation was important.

I knew that I would have to do some considerable research into all this to find out just what would and what would not work in a small boat at speed. A very big learning curve was involved. Even finding the right route was not going to be easy, not considering the icebergs and fog that are usual features of the North Atlantic in the summer. Nor could we afford to deviate too far from the shortest route. Time and fuel factors simply would not allow it. Then there was the weather, a vital challenge that could make or break the trip. In a 65-foot boat in the open Atlantic, we wanted the best weather possible. A major part of my navigator's role would be to find it.

Cougar. Founded in 1969 as catamaran experts, Cougar Powerboats today is run by multiple World Champion Steve Curtis.

There was the boat itself to think about too. Toleman had taken over the ownership of fast-boat builder Cougar - and as they specialised in catamaran designs and wanted to use this project to promote their technology, this record boat had to be a catamaran. These were uncharted waters. Nobody had much experience of high-speed catamarans of this size. Nothing was known about operating power catamarans on the open ocean either. On top of that, the boat was to have surface propellers, reckoned to be more efficient than conventional systems at the speed we were aiming for. But this kind of propulsion was new as well. The whole project was a voyage into the unknown, with plenty of doubters to say it was not possible. Which made it exactly the kind of challenge I liked, with lots of research working out just how it could be done, or whether indeed it was possible at all and whether the risks were too great.

I made an important breakthrough on the navigation side when I discovered the Argos Beacon. This was a gadget that you simply bolted onto the boat. It had its own batteries so it was totally self-contained, fully waterproof too, as it talked to satellites that automatically sent the position of the boat back to a central monitoring station on shore. It would not give us our position on board, but it looked like a great back-up system if any of my electronic navigation systems stopped performing. All I had to do was get on the radio and talk to our shore base who would be able to tell me our position to within a couple of miles. This would be accurate enough for positioning in mid-ocean and for finding the refuelling ships. It would also keep the shore team fully informed about where we were, which was a good safety feature. From my point of view it was the essential back-up if all the other electronic navigation systems went down.

The list of problems that we had to solve continued to grow. Things like safety and being rescued in mid-Atlantic had to be considered.

What would we do about food and drink at high speed? What about refuelling in mid-ocean? What about high-speed toilets? At times the problems seemed insurmountable. One by one, we found what looked like viable solutions. Much of this problem-solving had to be done under the gaze of the TV cameras that were starting to take an interest in what we were doing, an added pressure we could do without.

Whilst all this was going on, construction of the hull was progressing in a shed in the Cunningham yard on the South Coast. Then came the day when the inverted hull was brought out to be turned over, so that work could begin on the deck. For the first time, we could first get a measure of what the boat would look like. The shell looked huge as it came out of the shed, though if anybody had to find us it would be a tiny nothing out on the ocean. This was the reality that we were going to cross the Atlantic in. Hanging there, suspended by its nose from the crane, we prayed that we would never see it in that vertical position again. How wrong could you be!

The bare hull was shipped to the Cougar yard on the Hamble for final fitting-out. The launch day was a private occasion and we took the boat out into the Solent for its first trials. It was just as well we were private. The highest speed we could coax out of her was just 10 knots - and she would not even climb onto the plane! We found that the problem lay with the new-technology

Surface propellers
Though they work only half immersed, surface-piercing propellers are more efficient than conventional drives.

surface propellers. These worked on the principle that the hub of the propeller was located at the waterline at high speed, so that the top blades were out of the water and only the bottom blades were doing useful work. The benefit of the concept was that you didn't have any drag from shafts and support brackets to create resistance, a vital issue at high speed. Getting them to work was a little more complicated, transitioning from fully submerged at slow speed to half out of the water at high speed as the boat lifted onto the plane.

What we found was that at slow speed we had to get forced ventilation into the top blades of the propellers to get the water to break away from the fully immersed situation as the boat started to lift. As soon as they were half out of the water, the propellers could work in their surface-piercing mode. We experimented first with a temporary ventilation pipe and found it worked. When we fixed a permanent solution, the speed quickly ran up to the expected 50 knots. That was more like it! At last we were on our way, that is until we filled up the fuel tanks to the brim to simulate the starting load. Low in the water, the boat was just too heavy and it would not lift onto the plane. It was back to the drawing board because we needed every drop of fuel those tanks could hold for the Atlantic crossing. Finally we found that with a delicate hand on the throttle, and all the crew standing forward on the deck, that the boat could be coaxed up onto the plane but it was a tricky balance. Another problem solved, but there were plenty more to come. For navigation I had decided we were going totally electronic. Like jetliners that also relied one hundred per cent on computers, that meant carrying back-up systems, and back-ups for the back-ups. To ensure the right degree of redundancy I wanted two of everything: two Transit satnav receivers, two Loran-C receivers, and two Decca Navigators, plus of course that vital Argos Beacon. I had worked out that we should be able to carry Loran reception for about

Two of everything
Electronics and water don't mix. So I doubled up on all our nav systems to allow for things going wrong. Everything had a back-up - and I had paper charts too.

two-thirds of the way across the Atlantic, even though its accuracy would be deteriorating the further we went from America. Then there would be a gap before we could pick up Decca reception, about 200 miles off the British coast, for accurate positioning along the final run home. Hopefully the Transit Satnav would fill the gap in between, though I had little conviction it would be effective enough at the speeds at which we would be running, at best it only gave intermittent positions. To cap this array of electronics, I had two radars. These would be our primary system for running in the fog that we expected off the Canadian coast. In those days electronic charts had not been developed, so I had work out ways to plot positions on the paper chart - never easy at high speed, but then I was not looking for the highest levels of accuracy in the open waters of the Atlantic.

As we made progress, so we went out on longer and longer sea trials, heading out to get our first taste of the Atlantic. This was when we realised what a small boat we had in a very large ocean. Running at night was a new experience, and it was a strange feeling being cocooned in the small pilothouse with nothing to see outside. It was as though the rest of the world had disappeared - except for the constant movement and battering from the waves, and the glow from the electronic screens. We realised that this wave-pounding was going to be our major

Richard Branson was born in 1950 and founded Virgin as a mail order record retailer in 1970. Not long after he opened a record shop in Oxford Street, then a recording studio, and Virgin Music was on its way to becoming one of the top six record companies in the world. The Virgin Group is now involved in international music megastores, air travel, mobile telephones, finance, retail, the Internet, drinks, rail, hotels and leisure, with around 200 companies in over 30 countries, including Virgin Atlantic Airways, formed in 1984, and now the second largest British long haul international airline. The attempt on the Atlantic crossing was to be the first of many record-breaking attempts by Branson.

problem, and we wondered whether we could stand it for three days and three nights.

As the summer of 1985 drew near, so the pace of the preparations increased - along with the public scrutiny. We learned to live with a TV camera watching our every move, all the time still searching for sponsors. It looked like the new Virgin Atlantic airline were very interested. They were, but playing it very close to their chest. The deal was getting so close that the Press were invited to gather at Gatwick Airport, with their passports, even though they had no idea where they were going. The sponsorship deal was only signed at around three in the morning, before the press conference. Then we all boarded the only Jumbo jet that Virgin operated at that time. This was when we realised how much of a showman Virgin's boss, Richard Branson, was. With 400 journalists on board, we took off and headed west, announcing the record-breaking project as we flew low over the Bishop Rock lighthouse in the Scilly Islands, our intended finish-line.

It was a brilliant piece of publicity, the big Jumbo flying at little more than 300 feet above the waves, its flaps and wheels down to reduce the speed. As we turned to head for home, there was panic at St Mary's Airport on the Scillies. Seeing us approaching at minimum height with our wheels down, they thought that we had an emergency and were trying to land. Their airport was so small we would have had a job to park a Jumbo jet there, let alone land one. Safely back on land, we had Royalty in the form of Princess Michael of Kent for the official naming ceremony at the Cougar yard in the Hamble. Then it was down to the final planning and shipping of the boat across the Atlantic to New York. With Richard Branson now a crewmember, the whole pace of the operation was speeding up.

New York was something else. We based ourselves up Long Island Sound at Mamaroneck, and made the final preparations for departure. The American Press did not quite know what to make of us, this little upstart British boat that was trying to take the record away from their last luxury liner, the SS UNITED STATES. We were too focused on studying the weather charts to be worrying too much about what they thought, and day after day as the synoptic charts came in from the Met Office in Britain, I became painfully aware of just what we were taking on. Trying to find a weather pattern that would promise slight seas and favourable winds over the whole of the Atlantic was going to be a major task. I knew I would have to compromise with the weather because it would never be entirely favourable over the whole route. We would probably have to accept a few hundred miles of adverse weather on our trip across if we were going to have any hope of making the record-attempt that summer.

After a month in New York, we still had no glimmer of hope on the weather front and were beginning to look like a lost cause. The whole project was beginning to look like a bit of a joke but I could not see a gap in the weather. Then finally, after six weeks of waiting, one series of charts started to look promising. We put everyone on alert, Richard flew in from Britain, the refuelling ships were put on standby, and 24 hours later with the weather charts still looking good, we took the decision to go. This was the moment of truth. Would all our planning and plotting work out in the unforgiving wastes of the North Atlantic?

You couldn't believe the turmoil that went on inside during the early hours of the departure morning in New York, when we were preparing to attempt something that no-one had ever done before. I thought that the long weeks of waiting for the

The Hudson River
Such high hopes we had when VIRGIN ATLANTIC CHALLENGER started out.

weather had destroyed much of our excitement and resolve. It was hard to believe in that early morning we were really off on the adventure of a lifetime, not just another exercise. It was only when we let go the ropes and headed down the Hudson River that reality dawned in the early morning light. We were really on our way and the challenge of the Atlantic loomed over the horizon.

Now all sorts of doubts crept in. Had I got the weather right? Had I

The Ambrose Light Tower is now unmanned so record timing is done by the Pilot boat.

planned my navigation carefully enough? Would the refuelling ships be where we wanted them to be? Most of all, untried and unproved, did we have the right boat for the job? VIRGIN ATLANTIC CHALLENGER felt awfully small that morning, much too small to take on the might of the Atlantic Ocean.

At the Ambrose Light Tower, we said our farewells to the boats that had followed us out. The crew on the Tower gave us a countdown to the start line as they were doing the start timing. Then we were on our way, roaring across the line at 40 knots, held back from going faster by the heavy weight of fuel on board. It surprised me how quickly we settled into out planned routines. Steve Ridgeway, who had supervised the building of the boat at Cougar, was on the helm. Richard Branson was alongside in the second helm seat. I was in the port-side navigator's seat and Eckie Rastig, the MTU engineer, was over to starboard, where he could monitor the fuel system and his beloved engines. Ted Toleman was there too, alternating with Richard. Chay Blyth was our other relief helmsman. Then there were three Royal Marines, on board to provide grunt at the refuelling stops and to hold our hands if things went wrong. It was crowded in that tiny cabin, with only seating for five and four bunks in the rear.

Our first point of action was five hours away, when we would round Nantucket Island. It was an easy ride until then, valuable time for shaking into our routines and getting settled down. The seas were almost calm, making it seem like a cruise along the coast. Around Nantucket Point would be our first taste of the open Atlantic. But before that were the notorious Nantucket Shoals. Of course we could have gone south and rounded the outside of the Shoals. But that would have added two hours to our journey time. We were trying to beat a record, so the shortest route was the one to go for. I'd spent hours poring over charts of the area, but saw no obvious route across the shoals and certainly no marked channels. The shoal depths ranged from nothing to 3 or 4 fathoms, and I thought that I could plot a fairly direct route by following the areas of deeper water marked on the chart. The worry was that these shoals changed constantly, making me wonder how much I could rely on the chart. If the channels had changed drastically, my backup was the swell that was always running over the shoals. I reasoned that shallow water ahead of us would cause breaking waves, which we could see and avoid before we hit them.

It was a high-risk strategy with the world watching. Any mistake would be the end of what I hoped would be a long and promising navigation career. It took an hour to cross the shoals, and by running at top speed we reduced the draft to a minimum, the lesson I had learnt from Fabio Buzzi going through Jack Sound. We made it and that was the first challenge over. It was only afterwards, talking to the

The emergency refuelling stop at a container ship in mid-Atlantic.

Canadian Navy's hydrographer, that I realised those shoals had not been surveyed for 50 years. No need he said, because nobody went there!

Only stupid fools like us.

Now we were really out in the Atlantic, heading towards our first refuelling stop off Nova Scotia. This meant we were still running up the coastline, although some way offshore now. The charts I was using were still for coastal regions, so there was nothing to show the enormity of open ocean that lay ahead out in the Atlantic. We lived for the short term, conditions were good, and our confidence levels were rising.

That first stop was some 20 miles off Halifax, Nova Scotia, where a harbour refuelling tanker had come out to welcome us. Sliding up alongside, they offered us hot food as well as fuel. In less than an hour, we were on our way. The first stop had gone off well, helping our morale tremendously for the long night ahead. We now moved into the high-risk area ahead. It was also starting to get dark. On the run up to Cape Race, at the south-east corner of Newfoundland, we could expect our first sighting of the icebergs which littered these seas, pushing south from the Arctic Ocean. It was already noticeably colder, and the cold brought fog. Now the easy part was over and the challenge was really beginning. Fog and ice were not a healthy combination when you were running at 45 knots, though we expected them and had plans to cope.

It had proved impossible to get detailed information about icebergs. You just kept clear of them was the general consensus. We were not so concerned about the main bergs themselves because they would show up on radar. What I was worried about was the small ice, the growlers and bergy bits that fell off the main mass and floated nearby. These 10-ton lumps of ice, lying just awash, could prove a real hazard to a small boat. But I could find no information about how extensive they might be. To get a clearer picture, when I was flying over the Atlantic in the Virgin Jumbo, I had been up in the cockpit to look down at the icebergs below. What I noticed was that the small ice was always upwind of the main berg. Of course the logic of this became apparent when you realised that the berg was well above water and so was affected by the wind. The small ice was always awash with no wind-effect on it, so all the small bits stayed upwind. This meant that if we passed downwind of the icebergs, we should be clear of the small ice. With this vital information and icebergs already showing up on the radar, I had to plot a course through them that would hopefully take us clear. It was night, so there was no way we were going to see the small ice. The radar was our only guide and it would not see the small ice either. My nerves were stretched. There was always a group of icebergs that congregated just south and west of Cape Race, where a current eddy held them up. It was an anxious time as we threaded our way through them, in the fog and the dark.

We were going to have to live with the iceberg risk for the next 500 miles. It would have probably been safer and easier to take a more southerly route, but we were trying to stick to the shortest Great Circle route, which was what brought us up here to the north. An earlier worry that had crept in to the calculations was fuel. That last refuelling stop should have given us a good margin to get to our next top-up, a supply ship attending an offshore oil-drilling rig on the outer edge of the Grand Banks. But now our calculations showed that we did not have enough fuel to get there. Frantic contacts by radio to the shore team in London persuaded the supply ship to move closer to us and shorten the distance. We made it on the last dregs of fuel left in the tanks, but now we were really worried. If full tanks were not enough to run the distance between planned stops, there would not be enough to reach to the next refuel in the Atlantic either. What had gone wrong?

We realised that at that first stop, the guys had stopped filling when the tanks started to overflow, which was normal. What they had not realised was that the overflow they saw was not the fuel itself, but simply surface foam frothing out of the filler. In fact the tanks had been far from full when we left the refuelling stop. It was a simple mistake, but one that was to cost us dear even with full tanks at this second stop. Now we would be hard pushed to get to the next stop because that second ship had come towards us, shortening the gap. As a result, the next leg would be longer. We were strongly tempted to end the run there and then, and go back to the drawing board. But of course, out there on the ocean, you couldn't give up that easily. So we set out from the Grand Banks into the cold wastes of the Atlantic, with hope in our hearts and worry in our minds. We had already covered the first 1,000 miles in under 24 hours, something that had never been done before. Already one record under our belts.

It was only 1,500 miles to the coast of Ireland now, but in our 65-foot boat it seemed like a million. From the forecast, we knew there was going to be around 200 miles of difficult seas ahead. Sure enough, we had a very rough ride into the night, forcing us to slow up until the seas died down and we could put on speed again. The lack of sleep was beginning to tell. I think that my voice over the radio must have showed my concern too, causing our London base to start thinking about a rescue. The next planned refuelling was from a tug that had steamed out 600 miles off the coast of Ireland. Mindful of our fuel problem, we tried to draw her closer to shorten the distance. Even so, it was doubtful that we could make it. We voiced our concerns on the link to London, to see what they might come up with. Outside, we had our first rendezvous with an RAF Nimrod aircraft that was using us as a training exercise. Flying low overhead, we told them about our fuel trouble over the radio.

'Hang on', they said. 'We will try to find you a ship'.

True to their word, they were back in 20 minutes.

'Follow us'.

Well, we followed as best we could, being a little slower than they were. Sure enough, a ship appeared over the horizon, stopped in the water and waiting to give us fuel. Such amazing service, to find a fuel station in the middle of the Atlantic! By coincidence, it just happened to be a sister to the container ship that had carried our boat across the Atlantic to New York. And as the shipping company that owned her was one of our sponsors, they had a vested interest in helping. First they tried to transfer three 40-gallon fuel drums by lowering their stern ramp. That was too dangerous, as we might have been trapped under the ramp by the swell. Then they lowered the fuel drums by crane, still tricky, but finally we had the drums on deck. We pumped the fuel by hand into our tanks. I thanked the Captain and offered to pay by credit card. They said it was a donation, so we went on our way rejoicing.

Now we could make it to the next refuelling ship. Our spirits rose, and we put on full power to make up time. Despite the drama and excitement, we were still on schedule to beat the record. Refuelling at the tug went smoothly, though again with barely enough fuel to make the finish, because she had steamed closer to meet us. With just 1,000 miles to go, it felt like we were on the final run. We knew of course, it was not going to be easy and the fuel situation was a constant worry.

This time it was our London base that came up with answer. Just 300 miles from Bishop Rock Lighthouse there was a Royal Fleet Auxiliary ship, stopped and ready to give us enough fuel to reach the finish.

The hot food and fuel they provided were very welcome. Now we could smell success. There was just 6 hours running left to do, and more than 8 hours in which to do it. But talk about tempting the gods. The weather had deteriorated, now blowing Force 6 with some big seas running. Fortunately the wind was from astern and we found a relatively comfortable speed at a shade under 40 knots, fast enough to make the finish in time, but slow enough to keep the ride bearable. One more time, I did my calculations to make sure we were running to schedule. We were just 120 miles short of the finish, running about 50 miles south of Ireland. The ride was still rough and we were desperately tired.

Then there was a loud BANG, as we crashed into one more wave.

I will never know if we hit something in the water, or it was one wave too many for the boat. Whatever, we slowed rapidly, and one of the crew went below to see what had happened. The starboard hull had split open along the chine and water was pouring in.

The boat filled fast. So fast that all we could do was get the life-rafts ready and try to get off a Mayday distress call.

Cocooned in our own little space on board, we had been oblivious to the world outside. Without our realising it, the whole country was watching our progress on television, the hot news of the day.

Rescue in sight
Branson (left) looks hopeful but Chay Blyth does not look happy.

Apparently, our report that we were set to beat the record was the top item on the Six O'Clock TV News. Then, right at the end of the bulletin, they announced that our distress message had been picked up. The country was on the edge of its seats, wanting to know what had happened.

You cannot imagine a bigger drama. My wife Cath was besieged by the local TV outside our house. In the meantime, we had put on our survival suits and taken to the life-rafts. We drifted off and watched our boat in its dying throes. It was like watching an old friend die. Now we had to think of our own survival.

What we did not know was whether our distress message had been picked up by anyone. Not knowing made it harder to cope and it was starting to get dark, so we prepared for a long night, hoping we could survive out there in the ocean. After an hour of being cold and wet, an aircraft flew low overhead. It was the Press plane that had been waiting in the Scilly Isles to record our arrival, out looking to find us. Then a ship appeared, and we knew that rescue was imminent.

The GEESTBAY did a brilliant job of parking alongside our two life-rafts. In minutes we were on board, enjoying a glass of brandy, with invitations to stay for dinner. Pleasant though it was, that was a problem. The GEESTBAY was westbound, back across the Atlantic we had just crossed. The clock was still ticking too. Both the Royal Navy and RAF sent out helicopters which winched us up to land us in the Scilly Islands, still in time for the record! There was one slight drawback. You had to do the whole trip by boat to qualify, so that was the end of that attempt.

The first people to greet us were Customs and Immigration. We did not have a lot to declare, just the clothes we stood up in - and me with my camera, still intact with the valuable film of our whole attempt. Just from my pictures in the life-raft, I made £2,000 selling them to a national daily as we stepped ashore. From St Mary's we were flown up to Portsmouth by helicopter, then hustled into the back door of our hotel to escape the Press waiting outside. Now it was midnight, welcome time for reuniting with family. Then a proper night's sleep, the first for several days. Our Press parade was next day, for the normal barrage of questions. After that, life took a long time to settle down again.

What an end to a year of planning and hard work! But we were not about to give up there. Even in the life-rafts, we had talked about how we would do it next time. We had come so close, sinking just three hours from victory. Against that, we had built up a huge fund of experience. It seemed a waste to let it all go and not make another attempt. First, of course, we had to sort out the aftermath of this voyage, claiming on the insurance and dealing with the thousand items of administration, handling the inevitable Press enquiries, it just went on and on. In our failure, we had become virtual heroes. Which taught me the lesson; that heroic failure generated more enthusiastic publicity than glorious success.

Then there was another phone call. Or rather two, this time.

CHAPTER 8

TAMING THE ATLANTIC

For glory alone
Though we were going for the Blue Riband, we were not allowed to claim it. We were not a commercial vessel embarked on business and we refuelled on the way across.

The first call was from Ted Toleman, but there was no helicopter on offer this time. He was planning another go at the Atlantic record and would I join the team again? Since I did not give up easily, there was no hesitation in my reply. I knew the time-scale would be very tight to design, build and sea-trial a new boat in time for the 1986 season. We would really have to get moving quickly if the project was to go. Ted did not offer much detail. He just said he had to get the team together first. I suggested that we should aim for a monohull this time, instead of a catamaran. He was noncommittal about that.

Then there was a call from Richard Branson, saying much the same thing. I assumed that this was the same project that Ted was talking about. Richard said that he had to get the insurance claim on the first boat sorted out, then we could go ahead. It was only a month later that I found out Ted and Richard had parted company in a big way. With never much love lost between these two, things had obviously come to a head when talk turned to the new project. Now both were planning their own record-breaking attempts. This put me in a dilemma. Obviously I could not be part of both projects. I decided to stay noncommittal until the situation crystallised. It was only when Chris Witty, Toleman's trouble-shooter at Cougar and now with Branson, phoned and wanted a meeting, that I had to make a decision. I did not hesitate in going for the Branson offer. It was the right choice, because Ted's project fizzled when he realised Branson was serious. He knew there could not be room for two.

One of the things I liked about working with Richard was that once he had made up his mind about something, he let you get on with it. He had appointed Chris Witty to run the show this time and the priority was first, to decide what type of boat we wanted, then find a designer and builder. This was in September. We had to have the boat on the water by the following May if we were going to find the right weather window. The designer was easy. Peter Birkett had worked on the first VIRGIN ATLANTIC CHALLENGER, doing a great job developing the hull structure and supervising the construction. That made it logical to use him again. I had a lot of regard for his talents and practical approach.

This time we wanted a deep-vee monohull. The catamaran had given us a very hard ride and we were not up to facing that again. The deep-vee concept was tried and tested, a conservative choice, but the right one to make, based on proven technology. To make doubly sure, we brought in Sonny Levi to produce the hull design, with Peter Birkett developing the structure and working full-time to supervise the construction.

With top-level minds working on the design, we brought in Pete Downie to develop and supervise the machinery installation. I looked after the electronics for navigation and communication, plus the

Sonny Levi signing the first Levi Drive 240 in 2003

Born in Karachi in 1926, the brilliant Italian-British designer Renato "Sonny" Levi began designing boats for Cantieri Navaltecnica. He first made his mark with his innovative A SPERANZIELLA in which he won the 1963 Cowes-Torquay-Cowes Offshore Race. As well as designing the hull for VIRGIN ATLANTIC CHALLENGER II, Levi is credited with the development of vee-bottom boats and the step drive, ultimately leading to today's highly successful surface drive that bears his name.

Brooke Yachts
Our second Atlantic attempt was to be a monohull, built in Lowestoft by one of the Navy's most respected shipyards. After a stab at the luxury yacht market, the firm was wound up in 1993.

wheelhouse design pretty much as before. With Chris in overall charge, we made a professional and able team. MTU supplied the power units again, their expert Eckie Rastig again supporting Pete on the engine side. Brooke Yachts in Lowestoft promised they could build the boat on time at the right price, so everything moved very quickly from that point.

The big difference was that our every move was watched by the Press and TV. At least we had been through the project once already, so we knew what not to do. This time we could rule out a lot of the dead-ends that came up, allowing us to concentrate on getting the job done the right way. On the electronic side, the available systems were much the same, though now I knew I could rely on using Loran C for position-fixing most of the way across the Atlantic. Once again the navigation electronics were from Racal Decca, which this time included their MNS 2000, a single unit that had Loran C, Decca Navigator, Transit Satnav and Omega all together in one package. With two of those on board, we should have had every base covered. Just to be sure, I added a separate Loran C receiver. If your two electronic positioning systems failed to agree, which one did you believe? With three systems you could go for the majority vote. For communications we had two high-frequency radios. At that time, satellite communications had not been developed to the stage where they could survive on a small boat.

This was an exciting and a nervous time. Exciting because we had a second chance to get it right. We had been so close before, in spite of the problems. Now we would build on that experience, trying hard not make the same mistakes again. The nervousness was because once I had analysed the first attempt, I realised how lucky we had been. We had pushed luck much too far - and I knew from racing that once you started to rely on luck, you were doomed to failure. So we covered every base, trying make sure only a tiny part of the success relied on luck. At least we knew where most of the problems were. We set out to eliminate them, one by one.

How we slept
The roar of the engines and the constant slamming of the hull against the waves made getting any rest almost impossible.

Key of these was our reason for going for a monohull. It was tried and tested, compared to the catamaran. We knew what we could expect from the electronic systems on board, particularly on the navigation front. We knew too, how impossible it was to sleep in those bunks on the first boat. Just getting into them was risky. First you were shoved hard into the bunk as the boat surged up. Then you slammed into the bunk above as the boat crashed down. With luck, you got to sleep in the short interval between the two impacts. This time we used reclining seats we could strap ourselves into, hoping to sleep aircraft-style. That was if sleep was possible. You were so keyed up anyway, sleep could never be high on your list of priorities.

Pleased that we were making good progress, we had the boat launched and made ready for sea-trials. This was in May 1986, right on schedule, and I had the privilege of taking the boat to sea for the first time. Eased into gear for that first outing, the boat responded eagerly. Then we were clear of the dock and out in the open sea, ready to open up to see what she could do. We agreed that we would go straight out,

Twice Royal
For the official Royal naming ceremony, Princess Michael again did the honours. Introduced here to Dag Pike. I was proud to meet her.

and give the boat full-throttle over the measured mile off the harbour. There could be no gentle approach if we were going to be ready in time.

That first run gave us 48 knots, so we knew we were on the right course. Fine-tuning the propellers gave us another 4 knots, so that, fully

The crew
(Back row L to R) Eckie Rastig, Dag Pike, Peter McGann, Steve Ridgeway
Richard Branson, Chay Blyth.

loaded with fuel, the boat managed 42 knots - everything reading just as our calculations had predicted. We had the boat, now we could get on with the rest of the project.

First there was the Royal naming-ceremony, with Princess Michael again doing the honours. This was doubled up to be the Press launch of the boat as well. And in the full glare of publicity, our lives were no longer our own. One of our duties was to drive the boat round to Liverpool, where it would be loaded on board a ship for the Atlantic crossing. Easy enough, but first we had a rendezvous with Live Aid in London.

The night before this function was to be our last night in Lowestoft, our project's home base. A quiet dinner at the Yacht Club seemed appropriate - just the crew and one or two others, splitting a couple of bottles of champagne to celebrate completing the first stage. Of course first one bottle, then another, appeared on the table as Club members sent good wishes to help us on our way. It became a full-on, rip-roaring

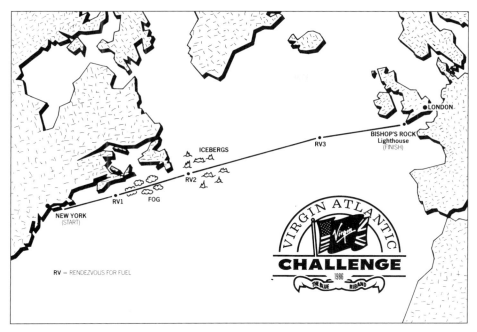

The route
2,800 miles is a long way. Out of New York from Sandy Hook, through the Grand Banks to the great iceberg field off Cape Race in Newfoundland, then by great circle to Bishop's Rock, the westernmost tip of Britain.

party. I might have got a couple of hours shuteye before heading down to the yard in an unwelcome dawn to get the boat under way. I stopped at the Yacht Club to pick up a couple of the crew, still sleeping on the floor. Then it was out, straight into the teeth of a gale, a rude awakening on our way to London.

It was not a happy voyage. Rough seas, sore heads and plenty of choice words. We met up with Simon Le Bon on his yacht DRUM at Tower Bridge, heading down river to Greenwich where another galaxy of Live Aid stars joined us for our promo runs up and down the river. With crowds lining both banks, it was a taste of what was to come, Richard Branson playing host to what seemed like half the British pop scene. Then it was on to Brighton for a much needed rest, before heading down-Channel to give the boat its first taste of Atlantic waters.

Rough seas, generated by the tidal race off Start Point, presented our first major set-back. Pete Downie, our engineer, had gone down below to do his routine check on the engines. Just as he came out of the engine-room, the boat hit a big wave. Poor old Pete went up, the boat went down - and when they met again, Pete had a broken leg. We diverted into Salcombe, the nearest port, where Pete was loaded first into the lifeboat, then ashore into an ambulance. At that moment we realised that our project was operating on a knife-edge. Just one mistake by any of us could have serious consequences. The accident had a sobering effect on the crew, bringing home the kind of risks we were taking. With Pete Downie out of action, we had to press-gang Eckie Rastig, the German MTU engineer, onto our crew. He was back-up we were certainly glad of.

This time round, we had a much smaller crew. Richard Branson doubled as money-man and helmsman. His cash had catapulted the project into the white-hot eye of public relations and he had proved himself pretty well on the first trip. Then there was Chay Blyth, who would share the steering, also there to raise the profile of the project. Unlike Richard though, he did not bring in any money. As our No 1 helmsman, Steve Ridgeway had done so much to make the first attempt work, his experience was invaluable. In the engine department there was Pete Downie/Eckie Rastig. I was navigator/communicator and weather man, and that was it. A professional team of six, with no room for passengers.

With the help of the Irish Navy, we practiced refuelling off Cork.

The magic of Cadgwith is alive, even in this photograph. You can imagine how it worked on me as a boy. And of course the boats were irresistible because you could walk up and touch them. It was so easy to picture them out on the ocean, doing those wonderful things that men did when they went to sea. You could feel it in the roughness of the ropes and the smell of paint. It was in the air too, in that sharp tang of salt. That same magic had worked its spell on countless sailors before me.

The siren's call of the sea cannot be denied, as I know many youngsters will experience in the future. Of course those old fishermen saw it working on me too. They knew I was hooked. I would go to sea and that would be my life. After all, it happened to them.

The RNLI was where I discovered the need for speed. When I arrived, the standard lifeboat was the Oakley self-righter. She handled like a brick and could make only 8 knots - far too slow when lives were at risk and seconds counted.

As Inspector of Lifeboats, I taught myself two things, handling boats in rough seas and handling boats that went fast. I had to push to get these ideas across. For instance the CHARLES DIBDEN was a pre-war design and very outdated.

This lifeboat, the WALMER was supplemented by an inflatable rescue boat I took there for evaluation, as I wanted them to have a RIB. I drove it around and left it with them to play with. A couple of weeks later, when I came to take it away, they would not let it go.

WALMER LIFE BOAT

When I started racing, it was nothing like this. Speeds were more moderate, and there was even time to enjoy the scenery. Not like the adrenalin rush of LA GRAN ARGENTINA here, which could do 115 knots and was more like a jet fighter than a boat. Because breaking records is more than the thrill of speed, there was a direct feed-back from designs like this into developing faster and better rescue craft. It made quicker rescues possible, shorter response times in getting to an emergency, a greater chance of saving lives. It served our modern life-style too, where time is money and we always seem to be in a hurry. Now wave-piercer designs are opening up new possibilities for high performance in rough seas - and I am involved with sea trials on one of the latest designs of this type.

CHRIS BAKER

This was our first Transatlantic record attempt, the experience of a life-time. Though VIRGIN ATLANTIC CHALLENGER felt like a big boat, she was a tiny nothing out in mid-ocean. She was the last word in technology though. Nobody had ever made an ocean-going catamaran that big before. Nor was there much experience with surface piercing propellers. It was only when we introduced an air duct into the top half of the propeller that we could get the boat to plane. Once we reached high speeds, navigation was critical and refuelling was vital. Everything we were doing with this boat had never been done before. Which made it exactly my kind of challenge. Could we maintain speed? Could we beat the weather? Would her hull hold up over 2,800 miles of constant high speed battering? We came so close, we were shocked when she sank..

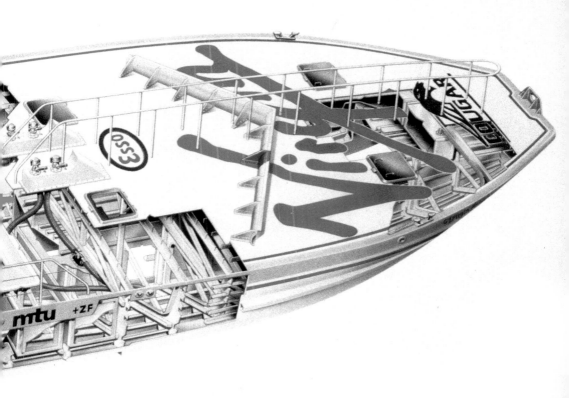

No. 1272   THURSDAY, JULY 3, 1986

DAG D

(with a lit

Britain may not be the greatest at football or tops at tennis; champions at cricket or knockout at boxing.

But when it comes to sailing, Britannia still rules the waves.

And with the entire country celebrating the record-breaking Atlantic dash of Richard Branson's Virgin Atlantic Challenger II, navigator Dag Pike has returned to his home town of Stroud with congratulations still ringing in his ears.

Sitting in his Lower Street office on Tuesday, decked out in blue ribbons by his secretary Gina Haines, Dag recalled the despairs and joys of the historic voyage.

"I have definitely had easier trips?" he said.

"When we started off the weather was calm, and for the first 36 hours there was quite a relaxed atmosphere on board. We were ahead of schedule, and in excellent time to take the record.

DISASTER

Then disaster struck — and the nation held its breath as the crew battled to drain five tons of water from the fuel tank following the second re-fuelling stop.

"It was very, very depressing. As the hours ticked by, we felt the record slipping away. We thought it was the end.

Last year, Virgin Atlantic Challenger I sank just hours from "home" — so the crew had already had one taste of failure.

The rest of the trip, though, was far from plain sailing.

In the early part of the voyage, the worst problems had been caused by one or two rather curious whales swimming within five feet of the power-boat.

But now the weather had deteriorated, and b

> DAG PIKE, navigator of the victorious Virgin Atlantic Challenger, gives an exclusive interview to "News and Journal" reporter Sandra Underwood.

the time of the third refuelling, the waves were blocking the view between Challenger II and the Irish Navy refuelling ship.

"The sea conditions were very unpleasant, and it was because of this that we decided to re-route the boat on a longer, but quicker route through calmer weather."

Suddenly, with the finishing line just around the corner, the sun came out and the skies turned blue, and it was full speed ahead for the Bishop's Rock Lighthouse.

URNAL

...ESTER COUNTY ADVERTISER

PRICE 17p

...DID IT!

...e help from his friends)

they passed the finishing line safely to a
...nt welcome from a harbour packed with
... and people, and several helicopters
...g above — one flown by Prince Michael of

...e welcome we had was fantastic. We
...ly realised how much the eyes of the world
... us, and how many people were willing us
...eed.''

...h champagne corks popping, and personal
...atulations from Prince Michael, Dag and
...ew — including Richard Branson — have
...eason to feel on top of the world.

SHRUGGED OFF

...culations surrounding the water-in-the-fuel
...y are shrugged off.
...it was sabotage, they didn't do a very good
...cause they didn't succeed'' — and no-one
...cares that the Americans are refusing to
...over the Blue Riband trophy to a "toy

...even in the elation of success — and
...g "the Blue Riband is a very great
...ement — Dag is looking forward to an even
... challenge.
...will be navigating a sailing ship across the
...c this winter in an attempt to take that

— but with his new book 'Electronics Afloat' to
promote, and countless celebrations to attend, it
will be a very long time before Dag's feet are back
on firm ground!

LONDON - MIAMI - EUROPE

The racing partnership with Fabio turned out to be a lifelong friendship. It was intense, professional and very successful - particularly when Fabio produced his masterpiece, *CESA 1882*, in 1986. This boat was phenomenally fast and utterly reliable - with unusual wings for stability and a winner all the way. In two years she won the Italian Championship and European titles, the Cowes-Torquay, Guernesey World-cup, World Champion American Power Boat Association, the Key West World Championship, and broke the speed record for the Nassau-Miami-Nassau. Later, in the hands of Stefano Casiraghi, she went out and did it all again. In admiration, Motorboat & Yachting magazine *selected CESA* as one of the hundred top boats ever built and her design has changed the face of offshore powerboat racing. Experience learned from her also enabled Fabio's craft to be the only ones in the world to set world endurance and speed records in every offshore class.

This was my 70th birthday present from Fabio, a breathtaking hydroplane ride on Lake Como in this gas turbine boat. In a previous life it had held the World diesel record, and for a sensation of sheer speed, it was unbeatable. Hardly surprising since Fabio was the first European to top 250 km/h in a hydroplane by the time I climbed into it - and it had won the Pavia-Venice Race at an average speed of 182 km/h. Talk about fast, the gas turbine power was incredible, and I needed to train on a smaller boat before I was ready. It was one of the most exciting boat rides of my life - before I started to hit the wash of the lake steamers. Still, I was doing 235km/h! I was on a high for days afterwards, probably because I survived. At speeds like that, it only took one mistake and you were history.

The complete opposite of power and speed, these Falmouth working boats are my latest passion and I just love racing them. So would any seaman worth his salt, they are the real thing. Originally designed for oyster dredging, they are heavy gaff-rigged craft around 30 feet long, with no modern equipment at all, although they do have cleats and winches. Everything about them is traditional and done the hard way, as you would expect with an original. WINNIE, the one I sail, is 107 years old. She brings me closer to the sea, which I have loved all my life. It's just man and the elements, reading the wind right, feeling it on your face and watching how it fills the sails. It's sensing the ocean, knowing what it will do and how to use the best of it - feeling more alive than any other activity on the planet.

Though she has not been in the water for ten years, *Virgin Atlantic Challenger II* still looks like a winner. She can still perform too, as she showed when her diesels fired up on only the second crank. She's slowly refitting in Majorca now, getting ready for perhaps more records. She's still performing and so am I, though these days I find consultancy work and being a marine detective for legal cases is where I get my excitement. Going to court as an expert witness can be as thrilling as 50 knots in the Atlantic during a Force 10 storm - fortunately people need fast boat expertise and the US Coast Guard chose me to write their Fast Boat Seamanship Manual. I advised the Singapore Police Coast Guard too, on high speed interception against smugglers. Now all I need is the Round the World Record.

After we left Salcombe, we carried on down-Channel in a more sombre mood, rounding Land's End towards the South Coast of Ireland, for a rendezvous with the Irish Navy. Once our record-attempt was running, they had bravely undertaken to do our third refuelling stop, somewhere out in the Atlantic. First they agreed on 200 miles out, which just would not fit our refuelling schedule. Then they agreed to 400 - still not enough. Finally they got permission to be on-station 600 miles out. For us it was the perfect location. We practiced refuelling off Cork that day, hoping things would go smoothly for the real thing out in the Atlantic. Then it was on to Liverpool, where the ship waited to take VIRGIN ATLANTIC CHALLENGER II across to America for the start of our epic adventure.

Our next meeting with the boat was in Halifax, Nova Scotia. It seemed a good idea to drop the boat off there and to drive it on to New York, giving us more experience over part of our actual record-breaking route in reverse. I managed to pick up a speeding ticket for the boat, driving around Halifax Harbour on a test run after it had been unloaded. I took it as a compliment. On the way to New York we stopped off in Boston to pick up Branson, who joined us for the final leg of the trip. Rather than risk crossing the Nantucket Shoals, I decided to take the boat through the Cape Cod Canal, a short cut into Long Island Sound. As we headed towards the entrance I called up the control station to say our top speed was 50 knots and ask what speed should we use to transit the canal.

Back came the reply, 'You can go ahead at full speed, Captain.'

'I said our top speed was 50, that's five-zero knots.'

'Oh, then I guess 15 knots would be about right, Captain.'

I think full speed through that channel would probably have emptied it. Whilst we had got used to operating this high-speed boat, it took others a while getting to grips with a craft of this performance. The shipping world was very conservative as we soon found out, the Americans regarding us as upstarts for trying to take the Hales Trophy - held by their SS UNITED STATES - in a "toy boat". We were under no illusion that we did not qualify for the trophy. Indeed, nobody attempting the record could qualify. There were no trustees of the trophy left alive to award it to anybody. Anyway, it was good publicity that people thought we might have a chance. So apart from trying to complete the necessary tasks to get the boat ready, we also had to make publicity appearances for parties and TV shows. It became a tough life of stretch limos and New York nightlife - with not a lot of incentive to

I studied the charts until I knew them by heart - studying any detail on board was almost impossible, bouncing along at 50 knots.

give up the high life and actually set out on a record-attempt.

That was of course what we had come for. And this time the weather became co-operative after only a couple of weeks. Once again I was nervous. Once again it was an early morning departure. During my racing career I had come to hate starts. You just wanted to go and get on with the job. It was only after you started that you could get into a routine and begin to feel comfortable. Before the start everybody wanted to talk to you, when all you wanted to do was focus on what lay ahead and get the job moving. All my life I hated waiting around. This

We left our berth in the New York dawn

start to our second Atlantic record-attempt was no different.

At last the TV cameras went ashore, the engines were fired up, and we left our berth in the New York dawn, once more hoping to cross the Atlantic in record time. This time we were better prepared. That did not make it any easier. Where was our send-off crew? One year on, the Ambrose Light Tower was deserted and unmanned, a victim of automation. So it was the pilot cutter that marked our official time of departure. Once more we roared off to our first marker at the Nantucket Light. We had got away with it last time, so I was prepared to push my luck, crossing the Nantucket Shoals again. Once more it was the right decision. But the repeat performance had one big difference - we were much earlier in the year. Our timing meant huge consequences for the weather along this coast. Though the forecast looked favourable as we cleared the Nantucket Shoals, the fog came down to stay with us for the next 800 miles.

Fog was prevalent along this coast. It was where the cold Labrador Current headed south and met the warm, moist air flowing north with the Gulf Stream. We picked up the fog as soon as we moved out into deeper water. Dense, but not thick enough to make us slow down. We could see ahead within our stopping distance. We also had to concentrate on the radar. I had my scope switched to the 3-mile range. The one across on the driver's side was switched to 6 miles, for early warning of approaching targets. Suddenly both radar screens were swamped with contacts. It looked like a rash on the screen, with over a hundred contacts within the 3-mile range. What to do? I did not think they could be ships or fishing boats, there were just too many. There looked like some sort of clear passage through them, so I thought let's get close to one and see what it is. We spotted one as it came out of the fog, a fishing marker-buoy with a radar reflector. Phew! Once we knew what they were, we could carry on at full speed, weaving our way through them. It was like running a video game, where you lost points if you hit one. On a more serious note, they were an early warning of difficulties to come. I knew the trip could be no easier than the last. I just did not know how difficult it would turn out to be.

At the first refuelling stop, once more off Halifax, the same tanker did a brilliant job, filling our tanks absolutely full. Now we were heading north, into iceberg territory again, all the time still running in thick fog. That whole night was spent glued to the radar. As we approached Cape Race on Newfoundland, there were the familiar iceberg shapes showing up on screen. In the pitch black fog, those blips were all we saw of them.

A moment of light relief came when we got a message from a British ship, heading out from the St Lawrence River into the Atlantic. 'Our route across the Atlantic looks close to yours. If you would like to stop alongside for light refreshments, you would be very welcome.'

It was a nice touch, but we were trying to break a record. Social moments had to take a back seat.

At the next refuelling stop, we were right on schedule. Another supply ship, servicing the Esso drilling rig on the Grand Banks. She appeared out of the fog as expected, and we tied up astern so that the fuel hoses could be passed over. Part of our plan was to have one of our own people on each refuelling ship, mainly to stop anything going wrong during our "pit stop". It just showed how wrong you could be.

Our refuelling went like clockwork. But when we let go and fired up the engines, we soon realised we had a problem. *Cough, cough, sigh,* nothing. Every time we switched on, the engines spluttered and wheezed. I wanted to call London with the words 'London, we have a problem.' Not being an astronaut, fame passed me by. We were too focused on the problem for levity.

Our hiccups were quickly diagnosed as water in the fuel. The supply ship had refuelled us from a tank that was over half full of water. Their routine was to replace water in their tanks as fuel was depleted, keeping them full for stability - not a problem because they had separators to filter the fuel before it got to the engine. We did not have that luxury. So now our tanks were full of half-water and half-diesel. Our only solution was to drain them into the bilges and start all over again. Even that was not as easy as it sounded. Our tanks were foam-filled to prevent surge.

The foam retained the water, but let the fuel through. That meant we had to wash the tanks through with diesel to clear the water. It was a long, slow process, all the time with the clock ticking. Our chances of the record were fast disappearing.

That was not the only problem on our hands. The weather was nudging us too. Logic suggested that our record-attempt should end at this point, that we should head for St Johns in Newfoundland before going back to New York for another try. Our weather-window was tight as it always was - and rushing up behind us was a big storm. Heading back would mean going straight into it - not the sensible option it first appeared to be. If we could get the fuel problem sorted, we could keep going to the east. But that meant committing ourselves to 1,500 miles of open sea. If we went east and did not bag the record, we were too far away for a fresh start. While we wrestled with the problem, Chay Blyth resorted to prayer. That did not offer a solution either. We decided that if we could at least get the engines running again - and there was still time - we would head east.

After about ten hours work, we had the engines running with what we hoped was relatively clean fuel in the tanks. Almost, but not quite. There was still water coming through with the fuel, building up in the filters and causing the engines to falter again. We stopped and started like this every half-hour or so, always hoping it would clear. We had been ahead of schedule at this stop, so we had time in hand. Now we were quickly running out of it. Replacements for the vital fuel filters were running out too. Our man on board the supply ship had been Steve Laws. To help with the fuel problem, we had taken him on board with us for the rest of the trip. He and Eckie Rastig did sterling work down in that hot and noisy engine compartment, constantly nursing the fuel supply.

We reported our fuel filter problem to London control. They tracked down replacements and managed to get them aboard one of the RAF Nimrods that was again using us as target practice. This time, it was no drill. Flying low, they dropped a parachute with the container holding the filters. It was a brilliant shot, landing just 200 yards ahead. Now at least, we could race non-stop again. I did the sums, and it looked as if we were still in with a chance. But we would have to push very hard.

We went on through that night, heading towards our rendezvous with the Irish Navy, now in place with our next load of fuel. This was going to be a night-time rendezvous, and I knew that the Loran C would not be very accurate so far away from land. I therefore planned to talk to them when we were about 100 miles away, so they could take a radio bearing of our signal. They could then work out a course for us to head towards them. It worked very well, and they shone their searchlight straight up into the sky, showing off their position as we got closer.

Once again it was a brilliant and efficient refuelling stop. With no added water problems, we were on our way within the hour. They refuelled us with Irish stew too, laced with considerable quantities of Guinness or Irish whiskey. It was a huge pot, and did wonders for our morale. Were our problems over, now that we were on the home straight? After our first VIRGIN ATLANTIC CHALLENGER experience, we could assume nothing.

With just 900 miles to go, the record was still a possibility. But now there was a problem with the weather. When you were planning the weather requirements a for a record-attempt like this, there was no way you could expect to get fine conditions all the way across the Atlantic.

Three days of fine weather across the whole three thousand miles of ocean was just not possible. To get away with it, you had to negotiate your weather-plot. And if you got it right, then things could be relatively fine wherever the boat happened to be during your crossing.

At any time though, quite close on either side of you, it could be really lousy, as we saw with the storm chasing us over the Grand Banks. Now, because of that fuel delay, we were ten hours behind our original schedule. That meant ten hours behind our weather schedule too. And ten hours was plenty of time for major changes to sweep across the North Atlantic. Our forecast ahead showed the weather was deteriorating rapidly.

What was now in front of us should have been behind us. But as we were no longer on schedule, we were out of step with the weather. And in a fast-boat, the last thing we wanted was head seas. I looked at the weather map. The team ashore had a good look too. Between us we decided we should detour around the worst of the bad patch ahead. It would mean further to go, but we would have better conditions. And as we were all so desperately tired, it seemed like the best thing to do.

Making that detour was really putting off the evil day. By heading south, we were skirting the bad weather, but to get to the finish line at Bishop Rock Lighthouse, we would have to cut across it at some stage. On our new planned route, the seas would be more from astern. This would give us a better ride and pander to our desperate tiredness. If you were tired you tended to look at things short-term, one at a time, like maybe the next fuel stop. Thinking ahead, the problems got bigger, so taking them one at a time was the best solution. If only. Unfortunately, I was the navigator and had to think ahead. At some stage, sooner rather than later, I had to get that boat to the Bishop Rock. And I could see trouble ahead - big, bad trouble.

As night fell, the seas got up. Soon we were running at full speed, with a Force 6 wind and waves that looked like mountains. In the dark, we could see little more than breaking crests. Something had to give, and the logical thing was to slow down. But with a record to break, we were running out of time. Against the clock, there was no room for manoeuvre. It kept ticking away whatever we did to make up time.

That was the worst night I have ever spent at sea. Can you imagine what it was like, running a 75-footer in rough seas in pitch darkness? All you knew was, it was going to be unpleasant. We tried to find a speed that would bag the record and give us the most comfortable ride. "Comfortable" of course, was a relative term - the snatched interval you felt as you held your breath between those bouncing, crashing impacts. Most of the time it was OK to run at around the 35 knots that we needed. But every so often there was a bigger wave, and the whole boat would fly out of the water. You knew it was going to be bad as soon as you went airborne. The engines would cut, and in the silence, somewhere close ahead, you knew there was going to be this monumental bang. So you held your breath, thinking you could not take any more. Then the next wave came, and the next. On and on and on. It was a long night before the seas moderated and we were through the worst. Afterwards, we all admitted privately we wanted to stop at that stage. The record did not matter, only survival did. But nobody wanted to be the first to give in. It would have taken only the slightest hint from one of us all to chuck it and cruise slowly home. But, as nobody said a word, we kept going. At last, towards daybreak on the fourth day, the wind relaxed and the seas reduced. Now we could really turn on the power and push for the finish.

The relief amongst the crew was fantastic, a real morale-booster. It was a great morning, we were running in more comfortable seas, and our ever-faithful Nimrod was overhead to see how we were doing. They called down on the radio for a position-fix, as their own instruments had packed up. By now I had the Decca Navigator component of the MNS 2000 up and running, so I was able to give them a lat and long. It was a very satisfying moment and I was relieved to be back in control of the navigation. Storming along, we were running at close to 50 knots, with the record definitely in our sights. Positive though this was, there was apprehension too. This was close to where we had failed the first time. I know I was listening to every vibration of the howling engines.

Any failure now could still dash the record from our grasp. The two on the helm were even more keyed up, totally focused on avoiding the floating debris that could have been our downfall last time. Tense and nerve-wracking, it was a time of absolute concentration. But underneath you could feel an easing-up too, a sense of letting-go as the finish approached. Experience reminded me that this could be a dangerous time. If mistakes were to be made this would be the time. Constantly, I kept checking all my instruments. Everything looked good. Now was the moment to focus on making the landfall.

I was confident that the Decca was doing its job and giving a reasonably accurate position. The horizon too was clear enough for a visual on the Bishop Rock when it came over the horizon. Even if the visibility closed in, there was the radar to pick up the lighthouse. It was fitted with a Racon beacon and would show up clearly. Touch wood, I thought I had everything in hand and under control. Then along came

Crossing the line, the wonderful sight of the lighthouse, right ahead.

Alongside in St Mary's. After all our trials and tribulations, we were about two hours inside the record set by the SS UNITED STATES back in 1952.

a violent thunderstorm and suddenly all my carefully laid plans were up the spout. In seconds, visibility was down to 100 yards in the heavy rain, with little chance of seeing anything. The radar showed rain and very little else. Sensitive to lightning generated by the storm, the Decca Navigator also decided not to co-operate. Suddenly, after 3,000 miles of ocean, we were running blind for the rocks at 50 knots. I could have cried. The Atlantic was not going to give up its record easily.

I could sense the others were starting to relax. Somewhere under that squall, they knew the end was just a few miles away. But I could not relax. Electronically blind and in the middle of a deluge, I did not know where the Bishop Rock Lighthouse was. We were just twenty miles out, and I desperately needed help. Fatigue did not help. I had been awake for three days and three nights. I blinked hard, staring out at the rain.

Whilst I thought we were on course for the lighthouse, I really wanted a visual - or at least radar confirmation. I was just about blurt out, *Slow down. This is crazy. We're running blind towards the rocks. I don't know where we are.* Then the skies cleared. I could see where we were going. And there was the wonderful sight of the lighthouse, right ahead. What a reprieve! Suddenly the air buzzed with helicopters. The

Facing the press, but it was wonderful to see Cath my wife, Cath my daughter, and Ben my son.

lighthouse was just a minute or two away. Then we were over the line. I have never known such relief.

The rest was a blur. John Nichols, the Isles of Scilly pilot, was out there recording our time over the finish line, as the Bishop Rock was now an unmanned lighthouse. Once he had confirmed our official record, he came on board to pilot us into St Mary's. Family and friends were out there in boats, and it was a wonderful homecoming. But first, once again, we faced Her Majesty's Customs and Immigration. There was some concern that we had seven in the crew instead of the six we had started out with. Where had the extra man come from? Was he legally permitted to enter the Kingdom of Great Britain and Northern Ireland? Eventually, it was sorted. Soon we were docked, tied up alongside in St Mary's Harbour in the Scilly Isles and finished with engines. Slowly, the realisation that we had actually broken the Atlantic record started to sink in. For all our trials and tribulations, we were about two hours inside the record set by the SS UNITED STATES back in 1952. We should have been jubilant. All I could feel was every part of me aching. Stepping ashore, I could hardly walk from the blisters and bruises. Elation would set in later. For the moment it was wonderful to see Cath my wife, Cath my daughter, and Ben my son. And, aah, a glass of English beer. We had a sort of impromptu Press conference, there on the quay at St Mary's. Though everything was low key and island-style, all I wanted was a hot bath and bed. It was wonderful just to crash - but nearly a week before I could get back to a normal sleeping pattern.

Of course, there was an anticlimax. An empty, nothing feeling now our huge project was over and we had achieved what we set out to do. OK, so we had a new Atlantic record. So what now? It was a hard act to follow. Yes, winning the Cowes-Torquay-Cowes powerboat race six weeks later was exciting. There was still a feeling of emptiness. It was a slow let-down too. Because the aftermath of our record-attempt carried on for some while. Talk about your fifteen minutes of fame. Aptly, our local Stroud newspaper summed it up the headline "DAG DID IT". It was strange being asked to open fêtes and give talks. Even stranger being recognised in the shops, and getting the best service.

Exalted company. The Prime Minister, Margaret Thatcher, came aboard and we ran up the river with her to the Houses of Parliament at 50 knots. Steve Laws (with moustache) was the extra man on board.

We took the boat on a victory tour around the coast. First stop was London, where we moored by Tower Bridge. Margaret Thatcher, the then Prime Minister came on board and we ran up the river with her to the Houses of Parliament at 50 knots. Then it was back to Lowestoft, where the boat had been built an eternity ago. What a welcome we had there! The harbour was lined with people. More of them, the police reckoned, than turned out for the Queen when she visited a few months earlier. Of course, the boat went back to the builders for a check. There were a few minor cracks in the welding. But everything had held together remarkably well, considering the punishment we had given her.

From Lowestoft, our first call on tour would be Bristol, where we had a date with HTV. They would meet us outside the port and cover us live as we went up the river Avon to the city. We had good time to make the long journey around the coast, but once more the weather intervened. Without planning it, we found ourselves sheltering in Dover Harbour with a westerly gale blowing up-Channel. It looked like that TV date would have to go. Then the forecast showed the wind easing for a few hours, before the next gale came in from the west. It was a small window, but there was a chance we that could make it. We left Dover at 2.00 am that morning. In a tribute to the remarkable capability of VIRGIN ATLANTIC CHALLENGER II, we had rounded Land's End by breakfast, having run down the whole English Channel. The forecast was right. As we rounded the headland, the wind was already up to Force 7. But once round, we were running before the wind, roaring up the Bristol Channel. We made our TV date with just 10 minutes to spare.

Just how lucky we had been on that Atlantic crossing was bought home to us later, when we were making a return visit to the Scilly Isles. Halfway across to the islands, both engines suddenly cut out and no amount of coaxing would get them going again. Surely we did not have to call for a tow in? That would have been worse than our rescue from the first crossing.

Over the radio, we put in a telephone call to MTU in Germany. After half an hour of drifting, they came back.

'Ve sink it is zee fuse.'

What fuse?

Apparently there was a fuse, tucked away on one of the computer boards, inside the control panel. We dismantled the computer and sure enough, there was the fuse. We replaced it with a piece of silver paper, fired up the engines, and everything was OK. So much for German design and efficiency. So much for their engine management system too. How could they put a fuse into a computer with no access from outside? Worst of all, how could they not even mention it in the engine handbook? It was a trend that worried me, the unstoppable switch to full electronic control. On boats these days, it was only the engineers who knew what was happening.

The victory tour lasted two months. Then, with the boat up for sale, it was south to the sun, where the brokers thought they could find a buyer. Once more, the boat showed its character. Leaving Plymouth in the late afternoon, we were refuelling in Lisbon by next morning. We did not think to make a record-attempt from London-to-Monte Carlo on that trip. That was to come later in my career. But VIRGIN ATLANTIC CHALLENGER II could have easily grabbed that record as well. In just two days of comfortable cruising, we were in the Balearic Islands. Perhaps we relaxed our guard too much, once we got to the Mediterranean. On the run up from Minorca to St Tropez, the forecast was bad. Since it promised nothing we had not already experienced, we set out on an overnight run. The wind was more on the beam and the boat took one wave awkwardly. Down she came on her side with a big bang. It was too much strain for the engine mounts. They gave way, forcing us to limp back to Minorca.

Temporary repairs took a couple of days, then we headed up to St Tropez at a more gentle pace. We had found a weak link in the design, and our approach to driving was a bit more cautious. But it was our arrival in St Tropez that made me realise just what we had achieved with our Atlantic record. Of course, St Tropez had seen it all, the rich, the famous, and the unusual. So were we surprised as we entered the Old Harbour at 9.00 in the morning and the whole port turned out to meet us! We stopped in the middle, to loud applause from the assembled boats and crews. That was something special.

The boat was sold to an Arab prince who kept it in the South of France, using it only on rare occasions. Fortunately he did not make too many changes to the design. But then she fell into disuse and the maintenance stopped. I used to see her lying in the harbour at Beaulieu when I went past in the train. It always brought a lump to my throat. But this was not the end of my association with VIRGIN ATLANTIC CHALLENGER II. She was to come back to my life years later. But now it was time to look ahead. There were new projects out there. And they were not slow in coming forward.

CHAPTER 9

RECORDS AND RACING

Now that I had a taste for record-breaking, I wanted more. I always found it amazing how quickly you forgot the bad bits of a project and focused on the good. There were certainly plenty of good bits about VIRGIN ATLANTIC CHALLENGER II. So where to next? Well, when the chance came up to get involved in an attempt on the Atlantic sailing record, I just could not turn it down. Now I was the holder of the Atlantic record under power, here was the chance for a double: the records under both sail and power. Nobody had ever done that before! I was wanted as navigator and weatherman aboard CHAFFOTEAUX CHALLENGER, and the chance of doing the big double

With Peter Phillips aboard CHAFFOTEAUX CHALLENGER. The crew looked experienced.

made me accept without my normal caution.

It was a mistake I would live to regret. And it showed how easy it was to get sucked into things without a valid enough reason to bail out. This sailing attempt was being put together by Peter Phillips, who had a lot of experience but very little funding. Both boat and the project had been cobbled together, but it looked viable. And the hard part, getting the boat built, was already done. The crew looked experienced and I thought it could fly. But sailing on early trials with the boat showed me just how different things were under sail. I had started my career in sailing, but this big, 80-foot catamaran was something else. You had to see it to appreciate just what the stresses and strains were on the hull and rigging of a big boat sailing at 25 knots. It was awesome how everything was so integrated and taut. I quickly realised that if any one part failed, the whole thing could collapse.

I got together my now familiar package of electronic navigation instruments, though only one of each because electrical power was at a premium on board a sailboat. To keep the batteries charged, we had to rely on a wind generator. And with the radio eating up the amps, everything else had to be in economy mode. Just the layout was a

The boat was sailed to New York, while I stayed behind to focus on the weather.

challenge, with the nav station located inside the cross beam of the catamaran. It had just 4 feet of headroom, a hatch in the bottom that served as the toilet or escape route, and an inflatable mattress for sleeping.

The target was to do the crossing in under 9 days, which meant averaging over 15 knots. That did not seem too difficult if I could get the weather right - and the boat was capable of 25 knots. This time I was looking at wind patterns with a fresh breeze instead of calms. As before, of course, headwinds were out. The attempt would be in April when the winds on the Atlantic were more consistent. It would also be very cold, as there was no heating on board. I relied on sailing performance figures from the early trials to make my weather calculations, and as I was to discover later, these were wildly optimistic.

The boat was sailed to New York by the rest of the crew while I stayed behind to get a focus on the weather. You needed to study the patterns for at least a week or two beforehand, to see how they developed and moved. As soon as I saw a likely break, I would jump on the plane to New York so we could be off the next day. There wasn't long to wait, though there was a strong element of guesswork in my weather assessment. Forecasts as long as 10 days in advance were far from guaranteed. No matter, once more I would be leaving New York on a record-attempt. Since this would be under sail, I should expect to be more at the mercy of the weather.

Finding a weather pattern for a sail-attempt was incredibly difficult. Computers would do the job today, but back then I had only paper maps that gave me the weather at twelve-hour intervals. This was the Atlantic too. And a lot can happen to fast-moving weather systems in twelve hours. What I was looking for was a depression that moved across the Atlantic at roughly the same speed and direction as we did.

There was little chance that it would be the same one all the way. Atlantic depressions did not travel conveniently along the route we wanted to take. Nor did they move at our preferred speed. That meant I had to look for following or beam winds that could take us all the way through to the Lizard Point, where the finish line was. Most other record-attempts under sail had failed because their forecasts were too weak at predicting conditions so far in advance. Everything came down to estimating the boat's speed in the winds forecast, for which I relied heavily on polar diagrams that Peter Phillips gave me.

Those diagrams were our downfall and far too optimistic. I knew the boat could sail at 25 knots in the right conditions, as I had been aboard when it had done this speed. What I did not know was that speeds like that were the exception, which made us a lost cause almost as soon as we left New York. We were simply not doing the speed that was needed to keep our place in the planned weather systems. Struggling from the word go, we still hoped that we could latch into a favourable weather system. It was a familiar route for me of course, though we kept further south than we would on a power crossing. By the time we were a 1,000 miles out we were right out of step with our chosen weather. Then a deep depression caught up with us and gave us hell. The wind screamed at 80 to 90 knots, and we were running at close to 15 knots even under bare poles. Though we were making good progress in the right direction, the speed was far too fast for the conditions, so we streamed warps astern to reduce the speed. On and on

The waves were so huge I was worried we would pitch-pole.

we drove relentlessly But we were moving so fast that the risk of pitch poling was very high. If our bows were driven so hard into a wave that they dug under, the whole boat could flip end over end. Not wanting to be caught below if things went wrong, I spent most of my time on deck.

At one stage the bows buried into a huge wave and the boat seemed to keep going downwards. I clung to the mast with the water up to my chest, convinced this was the end. Then the bows rose again ever so slowly, and we lived for another wave. Eventually the wind eased, and life became a little more normal. Not that it ever was really "normal" on board. It was bitterly cold on that ocean, in what was still virtually winter. We were completely unheated and most of our food was reconstituted dried food, or came out of tins. The noise on board was incredible as we pounded on our way onward. It had seemed a lot simpler on a power boat.

Then more disaster. Cracks appeared on each side of the cut-out sections of hull around the two cockpits. They seemed to grow longer by the hour, switching us quickly from record-breaking mode into survival mode. When the cracks started, we were about as far from land as you could get in the North Atlantic, which says something about Sod's Law. Now it was a question of nursing the boat to get to the nearest port, and any thoughts of an Atlantic record had totally disappeared. In such stormy conditions, it was hard to sail gently enough to reduce the strain on the hulls. Somehow we did what we could.

It was a lost cause. The cracks continued to grow until they were halfway around each hull. You could see the hulls actually bending as the boat worked in the waves. Water was coming in through the cracks, so of course this was the moment that the bilge pumps decided to stop working. We were forced to bail by bucket, for one hour in every two, to keep the water down. In a moment of black humour, we invented a novel bilge alarm system. This required one of the crew to be sleeping down below on an inflatable mattress. When he started to float and bump into things, we knew it was time to bail!

It was time to think about getting help, so we had a quick conference

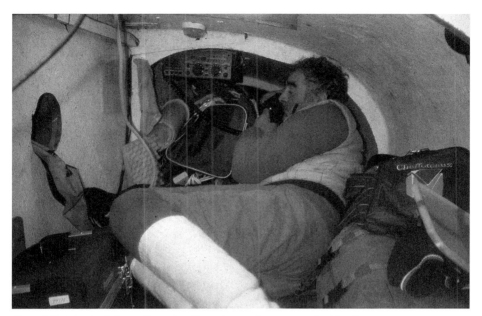

If we failed to clock in on the radio, then please chaps, come looking for us.

about what to do. Peter wanted to continue, but then it was his boat and he had a lot to lose if it was abandoned. The rest of us prevailed and with a storm already forecast to come up behind us, we decided it was time to get out whilst we still could. I got on the radio to alert Falmouth Coastguard of our predicament. In the dark, the risks were highest, so instead of requesting a rescue pick-up immediately, we determined we could survive until morning. I arranged with the Coastguard that I would call every hour on the hour, and give our position. If we failed to clock in on the radio, then please chaps, could they come looking for us. It was a vital arrangement to make. If the cracks got any worse, there was every chance that the boat would break in two and capsize.

That was a very long night at sea. Every time I got on the radio, you could almost feel the relief from all the other shipping listening in. You knew everyone wanted us to survive, a wonderful feeling of unspoken support. For me the hardest job was to keep my voice to a low, professional level, not easy with panic just below the surface. You wanted to scream for help, but had to pretend that you were in control of the situation. But we made it. Between bailing and radio calls, we survived the night. And in the early light of dawn, just as the Coastguard

The SEALAND PERFORMANCE coming to the rescue.
When she was launched in 1985, SEA-LAND PERFORMANCE was one of the biggest container ships in the world.

promised, there was this ship coming to the rescue.

It was a wonderful sight, except that a 250-metre long container ship is not the ideal rescue vehicle. Especially when its deck height alone is over 10 metres above the water. Anyway, they got us on board at the second attempt. Then we headed all the way back across the Atlantic to the US. Why are ships always bound in the wrong direction when they rescue you? Anyway beggars cannot be choosers, so we ended up in Charleston, in the US. It was a sad ending to an ill-fated project. It also persuaded me that maybe navigating in the world of high performance sail was something I should walk away from. Gut feeling told me I should stick to power in future.

I did not have long to wait. A writing assignment took me out to Viareggio in Italy. There I was to visit the Azimut shipyard and do a sea trial on one of their latest motor yachts. I had lunch with two PR ladies, who told me there was someone in the shipyard who wanted to meet me. When I was taken upstairs there were twenty or so people sitting round a table in a meeting. What was going on here?

Then Paolo Vitelli, the boss of Azimut stood up and said, 'Dag, we

Dr Paolo Vitelli is the founder and Chairman of the Azimut Benetti Group.

In 1969, just 22 years of age, Paolo Vitelli founded Azimut, a small company hiring out sailing boats. The following year, Azimut began to import and sell boats, mostly from Holland and Norway. After ten years of steady growth he bought the Benetti firm in 1985, one of the most famous mega-yacht builders in the world. At present, the Azimut-Benetti Group is the most important European motor-yacht builder and the leading mega-yacht builder in the world.

are planning to make an attempt of the Atlantic record, will you join the team as navigator?'

My immediate response was, 'Yes.'

Within half an hour, Paolo and I had agreed how much I would be paid and what my role would be. So there I was, taking on the Atlantic again. There was a significant difference. The AZIMUT ATLANTIC CHALLENGER was not only aiming to beat the record that we had set in VIRGIN ATLANTIC CHALLENGER II. She was aiming to make the crossing non-stop, with no refuelling. I was stunned. It was surely not possible to

85 feet long and built in light alloy, we got AZIMUT ATLANTIC CHALLENGER half-way across the Atlantic before engine trouble forced us to stop in poor weather conditions.

Two massive water jets were the only way to handle the difference in displacement between a full ship load and running nearly empty.

carry enough fuel for 3,000 miles of open ocean at 40 knots in a relatively small craft.

However Azimut's naval architect had designed a quite remarkable craft, an 85-footer that could carry twice its own weight in fuel and still get onto the plane. It was to be powered by four CRM lightweight diesels, coupled in pairs to drive two water jets. Water jet propulsion was specified because it was the only system that could cope with the huge difference in displacement between when the boat was fully fuelled and when she was nearly empty. Even so, the margins looked very tight. I had concerns from the outset that everything was a bit borderline, but that is the very nature of record-breaking. There was a fine balance between carrying enough fuel for the 3,000 mile crossing and having enough speed to make the record. It would

Navigation systems
Asked why he had a British navigator, Vitelli said, 'Because he is the best'.

have been nice to have a decent fuel reserve of, say, 10 per cent. However this was not a luxury we could afford if the challenge was to have some chance of success.

My job, as before, was to organise the electronic navigation systems and communications. I would also be using my previous experience to arrange the details of time-keeping and support facilities. To do that meant commuting out to Viareggio nearly every week. But it was an exciting project to get involved in. Once again I was setting out to achieve something that had never been done before.

The biggest problem with the Italians was their top-heavy administration. Those twenty people in the closed-door room were the organising committee, but there was little sign of anybody in overall charge. Vitelli was good, but he had an expanding shipyard and business to run. At the same time he had not really delegated authority to anyone else. Equipment and design changes were made without any consideration about their effect on performance. Inevitably the boat came out overweight, reducing our fuel reserves even further. But styling, that vital soul of anything Italian, had been conceived by

Arriving in New York for the Atlantic challenge, after cracked water jet inlet ducts nearly sank us.

Pininfarina. It certainly looked a stunner, even if it was short on the practical requirements for record-breaking.

The trials went remarkably smoothly. Then came the official naming ceremony in Viareggio, where it seemed all the great and good of Italy were gathered. This was an all-Italian project: Italian engines, Italian water jets, Italian electronics and Italian crew. That made me a very obvious odd one out. But when asked at the press conference why he had a British navigator, Vitelli replied, 'Because he is the best'.

Well, I could not have asked for a better endorsement than that. Now I had something to live up to.

This time the plan was first to drive the boat across the Atlantic to gain experience of her. We were going to take the scenic route from Italy, with fuel stops at Gibraltar and the Azores before arriving in New York.

This was going to be a record-attempt of sorts, for we hoped to set the fastest crossing from East to West, even though refuelling in the Azores would steal some of the lustre. Going for a record meant that we were to keep up the pressure, running at over 40 knots straight after departure from Gibraltar. It was luxury, record-breaking weather in this more southern part of the North Atlantic, with wall-to-wall sunshine and calm seas. Our relaxing ride was rudely interrupted when, without warning, the engine room started to flood with water. We stopped the boat and the bilge pumps emptied the water. Everything looked OK, but as soon as we started moving again, in came the water. Once again we stopped to bail, and the water stopped coming in. Once again when we got under way, the water came in. Here was a considerable dilemma. If we moved, the boat was actually sinking, taking water so fast that the bilge pumps could not cope. If we stopped, we stayed afloat, but could not go anywhere.

Our first priority was obviously to find the leak. Search as we might, there was just no sign of where the water was coming in. It was a real mystery. We found a temporary solution by re-routing the pipe-work of two of the other pumps, so they operated as bilge pumps. With all three pumps running, we could keep the water in check, allowing us to make forward progress at modest speed.

We turned back to Lisbon, where the boat was taken straight into dry dock. When the water was drained from the dock, the problem was clear to see. Water was pouring from one of the water jet inlet ducts. The welding round the aluminium fabrication of the jet intake had cracked, allowing water to enter. The crack only opened when the boat was under forward motion. When the boat stopped, the crack closed up. It was a relief to solve the mystery, but it did not raise our confidence levels very much. I had experienced too many record-breaking disasters to be inspired.

After repairs, we headed out into the Atlantic again, this time with no thoughts of setting a record. We refuelled at the Azores as planned, intending to cruise onwards to New York, just a couple of days away. This time it was the engines that did not co-operate. The oil consumption of the CRM diesels was rising at an alarming rate. The oil was being used up so fast that we would run out of lubricating oil long before we got to New York. Indeed it looked increasingly doubtful that we could even make the nearest land, in Bermuda, where we might be able to pick up more oil. In good VIRGIN ATLANTIC CHALLENGER style, we flagged down a passing ship and asked then if they could let us have some lubricating oil. Generously they did, and so we struggled on. By the time we neared Bermuda, we were down to just one engine, with the oil drained from the others to keep it running. Now it was my turn to worry, we had no charts of Bermuda to find our way into port. Luckily we were able to get the position of the Fairway Buoy from the Coast Guard by radio. By feeding that into the electronics as a waypoint, we made our way to the buoy, and from there we had a visual run in to harbour.

Finally we made it to New York, where we filled the boat with fuel and extra supplies of lubricating oil (more weight), ready for our record-attempt. American Tom Gentry was in New York at the same time, getting ready for his record-attempt. He was planning to refuel on the way across, so we were not really competing for the same record. Gentry's boat was his new GENTRY EAGLE, a larger version of VIRGIN ATLANTIC CHALLENGER II, also designed by Peter Birkett, but with power

Tom Gentry

boosted by a 5,000 hp gas turbine in addition to the two diesels. Two boats making record-attempts at the same time fired the imagination of the Press, which raised the publicity stakes considerably. Because we were both waiting for the right weather pattern, it even looked as though we might leave on the same day. Our routes were different of course, because Gentry's team had fixed refuelling points. We on the other hand could set our course however we liked, to get the best out of the prevailing weather patterns.

There was not long to wait. The weather pattern was a bit marginal, but if you didn't grab a chance on these attempts you could wait forever. The problem was, you didn't know if there wouldn't be even

GENTRY EAGLE
Like our VIRGIN ATLANTIC CHALLENGER project, it took two attempts before she broke the record.

better weather if you waited a bit longer. Our plan was to top-up our fuel over on the New Jersey shore just before departure. The tanks overflowed whilst we were doing this, and the Coast Guard refused to let us leave until the mess was cleared up. This took several hours, so we were late leaving. Not a serious problem, but not good for morale.

But, unbeknown to me, someone had authorised more fuel to be put in the tanks than planned. This was great for an extra reserve and peace of mind. It also meant that the boat was heavier, for which read "slower". I only realised this after we left, as we struggled to get the heavy boat onto the plane, and wondering why the speed was down to below 30 knots, too slow for our planned schedule. It was not a good start but we were off, settling down to our record-chasing routine.

This time there could be no cutting across the Nantucket Shoals. Leaving New York, we headed directly out into the Atlantic. With no refuelling stops to worry about, our only focus was the long run ahead of us. Then, because of our delayed timing, the weather started to turn against us, a combination of leaving late and slower speed from the increased fuel load. As often happens, the weather itself did not follow what was forecast. With the wind stronger than expected, our ride

AZIMUT ATLANTIC CHALLENGER's four CRM engines. One broken rocker arm out of 288 sunk our Transatlantic chances.

became rougher and rougher, a real roller-coaster. At times our still heavily-loaded boat was almost submerged, running into the back of the waves in front. At least the sea was running in our favour, even if the waves seemed huge. Our morale was boosted when we heard that Gentry had turned back from weather damage. We were not the only ones getting a rough ride! Then it became obvious that our roller-coaster antics were also making us burn more fuel than we should. Even with the extra load, at the rate we were using it up, it was going to be very tight to make the Bishop Rock at a fast enough speed to beat the record.

Berthed ahead of us in St Johns, GENTRY EAGLE had already abandoned her own record attempt.

Relief was at hand, but not the kind we wanted. Our four CRM diesels were among of the most complex engines on the market. Each had 18 cylinders in "W" formation, with four valves per cylinder. At several thousand revs a minute, that was an awful lot of valves going up and down, a total of 288. It was only one of the rocker arms, for only one of the valves, that broke. But that was enough to put the whole engine out of action. And with one engine out, there was no question of having enough speed to make the record, even if our fuel lasted.

At this stage, we were close to half-way across the Atlantic. With heavy hearts and the record looking difficult to achieve anyway, we turned back, thankful to escape from those seas. Newfoundland was only 400 miles away to the north, so that was the harbour to which we headed. Entering St Johns, we found GENTRY EAGLE already berthed there, where she had headed after abandoning her record-attempt. All either of us could do was lick our wounds and ponder the difficulties of running a small boat in the challenging Atlantic.

I left the boat there and headed home. AZIMUT ATLANTIC CHALLENGER was taken south and laid up at a shipyard in Rhode Island. GENTRY EAGLE had more excitement. On their way south, they ran ashore at around 50 knots - onto the rocky shores of Nova Scotia. The hole in the   bottom was large enough for the crew to climb through, an   unusual escape route ashore.

When the AZIMUT was shipped back to Italy, there were plans for another attempt on the record. Vitelli recognised the weakness of the organisation for the first effort and wanted me to take over as project director. We made plans to install a pair of lighter and more reliable V-16 MTU diesels to reduce the weight, giving us a boat that I thought could really do the job next time round. It was not to be. Without much-needed sponsorship, the project had to be abandoned.

Gentry went back the following year with the same GENTRY EAGLE, to set a stunning record with an average speed of 48 knots, but this was a refuelling attempt. Like us in VIRGIN ATLANTIC CHALLENGER II, he was

Donald L Blount. From a flying start in research and engineering in the field of hydrodynamics, Donald L. Blount moved to the Department of the Navy, Combatant Craft Engineering Department for three decades, serving the last nine years as department head. Founding his own company, he designed two vessels with speed capabilities of over 65 knots - Bravo Romeo Limited's DESTRIERO, the 220-foot (67-metre) gas turbine powered motor yacht that averaged 53.1 knots during a non-refuelled passage from New York to England - and FORTUNA, the 136-foot (41.5-metre) gas turbine powered motor yacht.

On 9 August 1992, DESTRIERO smashed the Blue Ribbon Atlantic record in 58 hours 34 minutes and 5 seconds, at an average speed of 53,09 knots.

another who had built on his experience from an earlier attempt, a very valuable commodity.

It was my own experience with Atlantic record-attempts that earned me the invitation to join another Italian team intent on grabbing the glory and going for the non-stop record. They had a whole new approach to the challenge, money being only secondary. The DESTRIERO project was spearheaded by the Aga Khan, but virtually everything about it was again, Italian. The aim was not only to set a new record for the non-stop crossing - they wanted to beat Gentry's record too. To become the undisputed champions of the Atlantic.

American designer Donald Blount was responsible for the concept. His solution for combining the high speed and long-range neces- sary for a record-breaking boat was

New territory
All-Italian, so I was not part of the crew, DESTRIERO's cockpit felt like a jumbo jet's.

to go big. Everything about DESTRIERO was on a scale that had not been seen before. Her length was 68 metres (nearly 225 feet), powered by a massive 60,000 hp to push her along. With a top speed of 65 knots, nothing that big had ever gone that fast before. Definitely charging into new territory.

The boat was built at the Fincanteri yard in La Spezia, Italy, installed with three 20,000 hp gas turbine engines, coupled to water jets. Essentially they were three Jumbo Jet engines,

The Aga Khan

adapted for marine work. The water jets were the largest that had been built at that time. Most amazing of all, DESTRIERO could carry 700 tonnes of fuel, which her engines burned up at 10 tonnes per hour. She was a far cry from the modest 2,000 hp power and 50-knot speed of VIRGIN ATLANTIC CHALLENGER.

With the plan for DESTRIERO to have an all-Italian crew, I was not part of the fun on board. My role was to plan the weather routing and manage the organisational details. This was a huge disappointment. It was not easy to sit on shore and watch them take off. However, with modern GPS positioning now available, the role of navigator on the Atlantic was not what it used to be. When you knew where you were with such accuracy all the time, it did not require the careful skill that it had in the past.

It was also much easier to plot weather routing from the shore, where there was access to the latest computer-generated weather information. At least I did get to ride in the boat. It was important to get a feel for the craft I was doing the weather routing for. Even so, I knew my job was not going to be easy: the design team's operational limit was for no more that 2-metre high waves at full speed. They might have wished for the moon. In the North Atlantic, 2-metre waves were virtually a flat calm. Hard, if not impossible to find, even when you had the magic wand of money to wave.

The boat was driven to New York, but only made slow speed across from east to west, so there was no new record there. When they phoned from New York to say they were ready, I turned round and said they should go immediately. I had been studying the weather for a week before, because you needed to

Richard Branson's Virgin Atlantic Trophy was a beautiful silver model of the Bishop Rock Lighthouse.

get a feel for what the weather patterns were doing, and it just happened to look good on that day. In good Italian style, they said they were not quite ready. I told them there was still a chance the following day, so that was set as the departure date. It was a delay they nearly lived to regret. Leaving later meant the weather window was tighter, and the margins that much smaller.

The prevailing weather showed a large but fairly stable depression, situated well north in the Atlantic. My plan was to route them round its bottom edge. It would not be easy to see exactly where the areas of 2-metre waves would be, and obviously they wanted to take the shortest route. I proposed that they angled up towards the centre of the depression, until the wave height reached the 2-metre limit, then turned east when the waves reached the set limit. In this way, they could feel their way around the depression, and combine this with taking the shortest possible safe route. It worked well until they were over half-way across. Then a small but vigorous secondary depression started off the coast of Spain, deciding it wanted to track north to join its big brother.

As the two depressions drew closer, it meant that the calmer seas between them diminished rapidly. I told the guys on board to go for maximum speed, hoping they could squeeze through the gap. They only just made it. Then the weather door slammed shut firmly behind them. It was a narrow escape. But if they had left the day before, there would not have been a problem. They broke the record by crossing in two-and-a-half days, averaging 53 knots, an amazing time. I flew out in Richard Branson's helicopter, to join the celebrations in the Scilly Isles and drive the boat back to Plymouth. Branson went down to present the crew with his Virgin Atlantic Trophy, a beautiful silver model of the Bishop Rock Lighthouse that he had produced after our own record-breaking VAC II crossing. Unlike the Hales Trophy, this one had simple rules. It was to be awarded to the boat making the fastest crossing of the Atlantic without refuelling. DESTRIERO still holds it.

It is worth explaining here the various trophies and records that are awarded for the Atlantic crossing. The first and most famous is the Blue Riband, a mythical self-awarded prize for the fastest crossing, and the one all the old Atlantic liners went for. Traditionally, the ship holding this record flies a long blue pennant, hence the name.

It was replaced in the 1930s by the Hales Trophy, awarded for the same thing, but qualified by the rule that the contender must be a passenger vessel. After the Hales Trophy was won by the SS UNITED STATES in 1952, there were no other challengers. As all the trustees of the trophy were now dead, the award itself was essentially dead too, locked away in the US Merchant Marine Academy. Of course, when we set a new record in VIRGIN ATLANTIC CHALLENGER II, we tried to resurrect the Hales Trophy. But it took a long time for the courts to authorise the appointment of new trustees and bring this famous trophy back to life. Now that the Hales Trophy is up and running again, the qualification is that the challenging vessel must have some commercial purpose instead of being a private craft or one built specifically for the record attempt.

As a result, there are now two major achievements to aim for. The Virgin Atlantic Trophy for the out-and-out record - and the Hales Trophy for the fastest commercial vessel.

Recently the UIM (Union Internationale Motonautique), the body that controls powerboat racing, tried to muscle in on the Atlantic records act, saying that they would recognise a record for vessels under 50 metres in length over a record course from the Ambrose Light to the Lizard Point, a slightly longer route. Quite why they felt the need to establish a new record over a different course, I do not know. It just makes for confusion in people's minds. Nobody has attempted that

HOVERSPEED GREAT BRITAIN
Sea Containers' first SeaCat, HOVERSPEED GREAT BRITAIN, took the record for the fastest crossing of the Atlantic by a passenger ship on the 23 June, 1990 with a time of three days, 7 hours and 54 minutes at an average speed of 36.6 knots, winning the prestigious Hales Trophy for the Blue Riband of the North Atlantic.

record so far, and I really feel that the UIM award is superfluous.

Somehow it seems the UIM just want to destroy 150 years of Atlantic tradition and be recognised as the new Atlantic authority. DESTRIERO is certainly a worthy holder of the Atlantic record, though I doubt whether we will see the likes of her again. When I drove her from the Scillies to Plymouth, the acceleration was just so impressive you were squashed back into your seat as she took off. Having 60,000 hp in one little throttle lever was an incredible experience. At full speed in such a large vessel, other ships seemed to zoom up over the horizon, then just vanish astern. I have been a lot faster than that in smaller boats, but it was the combination of size and speed that made for a very exciting ride. Because she had no commercial purpose, DESTRIERO did not qualify for the Hales Trophy.

Since DESTRIERO, attempts at the Atlantic record have been restricted to commercial vessels, mainly the big wave-piercer ferries. I worked with Hoverspeed when their wave-piercer ferry HOVERSPEED GREAT BRITAIN was the first to qualify for the Hales Trophy under the new trustees. Once again I was in the weather routing role, but with a much more seaworthy design the weather was not so critical and they set a date for departure rather than waiting for the right conditions. At 40 knots with a large 90-metre vessel you can do that, a very far cry from our early attempts.

To make some sense of all the different Atlantic records, it now wants one very high-speed vessel to qualify for all three records, then it can lay claim to being the fastest on the Atlantic, with no qualification - just like the Atlantic liners of old.

I have something in mind.

CHAPTER 10

FASTER AND FASTER

These Atlantic records were not my first attempt at record-breaking. Back in 1968, we had done a run down Lake Windermere in HOT BOVRIL to set a World Record for a Class I powerboat. Our speed was just 68 mph, which by today's standards is painfully slow. Many production boats can exceed that now, but at the time it was exciting stuff. Today, that same record stands at something around 170 mph, over 100 mph faster, a measure of how much fast-boat design has progressed in 40 years.

In between sessions of Atlantic record-breaking, I was the navigator on a little 28-footer that made a successful attempt on the Round Ireland record in 1987. This was just a 24-hour journey, made exciting by thick fog around the northern coastline, and drift-net fishing lines along the south. We left in the fog, thinking that we preferred the calm seas associated with it than the clear views and rough water alternative. Much of the navigating was done with one of the early little LCD radar sets, with a screen not much bigger than a small envelope. I was surprised at how well it performed. It was having this little radar that enabled us to navigate through the unlit and narrow rocky channel inside the Blasket Islands on the West Coast at night, which saved us quite a distance. The other guys in the boat were very dubious about this, but I said it could work. Coming out at the southern end of the channel, I told them to slow down.

'Why?' they said. 'We are clear of the channel now'.

But that little radar had shown up a patch of rough tidal race, and we were heading straight for it in the dark. The radar also worked well in the fog, but then there was not much shipping to worry about on the North and West Coasts of Ireland. Refuelling in the Arran Islands was a leisurely affair, with the local priest not prepared to let us have the fuel unless we stayed for a sit-down three-course meal that they had prepared for us.

A more serious project came along in 1991, when the drinks company, Drambuie, planned to make an attempt on the Round Britain record with a 45-foot US-built powerboat.

The year before, I had been knocked down by a car in France. I was walking on the verge of the road, when a car swerved off and hit me full-on. The police reckoned that from the impact, I travelled 30 feet through the air. I landed in a ditch full of stinging nettles, although I do not remember too much about it. I was taken to hospital, to be discharged the next day, thinking that my only injuries were severe bruising and a few cuts. Little did I know there was also a brain injury. A few months later, I lost all co-ordination of hands, feet and speech. That night, I was in hospital, undergoing an operation for a blood clot on the brain!

It was a pretty desperate situation, the clot growing so rapidly in size that the surgeon told my wife I would either come out of there dead, or as a vegetable. I am glad they did not tell me their prognosis, because I had other ideas. This was an operation under local anaesthetic, where they drilled holes in your head to relieve the pressure. It was almost as exciting as powerboat racing! Within three days, I was out of hospital, having made what the doctors thought was a miracle recovery. The problem was that they did not get it quite right. So I was back there a couple of weeks later, having the same thing done all over again. At that stage I think they gave me five hours to live. Nevertheless, the operation must have worked, and I remember spending Christmas Day in hospital with a tap in the top of my head. It seemed a novel way to drink my share of Christmas booze.

Brian Cummins, my brain surgeon, had done a brilliant job. The final test of my fitness on rejoining the outside world, was to give a talk about record-breaking to fifteen brain surgeons at a party in Brian's house. I think he wanted to show off to his peers all his skills in my recovery. I certainly became something of a celebrity in that hospital, because very few people ever made a full recovery from that type of brain surgery. I can joke about the episode now, but at the time it was very much a life-or-death situation. I was as surprised as anyone that I made it through without any long-term effects.

Anyway, I was out of hospital, and soon after I was at the London Boat

Show in the New Year, talking with Drambuie about this record-attempt. It was a bit of an act of bravado on my part. But when you went through a near-death experience like that, you desperately wanted to restore some sort of normality. Normality for me, was planning another record-attempt.

That first Drambuie boat had two Caterpillar diesels for power and was capable of speeds up to 50 knots. It was a heavy, but hopefully reliable boat, that should have been able to cope well with the difficult sea conditions around Britain. I was soon fit and well and ready to go. And that first Drambuie boat sat in St Katharine Dock in London, whilst I was looking closely at the weather charts, hoping for a break that would allow us to take off.

The weather patterns around the British Isles can be very challenging. When it is calm in the south, it can be as rough as hell up north. Then on one side, you could be under the lee of the land, while on the other, fully exposed to wind and weather. The strong tides and their effect on sea conditions also have to be taken into account. All of which requires intense study to get things right over a 1,200 mile route.

It took about three weeks before the weather started to look favourable. I proposed that we left on a summer Saturday, with an early morning start, to get the maximum daylight. In the summer, it is almost light for the full twenty-four hours in the north of Scotland, so we should have been able to do virtually the whole run in daylight, the safest way to go fast-boating. My proposed starting time was turned down however, because the project director was abroad at a motor race in France, and he would not allow us to start on our record-attempt without him to stage-manage things. I was beginning to find it difficult to take these guys seriously. If a record-attempt is to succeed, you have to be very single-minded. As it turned out, that was the one and only good weather window that whole summer, so we ended up making no attempt at all.

The following year, I got involved with Drambuie again, on what I hoped would be a better relationship. This time they had a new boat, a 50-footer called DRAMBUIE TANTALUS.

However, before the new boat arrived in Britain, I was involved in an

The first boat called DRAMBUIE

attempt on the London-to-Monte Carlo record. This was not too difficult, as there was no previous record to beat. But we still had to finish the 2,400-mile journey, and the Mediterranean can involve all sorts of difficult conditions. The boat was a catamaran motor yacht called ULTIMA, built in Germany with advanced styling, and owned by two German dentists, one of whom was the builder, Rolf Versen. The purpose of the record-attempt was to promote the boat and its capabilities, triggering sales for a production version.

We did some sea-trials with the boat out of Hamburg, then brought her across to London for the start. Again, I studied my weather charts. A promising window began to open up. We would have a bit of a rough ride to start with, going down-Channel, but reasonable prospects for the rest of the journey. We left the timing gate at Gravesend, to run down the Thames, and on to face the promised rough passage in the Channel, on the way to our first refuelling stop in Guernsey. We had problems with a fuel pump on one of the MAN engines, but the guys in Guernsey were brilliant, with the right spare available - and even someone to fit it, waiting when we got in. We went off for an excellent meal whilst the work was done, and I began to see that there could be a very pleasant side to record-breaking. Then it was inside Ushant, and on across the Bay of Biscay to the next refuelling stop at La Coruña, on the northwest corner of Spain.

Across the Bay, we realised that the fuel was going to be very tight to make port. So instead of La Coruña, we looked for somewhere closer. This turned out to be Ortigueria, a fishing port, where we begged for enough fuel to get us to La Coruña. The available fuel was only meant for fishing boats, so we had to convince them that ULTIMA was a new type of fast fishing boat. Eventually we got the fuel, then it was on into La Coruña, to fill the tanks brimful before our run down to Lisbon. As we left the dock after refuelling, the boat began to drift out. Unexpectedly I found myself half on our boat, and half on the boat alongside. I had to let go of one or the other, and swung back against the other boat with a loud crack. I thought I had broken something on board the boat. But it was me that was damaged, and it turned out one of my ribs had cracked. Now I had a difficult choice. I could go to a Spanish hospital, or I could stay on board for the rest of the trip, relying on the strong painkillers that the German dentists had.

The idea of a Spanish hospital did not appeal, so I chose to remain on board. It was a very painful trip. The painkillers made me drowsy, so I slept a lot. Getting up afterwards took an age of delicate negotiation with my body. The high speed movement of the boat did not help either. We refuelled in Lisbon where the police took away our passports. We had not warned them we were coming, so there was considerable negotiation to sort things out. None of this helped the way my body felt. But, as they say - no pain, no gain. So it was on to Gibraltar, then Palma in Majorca, then the final run to Monte Carlo when the pain-killers ran out. It was an epic journey, but we made it in three-and-a-half days, a record that stood for years. It would prove quite a tough one to beat.

A week later I was back with the DRAMBUIE TANTALUS, my ribs well strapped up and good painkillers to hand. There was quite a lot of work to do to get the boat ready for record-breaking. At one stage out on trials, the boat caught fire when the steering system overheated. This new boat was a 50-footer powered by four Caterpillar diesels coupled to individual

The first DRAMBUIE was powered by two Caterpillar diesels.

drives, a good installation for record-breaking because it meant we could keep on the plane even with only three engines running. Finally we moved up to Ramsgate, which I had determined as the best starting point for the record run. To give the Press time to see us off, it was planned to make a 12.00 midday start. This was not ideal, and I was not happy. All it would achieve was more running in the dark, something to avoid because it heightened the chance of mistakes. Anyway we set off, only to be called back when we were off Dover because one the Press had arrived late and had missed out on his photos! After this further delay there was a good chance we might get out of step with the weather pattern. Not the relaxed start I had hoped for.

Things got worse at our first stop for fuel at Plymouth. Water had got into the lubricating oil of one of the stern drives. That meant hauling the boat out, and thank goodness the marina was very helpful on that score. We found that the seal on the propeller shaft was damaged. Without a spare, all we could do was push it back into place and refill with oil, hoping that the drive would last the journey. We rounded Land's End and

DRAMBUIE TANTALUS'S problem
With a damaged stern drive, we had to haul the boat out at Plymouth.

headed up for our next stop at Holyhead, where it was planned to lift the boat out again to check the drive. Again we got excellent co-operation, considering that it was four in the morning. Then it was a long run up the West Coast to the Kyle of Lochalsh for more fuel. It really was exciting running at high speed through the islands and narrow channels on this coast, and despite the problems, we were keeping to a pretty good schedule. The weather did its bit too, with the whole Irish Sea staying virtually flat calm.

On we went, round the north of Scotland, a lonely stretch of sea. The Round Britain record course meant going round mainland Britain, so now we were faced with running through the notorious Pentland Firth. We had to pick a careful path through the tide races, but were not held back too much before reaching Aberdeen, our next refuelling stop. Here it became almost bizarre. I was met by car and whisked off to meet the Provost, before giving a speech at a promotional dinner specially laid-on for the event. It was lucky our timing was so right, making me wonder just what planet the organisers were on. What kind of a schedule allowed me to make a guest appearance at a dinner in the middle of a record-attempt?

The Drambuie people were so full of such plans, I was beginning to think this was probably one record-attempt too far. This came to a head when they suggested we stop for three hours out at sea. We were running ahead of their schedule and it would not be convenient to arrive back at Ramsgate early in the morning. I was not very polite about that, and suggested an alternative arrangement. We would keep going to the finish line no matter what, because surprise, surprise, we were actually trying to break a record. After we had crossed the line, we would happily wait outside the harbour if it was not convenient for us to enter until the reception was ready!

To add to the excitement of that final leg, we encountered a waterspout ahead of us in one of the narrow channels across the Thames Estuary. It seemed to fill the whole channel, so we turned round and ran away from it, trying to find another way through the maze of shoals.

I was skipper and navigator of that record-attempt and I don't think Drambuie were too happy with some of my comments. After the run they always insisted that the record was held in the name of the boat and not mine. Not surprisingly, we did not part on very good terms. When I got involved in a project like that it had to be done professionally if it was going to work. I just did not think that Drambuie, or at least their PR

DRAMBUIE's reception
After breaking the record, we actually offered to wait three hours until the official reception was ready!

people, had their priorities right on this one. OK, they wanted promotion and publicity. It still should have been possible to achieve that, and get the job done properly. Sadly in this case, there was too much tail wagging the dog.

Working with Fabio Buzzi was a very different story. After we had won the World Powerboat Championship back in 1988, Fabio switched to long-distance events. We did some exciting races such as the Venice-to-Monte Carlo and a 1,000-mile race around the bottom half of Italy. In 1996, I was with Fabio on one of the best races that we ever did, a Round Scotland Race. Daniel Scioli from the Argentine came across for this one, a true professional who I had raced with before in the Venice-to-Monte Carlo. The Round Scotland was really a race round the north of Scotland, starting from Inverness and transiting the Caledonian Canal, then heading up the West Coast, around the top end, and back to Inverness. It was wild country and wild ocean, familiar to me from lifeboat days and of course the Round Britain record with Drambuie. Up here, so far from anywhere,

Daniel Scioli. Current Vice President of Argentina, Daniel is certainly a hot performer. From Buenos Aires appliance distributor to world powerboat racing champion, he made it to Vice President in 2003. LA GRAN ARGENTINA was a boat for the very select few, with Daniel Scioli as its most regular driver - 3 times winner of World Champion Superboat USA and 4 times winner of Europeans Championships. With the boat modified in 2000 for long-distance record-setting, Daniel set the Miami-Nassau-Miami record at an average speed of 100 MPH!

you didn't want to mess things up. Any help required could be a long time coming.

By this time, Fabio was really into RIB building, so the boat we were using was his latest 42-footer, powered by a pair of 800 hp Seatek diesels. This was similar to the boat we had used on the 1,000-mile race in Italy. It was also more refined, with the kind of speed that would keep us towards the front of the pack. Obviously we did not race through the Caledonian Canal section although we did set another record. Across Loch Ness, we covered the 20-mile run in under 20 minutes.

In a briefing before the race, I told Fabio and Daniel there were going to be two very difficult, possibly dangerous, stretches of water. One was through the Gulf of Corryvreckan, where the chart showed a whirlpool. The other was through the dreaded Pentland Firth. Things were not going to be easy because this was a race, not a record. On a record-attempt you could choose your weather, and go when you liked. With racing, you started when the race started.

There were also some tough navigation challenges, running at high speed amongst the islands off the West Coast. Perhaps a hint of what lay ahead happened just after the main start at Fort William, when the chart plotter packed up. With no GPS positioning, we were back to paper charts and visual navigation, forcing me to haul out my rusty skills. When we examined that plotter afterwards, bits of the electronics had broken away inside - and this from a top-of-the-range unit! Fast-boats and electronics still had a way to go.

The tidal whirlpool at Corryvreckan proved to be virtually a flat calm, so I guess we just caught it right with tide and wind. Turning north, we were the first into Tobermory on that leg, then first again, the next day at Ullapool. By now the wind had freshened, and it was becoming a rough ride in the exposed waters. So we were not looking forward to the next leg, in open Atlantic waters and round Cape Wrath, for the run into the Pentland Firth. It was a long hard run, but again we were first when we stopped for the night in Thurso. The next day's run would take us through the Pentland Firth. Unbelievably, here too it was virtually a flat calm, in distinct contrast to that lifeboat trip years ago. It was great to see the Pentland Firth in a calm mood. By now we really had the race wrapped up. All we had to do was get to the finish at Inverness, which we did in quick time, to win overall. It was a great race into uncharted waters. It was also a pity we were going so fast, without time to linger and appreciate the wonderful scenery.

Another attempt on the London-to-Monte Carlo record came up a couple of years later. This time it was Dutch super-yacht builder Heesen who wanted to show what their boats could do. The record-attempt was to be made in a 60-footer, a lot smaller than their normal production yachts, but this boat had the power and performance to set a record. It was really a novel way of doing a delivery trip - Franz Heesen plus his regular trials skipper and myself making up the three-man crew. The record looked very breakable too, in this 50-knot boat powered by two big diesels coupled to Arneson drives. The forecast looked good, though we knew there would be some lively seas off Cape Finnestere, on the North-West corner of Spain. It would be rough for a distance further south too. Rough seas were inevitable at least somewhere on a record run.

All went well on the first legs down the English Channel and across the Bay of Biscay. After refuelling at La Coruña, we hit the promised rough seas and unexpected problems with the Arneson drives. You needed to have these drives trimmed up to get the engines running efficiently at speed, then you trimmed them down for slower speeds. The problems started when the boat was pitching, because then the propellers started to come out of the water altogether. You lowered the drives to keep the props in the water, but this overloaded the engines if you tried to run at any speed, threatening the engines with overheating. Our dilemma was that we could run at 30 knots, or we could run at 10 knots, but nothing in between. That was not too serious most of the time, because all we did was nurse the boat through the rough patches. But at the 30 knots we chose, it was something of a rough ride. The stresses eventually broke the mounts on the generator, which had never been designed for this sort of treatment. A generator wandering around the engine compartment was not something you wanted in rough seas, so it was slow speed into the nearest harbour in Portugal, and that was the end of that attempt.

By 2001, Fabio was going up in the world and had built an 80-footer with four 1,500 hp MTU diesels. Fabio had long had ambitions to tackle the Atlantic record, and this new boat might have been a feasible contender. However, after carrying out sea-trials, he realised that the boat would never have the fuel range for the Atlantic distance. Undaunted, we tackled a series of European records, starting with the Round Italy record, going on to the Monte Carlo-to-London, and finishing with a Round Britain record-attempt. It would be a unique accomplishment to achieve all three of these records in one year. But it was not going to be easy, not even with such a promising design, tailor-made for record-breaking. Part of the problem was the clash of personalities between Fabio and the owner, Hannes Bohic. Part was Fabio's assumption that going fast was all that mattered, and that the weather would sort itself out.

The boat would do up to 60 knots when empty of fuel. Fully fuelled with over 12 tonnes of diesel, it was down to 45 knots. The design was really an updated version of VIRGIN ATLANTIC CHALLENGER II, but crammed with more modern technology. The boat had plenty of speed for the records that we were after, and when we left Venice on the Round Italy record-attempt, it was in the easiest conditions I have ever experienced for record-breaking, with almost flat calms most of the way down the East Coast. By the time we were refuelling in Messina, we were well ahead of schedule and feeling relaxed. But the weather turned foul as we cleared the Straits of Messina, pitching us into a head wind that just got stronger and stronger. Running through the night, the conditions got worse and worse.

Eventually we altered course to head into Olbia, in Sardinia, to get a respite from the rough seas. As there was no previous record, the time factor was not so critical. The next day it was still rough for the run up to the finish at Monte Carlo, but Fabio cleverly got into the lee of the passenger ferry that ran from Corsica to Nice for an easier ride, peeling off to Monte Carlo towards the end. You would have thought that trip would make him take weather forecasts more seriously. It was not too be.

We were refuelled and ready for the long Monte Carlo-to-London record soon afterwards. This was a tough one as far as the weather was concerned, again doing battle with the Atlantic and the Bay of Biscay. Whatever the forecast said, you were always at the mercy of short-term weather changes. Indeed, Fabio and I had a falling-out about exactly that when our first possible weather window appeared. I thought the forecast pattern was just too tight, with not enough margin for small changes in our run up the West Coast of Spain. Strong winds were forecast about 100 miles offshore, but only reduced winds inshore. To me, that was just too small a margin to take chances with. But they, the forecasters, thought it would be OK. I was so unhappy at how it looked, I told Fabio he could go without me if he wanted to - the kind of shock treatment his Italian temperament needed from time to time. In the end he saw sense, and we waited another two weeks for better conditions. Even then, things were not easy. It was a long gruelling ride up that West Coast of Spain and across the Bay.

After negotiating the difficult Chanel du Four inside Ushant at night, our run up-Channel was in following seas, which gave us an easy ride. It was exciting, in our fast-boat, flat-out in the shipping lanes, overtaking these full-size ships as if they were standing still. Because we were over 20-metres long, we had to stick to the marked traffic lanes of the one-way system. There was so much traffic out there in the Channel, the regulations were as strict as anywhere on land. So there was a dog's leg in the course, before we could turn up into the Thames Estuary and smell the finish line at Gravesend. Ideally, from a public impact point of view, the finish for this record should have been in the middle of London, at Tower Bridge. Unfortunately the authorities were not keen for you to run up the river at 60 knots. Respecting this, we even took the boat off the plane for the last five miles to Gravesend. The last thing we wanted after so many miles was a speeding ticket. It took us two-and-a-half days to make the run from Monte Carlo to London, well inside the record we had set in ULTIMA. Given the right conditions, there was no doubt it could have been a lot less.

Next on our schedule was the Round Britain record. Again the weather did not co-operate. In fact we had virtually given up finding a weather window that year. But when a gap suddenly appeared in mid-September, the Italians hastily jumped on a plane and we assembled in Poole for an early morning start. The forecast was quite fantastic. Nothing more that 5 knots of wind over the whole of the British Isles for the next two days. It was a rare opportunity and we crossed the start line at 6.00 am. At the same moment, to my horror, virtually all the navigation electronics went down. No, no, these were perfect conditions, it could not be happening! Out came the screwdrivers. Roaring down-Channel, we managed to coax some life into one radar and one electronic chart system.

The rest stayed stubbornly out, which made me very nervous about reliability. Anyway, the weather window was too good to miss, so we had to take the chance. I was relieved that I had done all my homework on the paper charts as well.

Unlike the Drambuie attempt, this boat could get us round Britain with just one refuelling stop - at Scrabster in the north of Scotland. Everything went well as we rounded Land's End, heading north in almost flat calm conditions. Then in the middle of the Irish Sea, one of the engines started to falter. A moment later, it caught fire from a fuel leak. There was no panic, but we wasted nearly an hour sorting things out. The engine was never a hundred per cent after that, though at least we were off and running at high speed again. Up through the Scottish Islands, it was exciting navigation in the dark, particularly through some of the narrow channels such as the Kyle of Lochalsh. The weather held round the top of Scotland and on to Scrabster, where the refuelling was very efficient. In under an hour we were on our way, excited by our progress. It was still only 11.00 at night, so we had covered over half the route in just 17 hours, including the delays. Just imagine leaving the South Coast of England in the morning and going round the top of Scotland that same night.

After leaving Scrabster, we first had to negotiate the Pentland Firth. Once more it was a virtually calm and I was beginning to wonder what all the fuss was with this stretch of water. We picked up a bit of a lively sea, heading down the East Coast, but it did not slow us much. This was an open water stretch, where I could get a bit of a rest. Up until then it had been virtually non-stop navigation, very different from crossing the Atlantic. At 60 knots in confined waters, you had to make instant decisions about where to go next - and you could only do that if you had everything well-prepared beforehand.

It was also a good job that one chart plotter kept going down the East Coast. Visual navigation there at high speed could be very difficult. Big and obvious, towering above the sea, the North Sea oil rigs gave us a good guide in some areas. Further south there were sand banks lying in wait, where you had to pick up the buoys that would guide you round them. Then it was on round North Foreland and into the Channel once more, again making a detour to keep legally within the shipping lanes. Now we were hanging on every beat of the engines, particularly the sick one, roaring through the Solent on the finishing stretch back to Poole. By lunch time we were there, with a heavy sigh of relief. Right round Britain, we had completed the run in a little over 30 hours, setting not only a convincing new record, but one that looked very hard to beat. Over the whole 1,200-mile route, our average speed was more than 44 knots.

That was a good note on which to end the season. It was difficult record-breaking and every triumph was hard-won. Looming over them was still the one that I had never done: the Round the World record. In fact no one had ever made an attempt in a smallish fast-boat. So when the chance actually came up, I grabbed it.

Steve Schidler from California had done many long distance runs in fuel-efficient trimaran designs, and had set his sights on going round the world. With my experience, I was asked to come along as navigator and planner. That year, at the Miami Boat Show, I had my chance to try this single-engined craft. It certainly looked different, the slim main hull

Steve Schidler's craft for a Round the World attempt certainly looked different. With a very slender hull and wave piercing technology, it was smaller than other record-breakers and I was not convinced it was up to the job.

stabilised by very narrow side hulls, with only very basic accommodation.

Was it up to the job? It was mean enough, though it looked tiny compared with other long-distance record-breakers. Departure was planned for two weeks later, February and March being the best months for Round the World weather, especially if you wanted to avoid the hurricane and typhoon seasons in the different areas.

I got worried about this project when I found that despite our two-week deadline, the communications and navigation needs had not even been considered. Steve wanted me to go round the boat show to see if I could scrounge donations from exhibiters to finish the fit-out. That was when I realised the whole thing was a long way from the adequate funding and planning that were essential to success. I decided it was time to back away, still offering whatever support I could. Daring was one thing, reckless was another. And I did not want to set off around the world in a boat that was only half-prepared. I know I made the right decision. Shortly afterwards, when I heard that they had passed through the Panama Canal, they ran aground off the coast of Costa Rica, wrecking the boat completely. Perhaps if I had been there, it might not have run aground. But it was more a failure of equipment than people, so I am sure I made the right decision to stay out of it.

With my seventieth birthday approaching, it was maybe time to stop whilst I was on top. However I have since set a couple of personal records that I am sure are worth recording. The first was in celebration of my seventieth. Fabio Buzzi and I share the same birth-date, although he is 10 years younger. For my birthday present, he offered me the chance to drive his new hydroplane. This was his latest, very high-speed design - a little 7-metre three-pointer powered by a 1,000 hp gas turbine. Fabio had used it to win the celebrated Pavia-to-Venice Race that year. This was a crazy race down the River Po in Italy, in which you could enter any type of boat you liked, as long as it was fast. This latest hydroplane was certainly fast.

Now, as I had never driven a hydroplane before in my life, Fabio offered one of his slower hydroplanes to do a warm-up run. This was to get me used to the high speed in this very small, and very different, kind of boat. I only got up to around 100 mph in that trial boat, but I found it a very exciting ride, roaring up and down Lake Como.

Now came the moment of truth in the turbine boat. I squeezed myself into the tiny cockpit, not much bigger than a Grand Prix racing car, and tried to get comfortable. You didn't get a chance to get used to handling and the learning curve was very steep.

The turbine was in gear when you fired it up and you were heading out into the lake picking up speed all the time. The black cliffs on the other side rushed up very fast. About then was when I tried to remember what Fabio said about turning this boat. You had to drop a little fin on the inboard side to help the boat to turn.

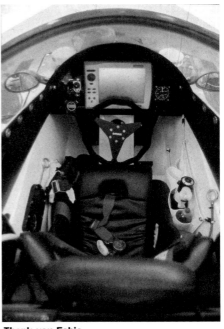

Thank you Fabio
My 70th birthday present was a fast ride in one of Fabio's hydroplanes. He was the first European to push one beyond 150 mph!

Simple enough, I managed this. Now there was a long expanse of lake stretching ahead. I put my foot down on the throttle to get the boat really moving and wow, it was a pure adrenalin rush.

At first I was cruising at around 100 mph, a really incredible ride, so I put my foot down further. The turbine responded immediately and just when you thought the boat could never go any faster it continued to accelerate. On one of the turns, my foot slipped off the throttle and got wedged between the pedal and a fixed part of the boat. Every time I tried to pull my foot out, the boat just went faster. When I snatched a glance at the dials, I was doing 145 mph. This was fantastic. Now I just wanted more and more speed. The boat responded.

But there was a downside. Lake Como in summer was a busy place, and I started to hit the wash of pleasure steamers that plied the lake. With the boat flying out of the water, I thought maybe this was the time to quit going any faster. But I did not want to stop, and it was only when the fuel got low that I headed for the shore. I don't think I have ever had such an exciting ride in my life. It put me on a high for days afterwards, possibly because I was still alive. At that sort of speed in a small boat, you only made one mistake and you were dead. The solution was simple, don't make a mistake. Thank you, Fabio, for the best birthday present ever.

The following year in America, I drove a 33-foot catamaran that went even faster. This was amazing for a production boat, one you could literally buy off the shelf. It was built by Nor-Tech and powered by two 1,100 hp petrol engines. We towed it to the launching ramp on its trailer and backed it into the water. The engines were fired up, and there we were, roaring across the harbour at Fort Myers, reaching speeds of 155 mph. It lacked the excitement and intimacy of the hydroplane ride, partly because the water was flat calm. But that was some production boat - and a personal record for me in terms of high speed. It was a ride that made me realise just how far fast-boat development had come since my early days.

CHAPTER 11

FAST AND FAMOUS

You met a lot of interesting people in racing and record-breaking. Offshore racing in particular attracted many of the rich and famous, and two of the people that I have raced with have since become kings and one has become a vice-president. I do not claim that I was in any way responsible for these elevations to high rank, but they did show that offshore racing could be a good stepping-stone up the ladder of fame. It was also a very good way to spend huge sums of money, one reason perhaps, why so many rich people were involved.

One of these was King Abdullah of Jordan. My association began when I was invited as a guest to Jordan, to help run a powerboat race in the Gulf of Aqaba. This was back when Hussein bin Talal was king, the

King Abdullah of Jordan (centre). He was still a prince when I first met him, at the helm of a 38-foot Aronow racing cat.

Father of Modern Jordan. The plan was to invite competitors from various nearby Arab countries that were taking up this new water sport for the first time. The Gulf of Aqaba had four countries bordering it; Jordan, Israel, Saudi Arabia and Egypt. The planned course would take in the waters of three of them. Because of politics, the racers would have to avoid Israeli waters, which were patrolled by a gunboat. This was to be the inaugural Three-Countries Race, held under the auspices of the King of Jordan.

I got the full royal treatment, starting with the flight out - First Class travel and VIP lounges all the way down to the town of Aqaba, where we set about getting the race ready. Not only was I involved in setting up, which was not difficult, I was going to drive one the King's boats in the race itself. Amongst his fleet of boats was a pair of 38-foot Aronow cats,

which each of his two sons was going to drive. I was allocated to Prince Abdullah, the eldest son who is now the King. With that, everything was set for the race day.

To make sure the race boats kept well clear of Israeli waters, we stationed a big Port of Aqaba harbour tug on the turning mark, so it would be visible from a long way off. This gave a clear indication for the racers to keep outside it, away from Israeli waters. Two teams from Kuwait had made the long road journey down with their small fast catamarans. After the start they leapt into the lead and disappeared

Prince Abdullah is son of the late King Hussein, known throughout the Middle East as the Father of Modern Jordan.

over the horizon. They knew they were looking for some sort of large craft, so when a big, grey vessel came into sight, they headed for it, to make the turn. What they did not realise was that their chosen turning mark was actually the Israeli gunboat. And from the Israelis' point of view, their fast approach did not look too friendly either. It could have been a disaster, and I think only their speed saved them from being blasted out of the water. As it was they carried on, quite oblivious to the political havoc they were causing behind them. It took some hurried international phone calls to sort out that incident.

King Hussein with his family. He took me on a personal helicopter tour of Jordan's most famous tourist sites.

Because they had rounded the wrong mark, these two very fast boats would be disqualified, even though they came in well ahead of the rest of the fleet. This meant the two King's boats would come in first and second, probably the best diplomatic move of the day. All in all, the race was a considerable success, so we were invited to the Royal Palace at Aqaba for lunch - after taking King Hussein and Queen Noor for a ride in the boat. Lunch was a wonderfully personal affair, and King Hussein asked if we had had much chance to see his country. When we said no,

Prince Albert of Monaco

we had been too busy organising the race, he offered to take us on a sight-seeing tour in his Black Hawk helicopter. And there it was, sitting on the tarmac outside.

This was the ultimate tourist experience, a personal tour of the country, in a helicopter flown by the King. As a result, we saw bits of Jordan that I was sure no tourist ever got to see. We landed up in the mountains for some magnificent views, then chased camels in the desert from the air. We saw all the usual tourist attractions too, including Petra, all from only a few hundred feet up. On arrival back at Aqaba, the two Princes were out fishing. So the King buzzed them from the air, doing wheelies in the helicopter above them. After that, no tourist holiday could ever seem the same.

The other prince now king was Prince Albert of Monaco. He was with us on the first of the Venice-to-Monte Carlo races, together with his brother-in-law, Stefano Casiraghi, second husband of Princess Caroline. Albert was new to powerboat racing, and as far as I am aware, has not done another race since. Casiraghi on the other hand, was

Stefano Casiraghi
The second husband of Princess Caroline of Monaco, Casiraghi was killed defending the World Offshore Powerboat Championship in Monaco.

Daniel Scioli
World Champion several years running, Daniel was one of the few with the skills sharp enough to take the controls of LA GRAN ARGENTINA, despite losing an arm in an earlier racing accident.

an avid racer, competing in the Fabio Buzzi boat CESA, only the year after we had won the World Championship in her. From CESA he went on to compete in a smaller Buzzi catamaran, and it was in this smaller boat that he was killed, competing in a race at Monte Carlo. I was close-by when it happened. It looked like he came around a turn mark, heading into lively seas that were running at the time. As he made the turn, the sun would have been right ahead, shining into his eyes. My guess is that he could not read the seas, and drove the boat straight into a wave at high speed.

This brought home in a very vivid way, some of the risks associated with fast-boats. It only took a split-second of misjudgement for things to go seriously wrong. Earlier that day, I had been approached by a group of Italian powerboat drivers including Casiraghi, who were interested in forming a consortium to make an attempt on the Atlantic record. They wanted me to add my experience to their team, but I think after Casiraghi's death this interest faded. Indeed it cast a pall over the whole of the offshore fraternity. I had had dinner with Casiraghi the night before he was killed, because he was interested in using CESA to attempt a Round Britain record. Of course, that did not happen either.

As for my Vice-President - well, Daniel Scioli is now Vice-President of Argentina. I first met him when he was part of our team, competing in the first Venice-to-Monte Carlo race. He was a very successful off-shore racer, teaming up with Fabio Buzzi in the American Superboat class, where LA GRAN ARGENTINA dominated the scene for two seasons.

Old Presidential yacht
Once the prestigious state icon of Argentina's president, General Juan Perón, the steam yacht TEQUARA was falling apart in Buenos Aires harbour by the time I got to her.

Scioli was the driver when we competed in the Round Scotland Race too, but it was only when I visited Argentina that I could see just how popular he was back home.

In Argentina, Scioli was racing with the then-President of the country in a local offshore race, when they had an huge accident. The President escaped without injury, but Scioli lost an arm. That could have been the end of his racing career. But ever since I have known him he has raced with just one arm, and been incredibly successful.

I was in Argentina to do a survey

General and Eva Peron
A touch of nostalgia from Perón's glory days, probably 1947. The president and his wife aboard TEQUARA before cancer claimed her.

on the old presidential yacht that was slowly rotting away in the harbour. This yacht was the setting for several voyages by General and Eva Perón, built in 1923. It was now well past its sell-by-date, auctioned off and bought by Juan Taylor, the Argentinean guy that I had raced with in that memorable event on Lake Geneva. There was a strong move in the country to get the yacht restored as part of the nation's heritage. In reality, it was falling apart, and I was the independent surveyor brought in to pronounce on its state.

It was an interesting trip to Argentina, not long after the Falklands War, so we British were not exactly popular. I was staying in the old Presidential Palace which had featured in the film Evita, continuing my Presidential association. Fallen from its glory, the palace now had rooms to let. Based there, I did the survey as requested. Then I met up with Scioli, and we spent a day cruising in his yacht up-river. The day ended going into a restaurant with Scioli, where all the diners stood and applauded him as we came in. That was before he became a politician. At the time he was a national hero, renowned for his offshore racing exploits.

Amongst other famous people I have gone boating with, Richard Branson must stand out as one of the stars. From the moment he came onboard with the Atlantic Challenger project, our lives were no longer our own. Part of the deal between Ted Toleman and Branson was they would have equal billing in any publicity associated with the event. The reality was no contest because Branson just had a natural flair for publicity. He could see opportunities when most ordinary mortals would never think there was any mileage to be had. This was brought home to me when we were rescued from the first VIRGIN ATLANTIC CHALLENGER, standing safe and on the deck of the rescue ship, enjoying a drink. Whilst we had been in the life-rafts, Branson had noticed one of the passengers on board filming the rescue. He went straight to him and immediately negotiated to buy the film, the only moving picture record of the actual rescue. While we were just standing there, grateful for being rescued, Branson was all business.

During all that time we were in New York, waiting for the weather on the first attempt, we would occasionally meet up with Branson for a drink in the evening. One day we were sitting in a street café in New York, and he asked what we had been up to that day on the boat. In return we asked him what he was doing in New York. Casually he said, 'I've just been trying to buy all the Beatles' songs.'

That must have been a deal worth many millions. He was a great guy to work with too. Once the main decisions had been made about the direction of the project and how it would operate, he just let you get on with it. And rarely was there criticism, provided you did a good job. But one day his enthusiasm for publicity got the better of him, and we had a huge row.

After we set the record, we returned to Lowestoft where the boat was built, where vast crowds were out to greet us. Branson wanted to put on a show for the crowd, and joined us on the deck of VIRGIN ATLANTIC CHALLENGER II from a helicopter off the entrance to the harbour. I took the boat through the piers and the bridge at slow speed and as we reached the Inner Harbour Branson said, 'Right Dag, go at full speed now up the harbour to give the crowds a show'.

At 20 knots, let alone 50, we would have probably sunk half the boats in the harbour. So I refused. Branson was furious and ordered me off the helm. Well, he was the boss and the owner. But I refused again, saying I was not in the business of killing people for a show. We continued at slow speed up to the harbour, with still Branson fuming. In his favour, he did have the grace to apologise afterwards, and thank me for not letting him do something stupid.

You got to know a guy intimately when you were on a boat like that for any length of time, so most of the time I had tremendous admiration for him. We even shared a hotel bedroom once in Brighton, though don't think for a moment that our relationship was that intimate.

After VIRGIN ATLANTIC CHALLENGER II, I was invited to play in his cricket team, made up mainly of pop stars from the recording studios near his Oxford home. These young kids really did not have much idea about how cricket was played, but those days out were always a lot of fun. Another event was a big party at his home that ranged over several fields, with bands playing and sideshows and whatever. It was strange meeting many of the pop stars of the day, relaxed and away from their publicity machines. We had a lot of them on board the boat at different times as well, many of whom I had never heard of. Of course my children always wanted me to get autographs. It was a strange world that was nice to visit, but I would have hated to get involved with it on any permanent basis.

Probably the most major collection of stars that I was involved with was when we did Richard Branson's TV presentation of *This Is Your Life*. This was in the days of Eamon Andrews and the Red Book. As the crew of VIRGIN ATLANTIC CHALLENGER II, we were involved in doing the pick-up with Eamon on board Branson's houseboat that was moored in the Regent Canal, north London. We were all dressed up as pirates by the BBC costume section in London, then bussed down to the canal. There a canal boat waited to take us to Branson's houseboat, his main office in those days. The BBC had thoughtfully placed a bottle of whisky on board to keep our spirits up, and the plan was to slide alongside Branson's boat where the pick-up would be made, and the Red Book presentation would take place.

Branson's attention was diverted by being interviewed supposedly for children's TV. We went alongside just forward of his boat, then boarded with cutlasses in our teeth, trying to look like pirates, which I did not find too difficult. We burst in on the false TV interview and the Red Book was presented. Then we all went back to the studios where the show took place, and one after another these stars came in to say their piece. The party in the Green Room afterwards was something else. But in the eyes of my children I disgraced myself when I was introduced to Phil Collins.

'Phil who?' I asked.

I never was much good at names.

Then of course, I worked with the Aga Khan on the DESTRIERO project, but he was very much the figurehead and not involved in day-to-day organisation. However there was a memorable party in Costa Smeralda in Sardinia to celebrate the record, where a notable sprinkling of famous names turned up. In good Italian style this was a pretty formal affair, so when Richard Branson arrived in his normal sweater, he was a bit out of place. I had to lend him a jacket and tie so that he could smarten up a bit.

On a final note in this name-dropping chapter, I taught racing driver David Coulthard to drive. I think he was pretty good at driving cars by the time I got him, but that was the day job. For pleasure he liked driving boats. When he bought a small fast sports boat, I was invited to spend a happy day showing him the finer points of fast-boat driving, then anchoring and going swimming, topped off by dining with him and his then-girl friend as company. It was a good moment when David dropped me off in the harbour at Monte Carlo. And certainly turned the heads of the locals.

CHAPTER 12

THE ART OF BEING RESCUED

It might seem a strange claim to fame, but I think that I am one of the most rescued people in the world. My tally so far, and I hope it goes no higher, is ten rescues. Now, you might think being rescued ten times shows a degree of carelessness. I like to think that it shows a degree of skill, because I survived all ten. Some of them were very serious indeed, as you may have gathered already from this book. Now for some detail about the actual rescues, to balance my successes with some of my failures. One strange thing about this modern world is that you are often more applauded for heroic failure than you are for hard-fought success. I have certainly had my share of heroic failures. So in recording these rescues, I hope there are lessons that can be learned should readers find themselves in similar predicaments.

There are two types of disaster at sea, slow and fast. With the slow ones, there is all time in the world to think what to do for the unexpected situation you find yourself in - if only you can get your brain into gear from the inevitable panic that goes with it. Slow accidents might be when a boat is sinking, or has run aground. Fast ones are more like a collision, or something that happens very suddenly. With a fast accident there is no time to think, you react mainly by instinct.

Time to think leads to all sorts of speculation, most of it not very positive. The future, for instance, can look very bleak when you spend ages contemplating it from the loneliness of a life-raft. For that reason, it's always best to find something that occupies your mind, not easy when you're waiting to be rescued. Those long hours of nothing do little to improve your situation. But nobody can dread the end of the world for ever.

So after a couple of hours, if things have not got any worse, you will find you cannot sustain this level of tension and more normal emotions will return. You will feel hungry and you will want to sleep. Life will go on, even though the risk may remain.

That reduction in tension is because your defence mechanisms switch in. I always find it amazing just how quickly you can come to terms with disaster at sea. It helps even more if you can find something constructive to do. Coping with disaster, or near-disaster, is never easy.

But the worst part is having time to think about things. It does not take a very vivid imagination to drop yourself into worst-case scenarios. And in these of course, you inevitably end up dead, or dying. It is your mental attitude that is most likely to make or break your survival chances, so it is best not to have too vivid an imagination. If you have a radio to talk to the outside world, that can help to put things into perspective. Which of course is probably the best help of all in any emergency situation.

By far the worst of these feelings of dread arise from sudden dramas, like collisions. Here you are thrown into a state of shock, reducing your ability for rational thought.

I have been involved in two collisions on the water, one between two ships, which coincided with my first trip to sea. That incident caused more surprise than damage. The other collision was a near-death experience, probably the closest call I have ever had on the water.

It started quite innocently. We were out on a photo shoot, taking pictures of a 65-foot, 35-knot power catamaran. Manoeuvring around and trying for dramatic angles put us in the wrong place at the wrong time, so that the catamaran rode right up over the top of us, even reaching and hitting our mast.

Our camera platform was a 40-foot sailing cat, a nice stable base to shoot from, and we were motoring in calm conditions on the River Crouch. I wanted to get some "wow" pictures looking down the tunnel of the power-cat, so we set up a dramatic angle as it was approaching from astern, rapidly overtaking us. Quite how it happened was a bit of a blur. Closing up on us fast, the cat's skipper was a bit indecisive about which side to pass. He left it too late and the power-cat hit us, rearing up over our stern, right where I was standing. Its speed on impact was probably around 25 knots, and the port hull hit me hard, knocking me

Disaster about to happen
At a speed of 25 knots, 30 seconds before impact. The catamaran rode up over our hull, knocking me down and carving a groove into the deck.

to the deck. The cat's keel, bearing down with all that weight and speed, chopped into us just two feet to one side of me, carving a groove in the deck. Not quite sure what had happened, I found myself lying under the cat's hull, which was still moving, just above my nose. A few inches the other way and I would have been dead, crushed under the cat. The noise was incredible, seeming to last for ever as the power-cat rammed itself further forward over us, only stopping when it hit the mast. Then, its engines still racing before somebody shut them off, it slipped slowly backwards into the water, leaving us in what looked like a battleground.

Still lying on the deck, I was too fearful to move, expecting to see broken bodies in the cockpit. Amazingly, none of us was seriously hurt, though as you can imagine, I was battered and bruised all over. Even then, my mind kept working, chasing priorities from long-ingrained reflex. I remember checking the bilges to see if we were sinking. It was hard to believe that the hull was intact and the engines still worked. The worst of course was the shock. I have a hazy recollection of getting the train home, then three days of shaking and feeling very unwell.

That accident still gives me bad feelings whenever I think about it. There was a lesson too. One that I should have had firmly in mind after all my years at sea. Never, never play boats at close quarters. It only takes one slip, one mistake, and disaster will strike.

That first rescue I had, when we grounded on a sandbank close to the entrance to Ramsgate Harbour, was a very gentle affair by comparison. We may not have had radio to communicate our plight, but we were well within visual range. We just had to wait until the lifeboat came out to tow us off. Plus, in those days, small boats tended not to have exposed propellers and rudders that got damaged in grounding. The only hurt was to our pride.

There are many rescue situations that are more routine than dangerous, though there is always the chance that they can escalate. Several of my rescues have been tow-jobs after engines have failed, a familiar hazard with racing boats, when engines were working under very high stress. Another tow-in I needed was when I was delivering a fishing boat, off the south Wales coast. I was running this small boat on my own when after only two hours at sea, I realised that the fuel was very contaminated. Dirt was building up in the filters so quickly that I had to strip and clean them every ten miles or so. This meant priming the fuel system each time before restarting, every time making the battery flatter and flatter. Eventually it failed altogether, with no chance of re-starting the engine. Fortunately I was clear of land and in no danger, so I could wait for a passing boat. Just sitting there with nothing to do made me realise how vulnerable you can be without a radio on board.

One of the worst machinery failures I experienced was on the West Coast of the US. This was on another record-attempt, running what was claimed to be the "world's fastest fishing boat" from Seattle to Alaska. The plan was to have breakfast in Seattle and dinner in Ketchikan, way up north. On the way we would pass through some of the most breathtaking scenery in the world, through narrow channels between the thousands of islands in the region. The 50-foot boat was called ORDER OF MAGNITUDE, and was powered by a 5,000 hp gas turbine with a small diesel installed as an auxiliary. Both of these engines were coupled to the same shaft, then to a single water jet. The boat was designed for catching Alaskan salmon, which for the ecology cycle and to preserve stocks, had a very short permissible fishing season. So short that the fastest boat to arrive at the fishing grounds got the pick of the catch.

We set out from Seattle at first light. A daylight trip was vital because these waters were littered with "dead heads", huge sections of tree-trunks that floated end-up, just above the surface of the water. If you hit one of those at 50 knots, you would be calling for help rapidly.

We made good progress through these dangerous waters, heading into Canada as we passed inside Vancouver Island. Suddenly there was a loud bang and the turbine screamed. Then everything shut down, leaving a still and very painful quiet. The main drive-shaft to the water jet had broken. As both engines were connected to this same shaft, we could go nowhere. Disappointed that our record-attempt was scuppered, we were now being blown rapidly ashore, onto rocks that did not look at all friendly. We put a call out on the radio, but these were not very busy waters. Still drifting shorewards, we got the anchor ready to drop, hoping it would hold us clear of the rocks. At that moment, along came another fishing boat. They did a great job of towing us into Nanaimo on Vancouver Island, and that was all I saw of the great tourist sights along the West Coast of Canada and Alaska.

Sinking on a boat in a blaze of publicity was another experience altogether, tracked minute-by-minute on television. You would think with half the world watching, there would be few problems to being found and rescued. It did not turn out like that. On our first trans-Atlantic attempt, when the first VIRGIN ATLANTIC CHALLENGER was still on schedule and just 130 miles from the finish line at the Bishop Rock Lighthouse, there was a growing feeling of excitement on board, even though we were desperately tired. Then BANG!! The noise made us instantly wide-awake. Powering along at 45 knots, the whole boat shook as we hit something underwater. We will never know whether it was a submerged object, or just one wave too many. What we hit did not really matter. What did matter was that water was pouring into the hull through a large split along the chine.

The end is the end
My photo earned me £2,000. But watching VIRGIN ATLANTIC CHALLENGER sink was like watching an old friend die.

This is no drill
When VIRGIN ATLANTIC CHALLENGER sank it was the real thing. And a liferaft at sea is a lonely place, as Richard Branson and Chay Blyth discovered.

Strangely, my first feeling was one of relief. All the banging and crashing of our hurtling, bone-jarring ride had stopped, and the fact that we were sinking did not seem to matter. Then reality switched in, and it was serious. With the bilge pumps unable to cope, "Abandon Ship" was our only option. My next feeling was cruel disappointment at having victory snatched from our grasp. My third was fear, as we got the life-rafts launched. It was a very big and lonely ocean on which to be adrift.

That record-attempt was a risky venture from the start, and we were going where no fast-boat had gone before. Because of this, we had practiced emergency procedures before we left, and the training quickly took over. We all had a job to do – mine being on the radio, to send out what was to become the most famous distress message on the Atlantic since that from the TITANIC.

In the loneliness of the Atlantic, we could have no idea how famous we had become. When news of our distress call hit the headlines, the country sat on the edge of its seats waiting for news. Meanwhile VIRGIN ATLANTIC CHALLENGER was sinking rapidly by the stern, we had the life-rafts in the water, our survival suits were on - we even had time to put stores in the life-raft. It seemed impossible to get a response on the radio, our weak signal beaming out on high frequency. Afterwards we found out that our call had been received, but I had not heard the reply. I also transmitted on the VHF radio, in the hope that there might be a ship within twenty miles or so. After all we were in fairly busy shipping lanes, off the south of Ireland. Then it was too late. The water was over the batteries and the radios went dead. We weren't done for ourselves though. The EPIRB (Emergency Position Indicating Radio Beacon) was bleeping away and I had also triggered the Argos Beacon to indicate our distress and position. Ashore they knew we were in trouble. But out on the ocean we did not know they knew, and this was our main worry. I was up to my waist in water, with the boat sinking by the stern, before I decided to get out and follow the others into the life-rafts.

We had two life-rafts, so we split ourselves between the two and tied them together. You cannot believe how immense and lonely that ocean looked from the life-raft. It was getting dark, and we faced the prospect of a long night out in the open with rescue nowhere in sight. That was what made you really scared, thinking about your prospects of survival. Out on the ocean you created your own little world, unaware of the impact ashore. Aboard the life-raft our world had shrunk to a tiny rubber capsule, the waves were huge and threatening. I watched them come one by one and was scared stiff.

From previous experience in life-raft training, I knew how bad the motion could be in such a small craft, so one of the first things I did when we started sinking was to take a seasick pill. It saved my strength and my sanity. Out of the nine people on the two life-rafts, only two of us did not suffer from seasickness. If you were seasick, you just gave up and survival was no longer a strong instinct. Of course I knew this from long ago on the MARJATA, and to this day I always have seasick pills with me every time I go to sea. In the small confines of a life-raft the motion was terrible, it was crowded and you were constantly irritated by what the others were doing. Everybody wanted to be at the small doorway in the life-raft cover, to get fresh air and to see what was going on. The awful hemmed-in feeling was not conducive to survival.

Apart from the seasick pills, the two most important things I took with me on that VIRGIN ATLANTIC CHALLENGER rescue were the portable VHF radio and my camera. Forget about flares and other distress signals, a radio beat them all. Not only could you call for help, but you also knew that someone had heard you and was hopefully responding. You could also indicate your problem and discuss how the rescue was going to proceed. The radio gave an enormous psychological boost and was your best friend in the life-raft. As for the camera, it gave me something to do, taking photos of the sinking boat and the life-rafts, photos that earned me £2,000 from a newspaper when we finally stepped ashore. Watching the boat sinking was another depressing moment. We had lived and breathed this project for over a year. Watching that boat slowly going down was like watching an old friend die.

Rescue came in just over an hour. The first indication we had that the outside world knew of our plight was when the Press aircraft found us. Their arrival was almost accidental. They were actually flying out to photograph us in the last of the evening light, on our way to the finish line. They got something of a scoop that day. And, much more important to us, we knew we had been spotted. Then came the wonderful sight. Not one, but two ships, coming over the horizon. It raised our spirits enormously and we felt that rescue was at hand.

However you were not rescued until you were standing on the deck of the rescue ship. So there were several anxious moments as the rescue ship parked alongside our two tiny life-rafts. This was a superb bit of seamanship. To this day, I remain eternally grateful for the skills of the captain of the GEESTBAY, our rescue ship. They fired a rocket line between our two rafts. It felt a bit scary, but with that line they could pull us alongside. We were nearly home and dry.

When they lowered the gangway, we could simply walk up. We had no women or children on board our life-raft, so I did not hesitate. I was first out, still in my not very elegant survival suit and life-jacket. There, at the top of the gangway, was a steward in a white jacket and black bow tie, with a silver tray of brandy glasses saying, 'Will you have a drink sir?'

What a wonderful return to civilization!

British ships certainly know how to treat rescued seafarers. The Captain was pretty insistent that we stay for dinner - but the two helicopters, one from the RAF and one from the Navy, were hovering overhead, waiting to take us off. We were winched up and taken ashore to a hero's welcome in the Scilly Isles. The memory of our time in the life-raft remains a vivid image. Dark, congested, scary - and very lonely. Ever since, I have managed to stay out of them. One experience is enough for a lifetime, thank you.

That rescue from VIRGIN ATLANTIC CHALLENGER was a pretty civilized and efficient affair. Our rescue from CHAFFOTEAUX CHALLENGER was very different. You will recall that this 80-foot catamaran started to break up because of cracks in the hull when we were attempting to set a new record under sail across the Atlantic. We had decided to abandon the yacht under the most controlled conditions possible in order to reduce the risks. That was why we decided to wait until daylight the following day. Rescue at night doubled the risks and we hoped that the boat would stay in one piece long enough for a daylight rescue. It was a difficult call.

SEALAND PERFORMANCE
The ship that rescued us from CHAFFOTEAUX CHALLENGER was the largest container ship in the world at the time, but not designed for rescue at sea.

Should we call for help immediately or should we wait and risk things getting worse? You did not want to make an unnecessary fuss, but you also wanted to get out, before things on board got too life-threatening. I still remember that dark and endless night. On top of everything else, we knew another storm was coming close.

Every hour on the hour, I called the Coastguard on the VHF link, giving our position update from a claustrophobic huddle inside the cross-beam of the catamaran, struggling with the reluctant radio. I knew that if the boat broke up it would be very sudden. I also knew I could be trapped inside that compartment. The hardest part was trying to keep my voice sounding steady and professional. All I really wanted to do was scream for help. At the same time, I knew all the shipping in the Atlantic was listening, so trying not to sound panicky was a professional priority. That worked both ways. You could sense the relief every time we came on the air. If they heard nothing, it meant we could well be dead, but please come and find us anyway.

On board we kept busy bailing and getting organized for rescue. Then next morning, the promised rescue ship came over the horizon. Whilst the SEALAND PERFORMANCE was a very welcome sight, you cannot imagine how scary that 900-foot container ship was, parking almost on top of us. It towered over our tiny boat, looking ready to push us under with its huge bow. Safe alongside of course, there was the relief that somebody else was taking over, that in a few moments we would be virtually home and dry. As it turned out, getting alongside was the easy part. Now we needed a rope to hold us in position.

I shouted up to the deck of the ship, 40 feet above us. 'Give us a rope!'

They stared back in fascination. 'We don't have any ropes on board this ship!'

Now disaster beckoned. We were drifting along the side of the ship, which was still moving ahead to keep steerage way. A projection from the ship's side caught in our rigging. As we slid past, the strain caused the rigging to snap, which brought the whole mast down, a ton of metal twisting and crashing onto the deck. We had survived our hull starting

Give us a rope
The deck was forty feet above us. But, modern ships like the SEALAND PERFORMANCE had no rope to help us.

to break up. We had survived the ship coming alongside. Now we survived the mast collapsing. But the worst was to come. And we were still a long way from being rescued.

Without its mast, CHAFFOTEAUX CHALLENGEr was just a low, flat platform. The ship still was moving ahead and we were still bumping down its side. As we arrived at the stern, the ship's momentum sucked us underneath the overhang. Right in front of us, the giant propeller was turning round ever so slowly. Remorselessly. I watched in horror as the bow slammed into that spinning, 28-foot chopping machine. It arced round like a giant bacon-slicer, slicing bits off the bow. It got worse still. As if not satisfied that the propeller would finish us off, the ship lifted on a swell, then sat on us, pushing us underwater.

It was like a scene from a James Bond movie. Except that Hollywood could never come up with such a nightmare. No amount of training taught you to cope with this sort of situation, nor was it in any handbook I had ever read. Thank God it happened so quickly that I do not remember being scared - just the feeling of total helplessness as the world slid rapidly out of control. Amazingly, none of our crew was injured. I dived for cover in the cross-beam that had been my refuge for the past week, trying to escape the thrashing cataclysm. Normally there was about four feet of headroom. It reduced to two as the ship sat on us, driving the whole thing underwater! With effort and a lot of luck, somehow I managed to wriggle my way out. It was great to see all the other guys were OK, dazed but still alive.

The sun never looked so good as it did when I came out of that flooded compartment. The fresh air was never so sweet. Incredibly, the VHF radio was still working. The Captain was amazed that we were still alive.

The 40ft side
SEALAND PERFORMANCE was like a mountain.

Climbing the side
Too tired to move, an electric hoist lifted us.

'Please don't do that again,' I said.

'I didn't aim to do it the first time,' was his reply, still astounded.

Chopped up and sat upon by a 60,000 ton giant, we were still no nearer to being rescued. We spent the next THREE HOURS on the radio, trying to talk ourselves out of this predicament. With its 40-foot freeboard and huge size, this container ship was far from the ideal rescue vessel. All the time we were in the water, the Captain was adamant that he would not risk his crew by lowering a lifeboat. This was not as callous as it seemed - more a matter-of-fact demonstration that many modern ships were just not equipped to carry out rescue work at sea.

Shipwrecked sailors in need of a drink
Polaroid photograph taken on board the GEEST BAY. VIRGIN ATLANTIC CHALLENGER'S crew with the ships Captain is dressed for dinner.

Our American rescuers from CHAFFOTEAUX CHALLENGER.
Wouldn't you know it - they took us back across the Atlantic, to Charleston.

Eventually, they found some ropes to hold us alongside. Then they lowered their pilot ladder, endlessly long and narrow, to climb up the 40-foot side. Thankfully it was fitted with an electric hoist. It was just as well. After all that time, I don't think any of us was in a fit state to climb the ship's side without assistance.

You can't believe how wonderful it was to stand on the deck of that ship. But still our problems were not over. It was an American ship, and the first thing we had to do was sign a waiver saying we would not sue them for the damage to our boat. It seemed there were lawyers around, even in the middle of the Atlantic. Next, and far more serious, we found that being American, the ship was "dry" - there was no alcohol on board. Of course you always wanted what you could not have, and I cannot remember wanting a drink so much at that moment.

Which means if ever you have any choice about who is going to rescue you, go for a British ship. If nothing else, the hospitality is so much better. And if I malign ships from other countries, I apologise, I have lived through too few rescues to make an exhaustive comparison of all nationalities!

That time we went aground with the Nourse Line ship TAPTI, early in my seagoing career, was a much more leisurely affair. Or perhaps I was more naïve in those days, less aware of the risks and dangers. We knew we were in trouble when the seas calmed down in the middle of that howling blizzard. That could mean only one thing. That though we could not see it, we were under the shelter of land. According to our planned course, we should have been a long way from land. But as we weren't where we thought we were, that did not help a lot, we simply had no clue about where we might be. The ship was in ballast and very high in the water, so she needed every ounce of power to keep her on course. It also meant that there was not a lot of stopping power to slow the ship down.

Nothing could quite describe the feeling of running aground on rocks. It had a terrible finality about it. And though you would love to have gone back five minutes and done things differently, it was too late for that option. Everything went seemingly silent, though the storm still raged over our heads. The ship stopped her restless rolling and pitching, becoming almost peaceful as she lay hard aground in the relative calm under the lee of the land. Of course we tried putting the engines astern to get the ship off. But hitting those rocks tore her bottom apart, and they were holding what was left very firmly in their grasp.

We sent out a Mayday - but as we were not where we should have been, we did not know which rocks we had hit, if you know what I mean. Because of the storm we had not been able to fix our position for a long time so we could have been anywhere on either side of the Minches Channel. Only when the blizzard eased later that night could we pick up a couple of distant flashing lights. We were close by the island of Tiree, where the lifeboat from Mallaig found us when it came to the rescue.

Fortunately, we were under the shelter of land when we hit the rocks, so there was no immediate danger. Our rescuers found us by taking DF (Direction Finding) bearings of our radio signals. Once again, the sensible option was to stay put with the ship until daylight, when a lifeboat could see to rescue us safely. That night was not as frightening as it was on CHAFFOTEAUX CHALLENGER. The ship was sitting pretty comfortably on the rocks, with not a lot of risk that she would break up in the short term.

It was, of course, a huge relief to see the lifeboat arrive the next morning. At the order "Abandon Ship", we lowered ourselves in the ship's boats to the water, so that we could transfer across at sea level. It was only when I read the reports of the lifeboat crew's heroism and the awards they received for their bravery, that I realised how much more serious our plight had been. They must have been fantastic seamen to get in alongside us and take us off like that. Perhaps my relief at being rescued made it seem easier than it was. By now the blizzard had eased, and we had what seemed like a relaxing trip back to Tobermory, where we were landed and I made my way home. It's still a wonder to me that after four years of serving aboard MARJATA, a ship that endured all sorts of near disasters, the one time we had to be rescued was when I transferred to her sister, TAPTI. Some ships were just born lucky.

So, with all this experience behind me, I can claim to be something of an expert at being rescued. To put it into perspective, I should also point out that I have been the rescuer of other people nine times, which almost sets the balance right. I only need a volunteer for one more rescue to set the books straight before I retire. Being a rescuer is very satisfying and there is a warm glow of achievement. There is not the same buzz when you are the person being rescued just a very scared feeling. Any rescue takes a great deal of thought and planning. You simply have to get it right because there may not be a second chance. The consequences of getting it wrong do not bear contemplating.

Thanks to my years with the RNLI, I have considerable experience of dealing with rescues and analysing people's actions. It is so easy to be wise after the event, but when you are thinking on your feet and everything is happening right in front of you, you do not always come up with the best answer immediately. There is a great tendency for the victim to think that the rescue ship or boat always knows best. Personal experience teaches me otherwise. They can be just a frightened as you are.

My tally of ten rescues has happened largely because I have pushed the envelope, trying to go fast in offshore racing boats, trying to break Atlantic records, trying to do things that have not been done before. Some would call this stupid, I would call it exciting. I have always been conscious of the risks and I have learned a lot, so that hopefully I will not make the same mistakes again.

CHAPTER 13

CRUISING WITH A DIFFERENCE

Whilst much of my life has been spent racing around in high-speed boats, I equally enjoy slower speed cruising. The snag with cruising is that it takes up a lot of time. There are not always enough holes in a busy schedule to relax. Then again, I tend to look for adventurous cruising - much more fun than the regular drift from marina to marina. Since my first four years at sea as an apprentice took me to many places off the beaten track, I keep looking for cruises in the more remote parts of the world, or which have the tingle of adventure about them.

When I was first involved in the development of RIBs all those years ago, I never imagined that they would become a boat for long-distance cruising. I think we started this trend way back in the 1970s, when three RIBs set out from the Bristol Channel to cruise out to the Fastnet Lighthouse, off the South West corner of Ireland, then back up the English Channel to Poole. These were relatively small Delta RIBs of 6 metres in length, and the plan was to stop each night in a hotel and really enjoy the trip, although we could expect some tough open sea sections along the route. Safety was pretty well covered by having three boats together. As the boats were very seaworthy and reliable, we did not have too many worries on that score.

We launched from the old ferry ramp under the Severn Bridge, and the run down the Bristol Channel to Milford Haven was achieved without incident, apart from the lively seas. Along this route we were in touch with the land the whole way, which gave a sense of security. But once we left Milford it was open sea all the way to a landfall in Ireland. At that time we were relying on a Decca Navigator for positioning, and it certainly did the business. After a few hours we ran into Dunmore

East and a warm welcome at the local hotel. Then it was back to coastal cruising, along the coast of southern Ireland to Baltimore and the Fastnet Rock. It was at Baltimore that we encountered the first problem with the boats being sabotaged - Baltimore West Cork that is, not Baltimore, Maryland! This sabotage put a new and unpleasant dimension on our cruising - a very deliberate attack with sugar in the fuel tanks and both Decca and radio antennas cut. It was difficult to imagine who we might have upset enough to have caused this damage.

The police thought that it was probably the work of drift-net salmon fishermen who operated off this coast. It appeared they might have thought we were some sort of official team come to monitor their activities, which were largely illegal. Presumably by stopping us from going to sea, they would have prevented us from monitoring what was going on. The locals were extremely helpful in helping us get sorted and back to sea again.

Fastnet Lighthouse
A friendly sight in a lonely ocean.

Our delay cost us a day, then we went off around the Fastnet Lighthouse and headed back to the Scilly Isles. This was a long open-water trip, wide open to the Atlantic. It got very lonely out there in our tiny RIBs, and we were well outside VHF radio range if we had needed to call for help. It was a great moment as we sighted the Round Island Lighthouse in the Scillies and headed into harbour after a very long day at sea. The sea conditions on that run had been relatively good, allowing us to keep up planing speeds. The next day there was a new challenge, thick fog, and not the kind caused by our hangovers. We did not have radar, but in a small manoeuvrable boat like a RIB, the lack of radar was not a serious problem. We were relying heavily on the Decca to get us safely to our landfalls, when we planned to slow down and creep carefully in to sight the land. First Land's End came up on cue, then the Lizard Point. At the Lizard we negotiated our way through the rocks off the headland rather than going well outside, something you could do safely in a RIB if you were careful. The next stop was the Eddystone Light, which began to turn the trip into something of a tour of remote lighthouses, like a return to my Trinity days. Finally we made Poole to end our seven-day pioneering voyage, a real adventure out there in small boats. Since then, RIBs have made all kinds of extensive cruises across open water. We just happened to be the pioneers of a whole new adventure sport.

A very different way to go cruising in inflatables was Camping Nautique. Here you cruised in inflatable boats, to land on a beach and camp out overnight. My introduction to this was on a trip in the Greek Islands, where the warm waters were an essential ingredient to this type of "back to nature" cruising. It was great fun cooking over an open fire on the beach in the evenings, and going out by boat to buy fish from passing fishermen for breakfast.

New Orleans
The Otech RIB took us fast round the Florida panhandle - where we saw the leaning lighthouse at St George before hurricane damage toppled it.

Back to RIB cruising, several years later I did a run from New Orleans to Miami in an Otech RIB. These were new waters for me and we had an easy, early morning start running along the Intracoastal Canal to Mobile before we headed out to sea. We did not have enough fuel to make the crossing direct down to the tip of Florida, so the plan was to hug the coastline, travelling from one refuelling stop to the next, usually refuelling twice a day. We stopped overnight in hotels, then headed out again the next day. The land along this coast was all low-lying, so the scenery was not very spectacular. Of course, the leaning lighthouse at St George was an interesting feature, and it was always exciting going into harbours that you had not visited before. It was a pretty lively ride, so we were glad of the refuelling and overnight stops as a break. The trouble was, it got harder and harder to leave harbour once we had stopped in this way. One of these refuelling stops was up the Suwannee River in the Florida Panhandle. Once we found the fuel-dock up a little side creek, this guy came strolling down scratching his head.

'Ain't never seen a boat like that before,' he commented. 'Ain't gonna sink is it?'

This was backwoods America, where they had never seen a RIB. At that time RIBs were still quite new in the US, and there weren't many about. Now they have really cottoned on to the virtues of RIB design, at least as far as yacht tenders are concerned, though they still have a long way to go to catch up with Europe. Anyway we hastened on, stopping at Fort Myers, then on through the Everglades to the Florida Keys. Navigating through the Everglades was a nightmare, with literally hundreds of confusing posts and marks to direct you through the torturous channels. Coming in from seaward, it was a job to pick out the right ones. The run up the Keys was interesting, with some good places to stop for lunch. Altogether, it took us just three days to make the whole trip to Miami, which must have been some sort of record.

Another shorter RIB trip was from just north of Belfast out to Rathlin Island off the North Coast. This was in a Storm Force RIB and the name proved to be very appropriate. The trip up was fine, and took around three hours. But it was blowing quite hard by the time we tied up in Rathlin Harbour. We had lunch in the local pub and one of our crew asked the landlord, 'How many people live on the island?'

Back came the reply, 'Well, I think they're all living at the moment'.

Getting back to the boat for the return trip, we were just in time to catch a weather forecast: winds of storm Force 10, imminent for our sea area. That was a pretty serious wind when you were in an 8-metre RIB. But as it was coming in from the west, we would only be exposed to it

Rathlin Island
'How many people live on the island?' we asked. 'I think they are all living at the moment,' was the reply.

for the first part of the trip. Then we would be under the lee of the land. We just made the open water section before the wind started really howling, arriving back safely. A rare place, wild and beautiful, Rathlin Island looked like one of those dreams where you could quite happily disappear off the face of the earth for a day or two. If you had to get weather-bound, that would be a good place to do it.

Another adventurous but very different cruise was to Stewart Island, to the south of New Zealand, the last bit of habitable land before you got to the South Pole. This was a scary place in the great Southern Ocean, the preserve of tough sail-boats and brave sailors embarked on round-the-world sailing adventures. It was also an area of powerful gales and rough seas, not the place for powerboats to venture without good reason. But there we were, heading south from Christchurch in New Zealand, preparing to stick our noses into this mighty ocean in a motor yacht.

Stewart Island deserved to be better recognized than it was, because here in the Roaring Forties at 47-degrees South, it forms one of the three major Capes that jut out into the Southern Ocean. Cape Horn and the Cape of Good Hope were both well known as major milestones on the shipping routes of the world. But the prosaically named South Cape, at the southern end of Stewart Island, was never on the main shipping routes because every sensible sailor headed north of New Zealand into the warmer waters of the Pacific. Since the world passed it by, it did not even justify a lighthouse, and from one year to the next few people ever passed this way. With such a remote reputation, Stewart Island was virgin territory and we were not disappointed. Here you entered natural harbours as if you were the first ship ever to visit. There was no sign of human habitation anywhere, just an eerie feeling of isolation and silence that was almost overbearing.

Stewart Island had a tiny 600-strong population to inhabit its 500 square miles, all concentrated in the one small township of Oban. Just

The Awesome cat at Stewart Island
It was awesome in rough seas too.

five miles of road linked these people, after that it was wild country with virtually no influence from man. Here you needed to be completely self-sufficient to survive. The incredible beauty of the scenery was matched by the wild ferocity of the weather, not surprising as the island lay directly in the path of the westerly gales that swept the Southern Ocean. We made this voyage of exploration in a 72-foot Awesome power catamaran. It was matched by truly awesome country, a place where only the best of boats and real seamanship could survive.

Whilst Oban offered a bar and restaurant, our real destination lay further south. First we called into the appropriately named Port Adventure, to have a look around. Finding little to keep us there, we continued on to Lord's River where we found a comfortable, well-protected night anchorage in the narrow channel. There was just room to anchor and we ran a rope ashore to a tree for added security.

The next day we headed south again to Port Pegasus, a large inlet close to the southern tip of the island. The uncontaminated air here made you breathe deeply. Under the boat, the water was clear enough to see the bottom at 30 feet. You could even see the fish you were going to catch. We anchored off a pristine white beach and went exploring by tender, heading up a river that had something primeval about the way the trees and bushes grew out over the water. It was so wild and lonely, there was a great sense of relief as we got back to the yacht. In the northern arm of this large natural harbour, up another creek, we found the remnants of an old whaling station. All that was left was a small slipway, where the catch would have been hauled up for flensing.

Wondering where the wild weather of the south had got to, the answer hit us with a 35-knot squall, screaming in from the southwest. Suddenly it was decision time, our original plan of going round the Island disappearing as strong winds streamed in from the cold south. Determined nevertheless, we motored out of Port Pegasus and turned south, so at least we could say we had been to the bottom end of New Zealand and the South Cape. As soon as we cleared the land, the Southern Ocean hit us full force, with a huge sea running. We had to make do with a distant glimpse of the Cape, before turning back north to head for Christchurch. We thought we would soon be under the shelter of land on the east side of South Island, but the wind had other plans. First it swung round to the north-west, which was fine as long as we kept close-in under the high cliffs. Then it edged further to the north, and before we knew it, we were struggling with a big head-sea that promised a rough ride all the way home.

This was a tough test for the Awesome, with airline schedules to meet at the other end. The wind swung round even more to the north-east so that it was right on the nose. The battle began. The Awesome was a displacement catamaran with long narrow hulls underwater, which certainly made it efficient. The twin 600 hp MTUs gave a top speed of over 30 knots, which for a 70-footer was pretty impressive. These same long, thin hulls also gave good seaworthiness, slicing through head seas rather than slamming over them. This was our first serious trial and the boat's excellent seaworthiness gave us hope for a fast run home in the 25-knot head winds.

We were not disappointed. Even in 8-foot seas, the Awesome marched on. Speed came down to 15 knots in the worst seas, the occasional thump of a wave under the cross-deck warning when the throttle needed easing a little. I had never been attracted to catamarans for power cruising, but this trip changed my mind. It struck me that here was the perfect boat to reach those parts the others couldn't reach, that could extend your cruising to the wilder parts of the globe. And one final accolade, from a long-time sufferer of seasickness - despite the rough seas, I did not have a hint of seasickness on this voyage. That was the best compliment I could give any yacht.

Another trip in New Zealand was much shorter and much faster. I was visiting Hamilton Jets in Christchurch, who were one of the pioneers of water jets. To demonstrate the prowess of their jets, they organised a wild river trip in a jet racing boat for me. They had this crazy sport in New Zealand where boats raced down untamed rivers at very high speeds, often with only of inches of water under the hull. We went up-river at a fairly leisurely 60 mph, powering through rapids and deep gorges up to the plateau. Waiting for us was the then-New Zealand champion of this sport, with his little 18-footer powered by a "little" 900 hp engine. I strapped myself in under the roll bar and was told whatever I did to keep my hands inside the boat. Apparently rolling over happened all the time.

We set off down river with the roar of open exhausts resonating off the rock walls. What a ride! We tackled the winding channels of that river at speeds up to 100 mph, twisting and turning to keep in the channel. At times we headed directly towards the walls of black rock, only to veer away at the last second. In shallow stretches of river, stones rattled against the hull bottom like bouncing ball bearings. It was such an exciting ride it took just 20 minutes to cover 20 miles, me just sitting there as a passenger, clinging on for dear life. At the end the driver turned to me and said, 'If I'd had my regular navigator with me, we would have knocked 5 minutes of our time!' The navigator on those racing runs was the one who did the spotting for where to find the channels.

At the other end of the world, I spent a week cruising off the West Coast of Scotland. It was a great change not to be rushing through this area at high speed, to have time to appreciate the fantastic scenery. Twenty-five years ago, on a sailboat charter, that coast was almost as remote as Stewart Island. The cruise was certainly memorable. One day it was blowing hard, so we dropped anchor in what we thought was a little sheltered cove, near Kyle of Lochalsh. No sooner had we anchored than the wind started whistling down off the mountains, in violent white-water squalls that threatened to take us with them. It just showed that even in the lee of the land, you could not always find the shelter you needed. It was time to up-anchor and find a better place, over on the other side of the loch where the wind was still strong, but blowing more steadily without the fierce squalls.

After a nice meal, I came up for a last look round before going to bed. I blinked. The shore lights were drifting past. That meant our anchor was dragging, so we would have to haul it up and find a more secure location. That was just the start of our troubles. Try as I might, I could not lift that anchor, yet we were still dragging! This was definitely one that the text books did not cover. I wound that windlass till the bow was almost down to water level, but still the anchor would not budge. Still we drifted. According to good seamanship practice, I had attached an anchor buoy before laying out the anchor. Heaving on

Our seaworthy motor cruiser
Snug inside when it was minus-5 and more.

that got me nowhere either. After three hours we were starting to get exhausted, so I decided on one last attempt. After that we would cut the anchor chain and get the hell out of there. But all this time, I could still not work out how we could be dragging but unable to lift the anchor.

Heaving on the anchor windlass, I had the bow right down to the water. Then I saw a huge mass of kelp break the surface, with the anchor chain wound round and round it. At last I could see the problem. The weight of the kelp, and stones that must have been in it, was too heavy to lift. Yet it was slippery enough to slide across the seabed. Knowing the problem made the solution easy. Securing the chain and towing our big anchor burden, we just powered out into deep water and headed for the shelter of harbour. The wind was still screaming, the seas were rough, and it was the movement of the boat that freed the kelp from the chain.

At last I could wind in the chain and secure the anchor. It was 5.00 in the morning before we tied up in harbour, tired and exhausted, but

Steering outside, inside
One small failure brought us close to an emergency situation

safe after one of the longest nights. After 55 years at sea you still came up against the unexpected.

Further south on the West Coast of Scotland, I was to make a trip with a fine and very seaworthy motor-sailer from Largs around to Chichester. This was a winter trip, but on a motor-sailer you could get nice and snug in the wheelhouse, so it sounded like fun. I should have known better when we had to break ice to leave the marina. It was bitterly cold, down to minus-5 degrees or more. Doggedly we went south in a rapidly freshening wind. Everything was fine, even when the wind reached gale force. We had a good boat underneath us and the engine purred away reliably. Then, as so often happened when things were going well, the steering gear stopped working. After experimenting, we found we could still steer by using the secondary steering position outside. It only wanted one thing in bad weather to switch us from comfortable cruising to a near-emergency. This was that one thing. Steering outside was fine except for the bitter cold and wet. We wondered how long it would keep working. It was time to give up and seek shelter, so we crawled into the Isle of Man early the next morning for repairs. I left the yacht there and went home. That experience was equally hazardous. All over the country the weather was so severe that blizzards had caused travel chaos.

Cold though it was, that trip showed that cruising in the winter had its pleasures and its excitements. It also had its dangers. Several years ago, I flew across the Atlantic to join a delivery trip taking a boat from Rhode Island right down the East Coast of the US to Florida. I had always wanted to do this trip, partly because you could see a lot of America when you ran down the East Coast. It also meant I could experience the Intracoastal Canal, which ran for virtually the whole length of the route we planned to take. This canal was largely built in the 1930s to provide employment during the Great Depression. It provided a secure trade route that was resistant to attack in time of war. These days, pleasure craft use it as much as commercial traffic, maybe even more. It is a remarkable feat of engineering, combining stretches of sea, rivers and man-made canal. Not only did it extend down the East Coast. You could also cross Florida, then carry on round the whole of the Gulf of Mexico.

Winters in North America can be severe. Even so, that winter was exceptional. After the trans-Atlantic flight into New York, the local flight

Coming into refuel in New York. Even the cockpit was filled with ice
We found shelter between the towns of Jerusalem and Galilee.

up to Providence was delayed. On top of all those hours hanging around waiting, by the time I made it, my luggage didn't. I took a taxi to Portsmouth in Rhode Island and booked into a hotel for the night. It was bitterly cold and I had just the clothes I was wearing for the flight.

That made it easy for me to be picked up the next morning for our 6.00 am start. The other guys lent me some warm clothes, and we spent an hour trying to get the ice and snow off the boat. We got some heat into her, then had to break her out of the ice in the frozen marina before heading for open sea. Not much else was moving on the water. Perhaps they knew better. Any spray we shipped aboard froze instantly across the windscreen, obliterating our view. It was so heavy, the fan heater we set up to blast it off could not clear it. Then, as we reached open water at the entrance to Long Island Sound, the spray froze on contact all over the boat. First it covered the GPS antenna, coating it so thick with ice it stopped working altogether. Then the radar went down, heavy ice locking the scanner and freezing it solid.

Very quickly, we were in serious trouble out there. Even the cockpit filled with ice, every surface so slippery that it was treacherous to be on deck. It was time to get out of it. We turned and found shelter believe it or not in "Snug Harbor," with the town of Jerusalem on one side and Galilee on the other. Thankful though we were, there was no religious experience to be found, just a sense of relief that we were safe in harbour. Where we were, tied up in the marina, we were only 25 miles from our starting point - a nightmare start to our trip south.

Two days later, with my luggage retrieved, we set out again. It was still bitterly cold and all our likely refuelling stops down Long Island Sound were closed because of ice. Finally we made it into New York, which was exciting. For our own safety though, we had to focus on the huge ice floes coming down the Hudson River rather than enjoy the scenery. We forced our way through the ice, into a refuelling berth. Then all topped up, we bid farewell to New York, on our way to our planned overnight stop in Atlantic City. Here again, we had to force our way in through the ice, to get to a berth in the marina. Luckily, the boat we were travelling in was a Little Harbor 44 Whisper Jet, so named for its triple water jets, a propulsion system we blessed for getting us through the ice without damage. No sooner were we berthed than down came a blizzard, forcing us to hole up there for two days. Even now, I could not think of a more depressing place to stay. Atlantic City's only entertainment was gambling and it was full of sad people. We were glad when we could get underway again, out to the open sea.

Now we had a run down to Chesapeake Bay, and by this time we had had enough of open waters and rough seas. It was time to head inshore and take to the canal route. Though the canal was open, the severe cold had created a film of ice over the water. This was exciting, cracking through the thin layer of rime ice as we ran at 35 knots. This had to be one of the few canals where you could run at speed - as long as you did not disturb other people, either on the water, or on the banks. Now we stayed with the canal for a long way south, only hitting open waters where the Intracoastal route used rivers and estuaries as part of its route. Even further south, we came back out into the open seas to make faster progress. That was a mistake because we underestimated the conditions. Fine though it was, running in the out open sea, we had to pass through shallows to get to our refuelling point in St Augustine, in the north of Florida.

With a big swell running, the seas were breaking in awesome fashion in the entrance channel. And just to compound the problem, there was thick fog. We were running out of fuel, which meant we were also running out of choices. Whatever we did, we had to get into harbour.

The entrance channel to St Augustine had a couple of right-angle turns. This meant that we had to find the marker buoys to keep safe in the big breaking waves rolling in from seaward. If we missed one buoy in the fog, there was every chance we would be rolled over in the breaking waves, to be washed up in pieces on the beach. It was a nerve-racking few minutes, taking every ounce of skill to drive that boat in the big following seas, at the same time trying to negotiate the channel. There was a huge sense of relief when we got to the calmer waters inside. We were safe, but the experience showed just how quickly - and how dangerously - a situation could escalate. And it underlined a lesson we already knew: always to have enough fuel for an alternative port when you were running along a coastline. Running low on fuel was careless enough, the added hazard of fog plus the heavy swell could easily have been the end of us. I was angry with myself for not having anticipated this possibility. Coming out again after refuelling, the fog had cleared. It was still a lively ride around the shoals of Cape Canaveral, where we could see the Space Shuttle waiting on its launch-pad for take off.

Only now, as we hit Florida's warmer weather, was the ice disappearing from the boat. It had been freezing virtually all the way south - one of the worst winters along that East Coast ever. After an epic ten days, we finally made it to West Palm Beach, where I was pleased to step ashore with the warm Florida sun on my back.

Another marathon journey, by river and canal, was an overland delivery trip from a shipyard on the River Danube in the south of Germany, to the sea at Rotterdam. This trip was in an 80-foot motor yacht, the first large yacht to make the journey since the opening of a canal that linked the Rivers Danube and Rhine via the River Main. I was used to voyages that measured progress horizontally. But on this trip, in a big yacht, our most impressive progress was measured by altitude, on a pioneering excursion that took us to 1,200 feet above sea level - the highest you could go in a sea-going yacht anywhere in the world.

On the upper reaches of the River Danube, there was a monastery where a cross on the ground marked the centre of Europe. A few miles east of this cross, there was a shipyard that built luxury yachts, an

NATALIE **through rivers and canals,** 1,000 miles overland, then 1,200 feet down to the North Sea.

unlikely location with an unusual choice of routes to the sea. If you headed east it was 1,500 miles down the Danube to the Black Sea. To the north and west, it was 1,000 miles to the North Sea. When I joined NATALIE on her maiden voyage to the deep blue ocean, war-ravaged sections of the River Danube were no place for luxury yachts. That meant our route to the sea was to first climb up through the new Rhine-Main-Danube Canal to the watershed that divided the two main rivers of Europe, then drop 1,200 feet down the Rivers Main and Rhine to the North Sea, where NATALIE would get her first taste of salt water.

Big though she was, NATALIE was dwarfed by the scale of the lock structures on this canal, so deep that day seemed almost night under the 70-foot high dripping walls. As the lock filled, the yacht rose up to a new vista of rolling, rural countryside. This was the very cradle of European history, steep-sided valleys providing a route for invading armies from both directions. Dotted across them, old towns and castles were testament to historic quarrels over the centuries, making the climb to the summit level full of interest.

The canal was designed primarily for commercial traffic, so we kept company with a barge heading north, sharing the locks to conserve water. The locks were unique, with the top gate rising up out of the water to seal the gap, while the mighty bottom gates dropped like a guillotine to hold the water back. It all operated with German efficiency, each lock taking around 10 minutes to fill and climb to the next level. By the afternoon of the second day, we passed through the final lock on the canal at Bamberg, into the River Main. This was the toughest section of the route, with over 50 locks to transit to reach the mighty River Rhine. It was test of patience and driving skills too, commercial traffic always had priority because they paid to use the locks. We didn't.

Each night we would tie up and celebrate the day's run with the traditional bottle of brandy, throwing the neck overboard to placate the water gods. Our slow progress seemed to be in sympathy with the rolling rural countryside. Once while waiting at one lock, the skipper's wife on the barge ahead jumped overboard with a scrubbing brush to clean the hull. There were no volunteers on NATALIE to polish our own gleaming sides.

After days of narrow canals and rivers, nothing prepared you for the scale of the Rhine. At Mainz, where we left the River Main behind, the Rhine was a majestic river, busy with traffic, where a powerful current hurried down to the sea. In this largely uncontrolled river, we had to keep to the buoyed channels, which in places were quite narrow and often wandered across the river. Ahead, the hills closed in. We were entering the famous Rhine Gorge, its entrance marked by the magnificent Niederwald statue on the hillside opposite the town of

Bingen, built to mark the re-establishment of the German Empire in 1883. The channel buoys were barely awash in the 5-knot current and rapids formed in the river. The tower of Mäuseturm in the centre of the river marked the entry to the Gorge proper. Here the traffic increased more than double with the large number of tourist boats out to view the dramatic scenery. On the water, it got exciting. Rushing downstream, sometimes at close to 20 knots, there was a very busy traffic flow to contend with in the twisting channel. To keep you on your toes, traffic going upstream had priority, switching from side to side to avoid the strong current. Adding to the confusion there were barges under tow, long hawsers separating them from their manoeuvring tug. Passing between them was a fatal mistake to make.

At Cologne we halted our headlong rush down-river. Time to stop for the night, at a berth in the Rheinauhafen Marina, with just six inches clearance under the swing bridge at the entrance. From here our route to the sea went on down-river, past Düsseldorf and industrial Duisburg, on into the flat countryside of Holland and the largest port in the world, Rotterdam.

That voyage pioneered a route across Europe for motor yachts, an

Canal boats
Calm water and taking your time, a contrast to the restless sea.

227

alternative but very long way of getting to the Mediterranean. It required a degree of courage to mix with the heavy commercial traffic, but the stunning scenery made it well worth the effort. For excitement, it rivalled any of those I had made across the Atlantic.

I like cruising on canals and rivers. Perhaps the appeal lies in the calm water, a contrast to the restless sea. There is always interest along canals, plenty of history too. Apart from owning a canal boat at one time, I have cruised on many.

One of the more interesting was the Erie Canal that linked the Great Lakes with New York in America. Like most canals this one was now mainly used by leisure craft, but all the locks were manned, so you had a pretty easy passage. We had a charter boat and tied up one night just short of a lock. It was a bit of remote spot, just outside a small town, and the lock keeper came strolling down to chat. He offered us the loan of his truck, so that we could drive into town - as long as we were back by ten, when he finished work. What hospitality! But that was the sort of thing that seemed to happen on canals. It always surprised me how friendly and helpful people could be in America.

Rivers and canals themselves often surprised me too. Just north of Bangkok was the largest brewery in Thailand. And inside the brewery grounds was one of the most modern boatyards in the country. Its existence helped explain how I found myself being driven from the airport at Bangkok in some of the densest traffic in the world. The plan was simple, help navigate the prototype Ladenstein 2000 from this boatyard in Bangkok down to Singapore, where it was going on display at the Singapore Boat Show. The river was to be our route to the sea, on the first modern luxury motor yacht ever to be built in Thailand. Unlike many other cities that turned their backs on rivers, Bangkok used the Chaophraya as a major highway, with a unique range of boats providing transport for tourists, commuters and cargo. Cruising down this river was to prove both interesting and exciting, opening a window on cruising that few have experienced.

You normally would have to drag me past a brewery. But I was eager to see the yacht that was to be our home for the next few days. Stocking

Thailand's long tail boats
Egg whisks powered by truck engines, and a manic desire for self-destruction.

up with drink was easy in such a location, but food was more difficult. Then we set off into the river, into traffic that got busier and busier as we approached the centre of Bangkok, a place where contrasts were dramatic. Slow, stately ferries crossed the river every half-mile or so, narrowly missed by high-speed commuter boats that whisked passengers upstream and downstream. There was plodding barge traffic too, heavy with cargo, and in a fever of thrusting, racing excitement, the unique long-tail boats which plied as water taxis.

These long-tail boats were a remarkable example of marine evolution. Developed from the long, narrow-hulled river boats that were designed for easy rowing, they were mechanized by the simple expedient of mounting a large truck engine and gearbox on a swivel bracket at the stern. The prop shaft was a long tube extended out from the transom. Some ten feet astern was the small two- or three-bladed propeller that worked like an egg whisk. It seemed that a manic desire for self-destruction was the main qualification for driving these boats.

Speed was king on the Chaophraya River, and the faster you went it seemed, the higher the priority you had. So the slow ferries that crossed the river trod a tentative course, weaving through the faster traffic that used its strident horns to demand right of way. There were no rules of the road, it was survival of the fittest, and it worked. The commuter ferries with their graceful swan neck bows fought for space at the landing stages. The long tail-boats knew their place and sneaked in when there was a gap. Between them all somehow, the cross-river ferries found a space. Passengers had to be quick, the ferries only staying alongside for twenty seconds or so, as marshals with loud hailers harangued the crowds to jump aboard quickly. It looked like organized chaos, and the city thrived on it.

It was quite a relief to pass the last of the bridges away from the downriver shipping terminals, and head out to sea. It was perfect cruising weather, and we settled down to a smooth 25 knots, the twin 1,200 hp MAN diesels murmuring with a quiet hum for the overnight run to the island of Ko Samui, almost due south. Ko Samui was such a contrast to Bangkok, you could be in another world. Here everything was peaceful, with none of the hustle and bustle that characterized Bangkok. This was "take your time" country and we came into the pier at Hat Bo Phut to pick up another crewmember who had flown in. The airport terminal had a thatched roof and open sides, with the jungle encroaching close by. Apart from picking up the extra crew, our reason for coming was to visit the nearby Ang Thong National Marine Park. This was a spectacular group of islands that combined high undercut cliffs with brilliant white beaches, a true tropical paradise in the process of opening up to tourism.

After cruising the islands it was time to head south again, to our first refuelling stop at Songkhla. As we had stayed in Ang Thong longer than planned, it was dark when we arrived off Songkhla, for our first and nearly final problem. The chart showed the entrance channel lined by lighted buoys, but none of the lights we could see conformed to anything on the chart. There were tiny islands too, on each side of the entrance. We should have picked them out on the radar, but they were lost amongst the ships at anchor. The harbour was a river entrance protected by breakwaters. As the chart showed plenty of water for us, we decided to head in, expecting to pick up the open entrance between the breakwaters on the radar.

I was down below, concentrating on the radar, whilst the rest of the crew were up on the flybridge. As we closed the land, I could see what looked like the opening between the breakwaters, so we set the course for this. This opening looked clear and inviting on the radar. As we closed it, and I still busy with the radar, I was suddenly aware of shouting. With a sudden roar, the engines went full astern, bringing the yacht to a rapid halt. There, 50 yards in front of us was a very solid looking breakwater!

I could not understand this, as the gap was still showing on the radar. Then it dawned. The radar antenna was set very low on the arch mast towards the stern. Those three stalwart crew standing on the flybridge had blocked the radar beam, creating what I thought was the "gap". Once they sat down, we followed the breakwater to find the real gap, and entered harbour.

After taking on fuel and food, we set off after midnight, for the long run down the coast to the next stopping point, in Malaysia. It was an amazingly clear tropical night, with calm seas and stars right down to the horizon. The night became more surreal when my cell phone rang. There I was, cruising under moonlight in the South China Sea, doing a radio interview for the BBC in London. Life did not get more bizarre than that. We kept a little way off the coast to avoid the many small unlit fishing boats. It was sad to miss those beautiful off-shore islands in the dark, but we had a deadline to meet. By dawn we were well south.

Our next stop for fuel was Mersing, a small fishing port and ferry terminal serving the many islands offshore. This was busy tourist country in the mini-state of Jahor, though Mersing retained a lot of its traditional fishing atmosphere. The main tourist activity was out of town, concentrated down on the beaches. It was like carnival day when we arrived, with crowds around the harbour. Our arrival had coincided with a holiday and people were thronging for the island ferries to spend the day offshore.

It was like Bangkok all over again, but on a smaller scale. Dead slow, we literally nudged our way into port. The trouble with a beautiful white yacht finish - one that had yet to be bought and paid for - was that you could not afford to touch anything. So we played it defensively, squeezing our way into the refuelling berth. There was just time for a quick run ashore, then we were off again and heading south to Singapore. Late that afternoon we rounded the south-east corner of the Malay Peninsular, slap into perhaps the busiest shipping channel in the world.

What a contrast between sleepy Mersing and the busy high-rises of Singapore! It was like snatching open the door to another world, fast and urgent, where commerce ruled. There were ships everywhere, many at anchor waiting for cargoes, small craft rushing in between. It was as busy as Bangkok, but a lot more organized and disciplined. We nudged our way into our allotted space, in the marina inside Sentosa Island, near the centre of Singapore. I had a special call to make. When I first went to sea all those years ago, a young, impecunious apprentice on a tramp ship, I remembered peering through the windows of the famous Raffles Hotel. In those days it was the centre of the British Colonial Empire, with rich men in white suits dividing the world between them. At 17, I did not have the money or style to go in. Now was my chance. Strolling nonchalantly into the Long Bar, perhaps the most famous in the world, I ordered my gin sling. Sipping it slowly, I settled back into a cane chair, watching the world go by and reminiscing about a very exciting voyage.

It is not only cruising to interesting places that I find exciting. I am fascinated by new concepts in fast-boats. In my writing career, I have made a speciality of seeking out and testing new types of boat. And you would be surprised at how many turn up around the world.

For instance, there was a new wave-piercer ferry developed in the Caribbean, to cope with the difficult Trade Wind seas experienced there. The passenger cabin was perched on top of two very slender hulls that went through the waves instead of over them, to give a level ride. It worked remarkably well, and it was an exciting voyage out from the

ULTIMATE LADY.
Launched in 1998, ULTIMATE LADY was the world's first wave piercer yacht, a catamaran and winner of the 1998 International Superyacht of the Year Award. Presented to Craig Loomes for his design in the 23 - 32-metre Power Category, this was the first time that a New Zealander had ever won the award, ranking him among the world's top superyacht designers.

building yard in the US Virgin Islands, first to St Maarten, and then on to the tiny island of Saba. Saba is literally an extinct volcano and not much else, though it has a small tourist industry. Being well off the beaten track, it attracted the extrovert tourist, and our boat was a design that could make the 20-mile crossing from St Maarten a pleasure over the purgatory of existing small passenger boats.

Whilst big wave-piercers are dominating today's fast ferry industry, smaller versions are making inroads into the yacht market. I went out to New Zealand to test the first 27-metre version, and what a revelation in sea-going performance it was. This Craig Loomes design has since been followed by more, Craig being very much a pioneer of wave-piercing designs, in catamaran and trimaran form. Proof of Craig's superior trimaran designs will come when I go out to Mauritius in 2006, to be trials skipper of a 23-metre trimaran yacht that has been built on the island.

Wave-piercing does appear to be the way of the future - if only wave-piercers could look like more regular yachts. Since yacht owners are not noted as pioneers, it was the military that took up the idea of a long, thin monohull design, the VSV (Very Slender Vessel). The 50-footer I am thinking of was developed in the UK for military

The first VSV (Very Slender Vessel) was conceived as a high speed power
boat to seat up to six and carry them across the Irish sea in relative comfort
in all but the worst sea and weather conditions. The MkI 30-foot VSV was
designed by Adrian Thompson for Nick Keig who owned and built the vessel.
The vessel was constructed from high tech composite materials and was
fitted with a petrol V8 engine and Hamilton waterjet drive system. The vessel
was launched and proved all the sceptics wrong when it was seen to be an
extremely fast and easy to handle boat. Many different variant VSV have
since been procured by military customers both in the UK and abroad,
including this MKIII in 1995. Designed by Paragon Mann, and built by Vosper
Thornycroft of the UK, the craft have a long slender hull shape with two large
chines to generate lift and dynamic stability. Limited interior space means the
craft is most suited to military roles where speed and stealth are required.

use by designer Adrian Thompson. I went out on sea-trials with the
Special Boat Service guys, to test this boat in the Portland Race. It
looked more like a missile than a boat, a narrow hull with wide chines
to help stability. It takes a while to get used to the idea of going through
waves rather than over them. But once you get used to the idea, you can
run at speeds in rough seas you would never have thought possible in a
regular deep-vee hull. Of course, shipping all that water and spray over
you, you cannot see where you are going, possibly a handicap. But then
submarines operate like that, and this boat was very similar - in the
mould of sinister stealth designs that the military love. That trip into the
Portland Race was a much kinder experience than the one I did during
those lifeboat trials many years ago.

A flying boat was another interesting experience. Well, not exactly a

WIG boat VT-01 in extreme ground effect
WIG means Wing In Ground, and a WIG boat is a craft with wings that cruises just above the water, floating on a cushion of high-pressure air between its wings and the surface. I thought at first it was like a hovercraft, but this cushion is created by aerodynamic interaction, ˙unlike the hovercraft's static air pad. This makes it highly manoeuvrable, but it does need sufficient forward speed to generate the cushion. 80 mph up the Rhine is a bit nerve-wracking, steering through all those barges.

flying boat, but a ground effect craft. Twenty years ago, the Wing in Ground (WIG) craft were still novel in the smaller sizes. Curious, I went to Germany to rest a two-seater sports version. This "boat" actually flew about six inches above the water and had short stubby wings, an air propeller and a rudder. To start with, I sat in the back and let the designer do the driving. But it would not fly with this weight on board, so he suggested that I take it out by myself. Never having flown anything before in my life I was a bit nervous. What the heck, it looked simple enough, with just the throttle and rudder for control. At about 40 mph, it took off. Immediately I felt a sudden loss of control, so I cut the throttle. I then realised that the loss of control occurred as the hull left the water and started to fly. There was no bite on the water. I gave it another go and this time persevered, getting it into flying mode at around 80 mph up the River Rhine, trying to dodge to those big barges coming downstream. In flying mode the rudder took time to respond, you turned the wheel and waited for what felt like an eternity before anything happened. You needed considerable anticipation to control these craft, a different kind of discipline, but it was an exciting ride to "fly" up the Rhine.

On a totally different level, I went out in what was billed as the "fastest super-yacht in the world". This 140-footer was built in Holland to a Frank Mulder design, and had something like 20,000 hp to push it along. My job was to be the official timekeeper - to verify the speed so that they could claim the first super-yacht speed record. We ran up to 65 knots, close to the predicted top speed of 70, but then the yacht spun out, turning rapidly out of control. That slowed things down for a bit, and it was back to the drawing board for the designers.

Another fast yacht for which I acted as consultant was the Wally Power 120. This dramatic looking yacht, with its all-glass superstructure, was powered by triple 5,000 hp gas turbines. We spent a long time trying to convince the engine-management computers to cooperate and let us run at speed. When we finally did, we achieved a creditable 64 knots - though as always, the designers were hoping for more.

The one sea trial that really stands out was with the very last of the famous wooden Aquaramas built by Riva. These magnificent craft had been the boat of choice for Royalty and film stars for years. This last one was kept by Riva at their yard on Lake d'Iseo in Northern Italy. There they had a small boat dock, built in under the offices. Inside this fully enclosed dock was the beautiful, gleaming varnished Riva, with men in white overalls, doing the last minute checks. I stepped into the boat and fired up the engines, the door of the dock was lifted and I roared out into the lake. The experience was a sensation of pure emotion, just feeling and driving this wonderful creation. It was with reluctance that I eventually took it back – I just wanted to go on forever.

A Riva on Lake Como
An absolute classic, the Riva Aquarama was a living legend. And by the 60's, Rivas were a world status symbol. Celebrities and the international jet-set all chose Riva. Nothing else had the exquisite lines, or the unmistakeable Riva prestige. Brigitte Bardot, Dino de Laurentis, Richard Burton, Sean Connery, Peter Sellers, the Shah of Persia, Prince Rainier of Monaco and King Hussein of Jordan all owned Rivas. Even today the magic still fascinates. Me especially.

CHAPTER 14

USING THE EXPERIENCE

Not long after I left the RNLI to work first in the fish business and then for myself, I got a call for help from one of the offshore oil operators working in the North Sea. Back in those early days, they were still struggling to find their feet. After accidents like the collapse of the Sea Gem oil rig, the stand-by ship regime was initiated so that there was always a ship standing by each rig in case of trouble. These ships carried rescue boats which the operators were constantly damaging during the launch and recovery process. My job was to find a better way of launching and retrieving these boats in relative safety. I had had a lot of experience with launch and recovery through Trinity House operations, so it was not too difficult to find a solution.

The Jack Up Rig Sea Gem.
Sea Gem drilled the fourth well to be sunk in British waters, becoming the UK's first gas strike on 30th September 1965. Then just after Christmas, it collapsed when preparing to move to another site. Whilst the legs were being lowered, two of them suddenly crumpled. No distress message was sent as the radio cabin was washed into the sea. Luckily the British cargo ship Baltrover was a mile or so away and saw the accident. By the time rescue helicopters arrived there was only a mass of wreckage and one of the legs sticking above the water. Of the 32 men onboard 13 were lost. New rules resulting from this tragedy brought the stand-by boat into being.

This escalated to another job aboard a ship in which they wanted to launch a 10-ton tug from the aft deck by crane. Again I found a way to make it a relatively safe operation. It was from these early jobs that I began a secondary career as a consultant. This work has now expanded into a full grown business, Dag Pike Associates. It has generated some very interesting jobs and landed me in some very interesting situations.

Dag Pike, the detective
Being an "expert witness" is work that I love

A lot of this work is as an "expert witness", giving an expert opinion in court cases. This is truly work that I love. Appearing in court is pure theatre. Although everything is slow-moving, the drama and emotion is real - and sometimes very exciting. Actually appearing in the witness box is a very draining and challenging experience, like navigating at very high speed, except of course in slow motion. I have spent whole days in the witness box, and come out feeling I have been through a washing machine.

Some of these cases got pretty exciting. At one stage I was involved with some work on behalf of the Customs. On a number of occasions this involved drug-smuggling, and though I was there purely as a navigation expert, I could not help being dragged into the drama. In one of these, I ended up as the main prosecution witness at the biggest drugs trial in Britain, a case involving £200 million worth of cocaine. It started when I was having lunch at the Dorchester Hotel in London, not something I do regularly, but this was a special presentation lunch. I had just got through the main course when I was called to the telephone. It was the Customs. They were about to raid a ship in the River Thames, could I get down there as fast as possible? They wanted someone with experience to check out all the navigation equipment and papers, immediately after they boarded.

I was on my way, arriving to find a Special Boat Service team with inflatable boats getting ready for action. I felt a bit out of place in my London suit, all the SBS guys were wearing bullet-proof jackets and carrying guns. The target was a Gulf of Mexico supply ship. It had just arrived in the River, and the Customs had a tip-off that there were serious drugs on board. Once the tough guys had gone in and found this big stack of cocaine, I climbed on board and went through every scrap of paper I could find. I collected the few charts that were there and checked out all the navigation electronics to ensure that they kept working. This would enable me to extract any positions still contained in their memory systems. Whilst the Customs had the tip-off about the drugs, they did not know where the ship had come from. My job was to try and plot her past movements from the information that I could find on board - much more exciting than lunch at the Dorchester.

Once all the evidence had been tallied and checked, I spent three weeks going through it. Gradually, I was able to piece together a picture of the ship's movements. They had left from the port of Morgan City on the Gulf of Mexico, sailed across the Caribbean, refuelling at a small island there, then headed across the Atlantic. They did not call into the UK on their first crossing. After stopping on the Spanish Coast, they went back across the Atlantic, presumably for another load, then made a return trip. There were quite a few anomalies in this plot, and I had to check out a history of weather conditions over the period, to see how many course alterations might be weather-related. And so it went on. It was real detective work and gradually I was able to tease out the truth, even to the point that I could tell where an air drop for drugs had been made, off the coast of Venezuela. The fuel log was a vital part of the evidence I had. To confirm everything, I had to check out how much fuel remained on board and what the fuel consumption of the engines might be. These guys had even converted some on-board ballast tanks to carry fuel, so they could increase their range.

Now I had to put all this into a report, then appear in court at the trials. First it was the crew of the ship that were in court. They got off because they said; yes, they had picked up the packages out of the sea, but as none of them were opened, they did not know they were shipping drugs! Then it was the turn of the masterminds behind the operation. They were sent down for 30 years, vindication I felt, for all the hard work I had put in. Of course, the money I got paid was good as well, and I was not even paid for results.

Another drugs trial also involved an offshore oil ship. This one had picked up their haul in mid-Atlantic, presumably from another ship, then sailed right round Britain before trying to land it. To avoid suspicion, we assumed they wanted to make it look as though they had come in from the North Sea. Arriving directly from the Atlantic might certainly have raised questions. Again it was a tip-off that led to the ship being stopped. They were boarded by the Navy and brought into Hull. Then it was my turn, and again my job was to plot their courses, to find out where they had been. This time there were some charts on board, though in these days of electronic navigation, it is surprising how little information people note down on paper. Despite this, I was able to piece their route together. The only problem was - I could not put a date on when they had travelled it. That was a worry. They could simply have said it was an old route. Finally, I was able to pin them down through a photo taken by the aerial photographers that monitored ships going through the Dover Straits. They took these pictures in the hope of selling them to the owners. So here they had a beautiful picture of the ship, with the date and time on it. More detective work. At that trial, police with guns surrounded the courts. There was a possibility that the defendants might be kidnapped.

Most of these legal cases were much more ordinary. But now and again, one turned up that was both exciting and high profile. One such involved a Greek ship owner who claimed insurance on the loss of his fast motor yacht when he and his crewman were thrown overboard in rough seas. That was his story. But the insurance company were not convinced. My job was to investigate the background to the claim, even going out to sea on a sister yacht in Greece. The story that came out was quite amazing. Apparently, the owner and his crewman were going from

Piraeus to one of the off-lying islands, where he wanted to pray in a special chapel for the safety of his wife, who was going into childbirth. That in itself seemed unlikely, particularly in the rough conditions that prevailed. Worse was to follow.

According to his story, they were some way into the trip when he saw that a fender had not been stowed properly. As a neat and careful seaman, he went out onto the aft deck to bring it in. But in doing so, he slipped, and ended up hanging over the side, clinging on to the fender rope. His crewman, who was on the radio, ran aft to help him. And promptly fell overboard as well.

Picture this boat, still on autopilot at 25 knots, with one person overboard and the owner hanging on by a fender at the stern. At this point apparently, the fender line broke, dumping the owner into the water as well, while the boat disappeared over the horizon into the dark never to be seen again. Amazingly, the crewman swam back and found the owner, who had since managed to grab the floating fender. The two of them then said they spent the next 10 hours clinging to it, before being rescued by one of the owner's own ferries the next morning! On top of all that, despite the accident happening in waters that were completely surrounded by land, no wreckage or trace of the boat was ever found.

As a survival story it was incredible, so extreme that it might just have been true. It relied on an amazing series of coincidences for everything to happen as suggested. Even when I analysed the story, there did not seem to be any one thing that could not have happened. The insurance company refused to pay up however, and so the owner took them to court to get his insurance money. The trial lasted three weeks, and it was only when the owner was in the witness box that he gave himself away. When asked how far was he from the fender when he went into the water, he pointed across the courtroom to show the distance. Suddenly, when I arrived back home that night, it clicked. I did a lot of calculations and worked out that even if the owner had been an Olympic swimmer, he could never have managed to reach the fender in the strong winds that were blowing at the time. It would have been moving much too fast away from him, downwind. Found out, the owner was told he would be reported to the police for criminal fraud if he did not abandon the claim. And that was the end of a three-year saga. Some expert witness work can be pretty gruesome when it involves personal injury claims, as so many of them do. Analysing what has happened in an accident requires a great deal of detailed thought, and it really stretches you. No two accidents seem to be the same, but they are always interesting. Though when you get a high profile case, there is the additional ordeal of facing TV cameras as you come out of court.

As I drift into old age, I am trying to sell the expertise that I have gained in over fifty years at sea, whilst I still have access to it. You might think that this work is nearly all done at an office desk, but some of the jobs have a strong element of excitement about them. With all the experience I have had of driving fast-boats, I get called upon to organise training programmes. I spent three weeks in Singapore training with the Police Coast Guard there when they introduced a fleet of new high speed patrol boats. It was certainly exciting having the fastest boats in Singapore, and running around at high speed with a blue flashing light for priority. Even more exciting was when we practised the interception techniques that are used to stop the bad guys. Here you powered alongside the other boat, pinning your boarding boat alongside to prevent escape, and dispatched your boarding party across. Doing this at night, in pitch black at 50 knots, was even more exciting. All this without lights, so that when you switched on beacons and sirens as the boat came alongside, the element of surprise was complete. Much more fun than powerboat racing.

I was doing something similar with the US Coast Guard when I spent a couple of weeks with them on a familiarisation exercise. This was at a time when the Coast Guard was introducing some new high-speed patrol boats, and against international competition I won the contract to write their *Fast Boat Seamanship Manual*. I guess I was a good choice, because a lot of people can drive fast-boats, and a lot of people can write, but there was a very limited supply of people who could do both. Part of the deal was that I would spend those two weeks looking at Coast Guard operations in several parts of the country. Down at the Brownsville Coast Guard Station in Texas, they have a major problem contending with illegal immigrants that come across from Mexico, and it was interesting work intercepting these small boats. Their speed was no match for the speed of the Coast Guard, but they were pretty wily customers, and it was a delicate operation to stop them without tipping their long, narrow boats over.

The Coast Guard have an advanced training base at Camp Lejeune in North Carolina which they share with the US Marines. This is a major base, home to the Marine Expeditionary Force, the 2nd Marine Division, the 2nd Marine Logistics Group, plus other combat units and support commands. I don't think I have seen so much firepower concentrated in one place, with tanks rumbling down tracks and helicopters buzzing overhead. It was quite a relief to get off to sea, to the relative peace and quiet of running fast-boats and practising interceptions. From the experience of writing that manual for the Coast Guard, I have written a similar book for fast-boat drivers in the leisure market in the US.

More recently I have been back out in the North Sea, looking at the offshore oil operations. This was under a contract I had with the Health and Safety Executive, to do a study of launch and recovery systems used for the fast rescue boats as well as the boats themselves - and to come up with ways to improve both the effectiveness of the operations and their safety. In some areas, things haven't changed a great deal in the 30 years since I worked out here previously. For instance, there is little incentive for oil companies to spend money on these safety facilities because they do not add to their profit. I found it quite scary the risks that these people took, knowing that if you ended up in the water out there in the depths of winter, your survival chances were not high.

It is one of those strange quirks of fate that as you get older and perhaps less able to cope with the physical side of fast-boats, people want you more and more. Coming up is some training work in South Africa on new fast RIBs designed for catching fishery poachers. Then it could be back on the drug-smuggling game with a proposal for training

Getting the boat back
Fast rescue craft launch and recovery is now very advanced. This system, designed in Finland, works over the ship's side in severe weather conditions, even while moving.

the crews of new fast patrol boats being built for a South American country. I think it is time to get an assistant who can do the hard work of these training programmes, whilst I stand on the shore and watch.

Consultancy work has many different facets, and every job that comes up is different from the last. It is always interesting and in many cases, exciting. The challenges may be very different from the rigours of offshore racing and record breaking, but whilst there is still fun and excitement to be had from it, I want to keep going. I am a great believer in keeping active, both physically and mentally as I drift into old age, and this consultancy work certainly offers its share of that.

CHAPTER 15

THE ULTIMATE CHALLENGE

I guess that most people when they get to seventy-three sit back and look at what they have achieved, not what they are going to do in the future. This book is a lot of looking back and nostalgia for me, but when people say to me 'You have done a hell of a lot in your lifetime,' I respond by saying that it is not what you've done that counts, it is what you are going to do. And I have plenty of things that I still want to do and make happen. Records are made to be broken. So when a British team broke our Round Britain Record last year, that gave a strong incentive to get out there again and take it back. Fabio Buzzi and I are talking about it and Fabio has the boat. So who knows? It might happen.

The Round the World record has always been a dream, and for me is a piece of unfinished business. The Jules Verne challenge of *Around the World in 80 Days* has been done, but it should be possible to at least halve that time. On water that is, not on land, or in the air. In fact I set my own mini-Round the World Record earlier this year in Dubai. They are building a replica World, creating 300 islands and a protective breakwater in the waters off Jumeirah Beach. This was too good to miss, so I borrowed a Pershing 62 and we went off and circumnavigated The World in just 25 minutes. The world gets smaller every day!

The Atlantic remains a constant challenge, and I would like to see the messy situation that currently exists with all the different records and classes involved sorted out. With this in mind, I have put together the basis of another Atlantic record-attempt, with a design that would qualify for all of the different categories that currently exist. Technology moves on, and we have come up with a design that not only could set a new record, crossing faster than the 53 knots average that DESTRIERO set, but also qualify in all the other categories. It would be under 50-metres in length so that it would qualify for the UIM record - going for which would mean getting the boat timed as it passed both the Bishop Rock Lighthouse and Lizard Point. To qualify for the fabulous Hales Trophy, it would need to have some commercial function, and what I am looking at here is the design of a craft that could carry high speed cargo such as courier packages on high speed overnight runs, providing a viable and cheaper alternative to air freight. Then it would have to be the fastest overall on the Atlantic, to qualify for the Virgin Atlantic Trophy. So we are looking at a vessel that could average at least 55 knots for 3,000 miles and carry cargo.

It sounds like an impossible dream. But that was what they said

A practical, cargo-carrying Atlantic record-breaker
To break all of the various records in one go, Peter Birkett and I have this idea for a mono-hull wave piercer powered by gas turbine and water jets. The pilothouse would be a separate pod, detachable by explosive bolts in an emergency, a self-contained escape capsule with its own small diesel and stern drive.

when we tried to set a new record in VIRGIN ATLANTIC CHALLENGER. I have worked with Peter Birkett who designed the Virgin boats, and we have come up with a design that can fulfil all these requirements and more. At present we are looking at a 45-metre deep-vee hull that would be long and narrow. By making the hull narrow, it is less sensitive to waves, so that it cuts partially through them instead of lifting over them. This can greatly reduce the pitching of the hull, the one thing that really slows a fast-boat down in rough seas. However if you go down that route, there will always be the risk of solid water coming down the deck when the boat cuts through a wave, burying the bow. This can happen when you meet one of those bigger than normal waves. And there are plenty of those out in the Atlantic. Solid water travelling down the deck at 60 knots can be very destructive, so you want to place nothing in its way. Accordingly, the deck of our design would be completely clear, with the pilothouse raised on stilts to offer minimum resistance to the water. There would be three of these stilts or pylons, incorporating the air intakes for the engines. Above would be the egg-shaped pilothouse. On the question of safety equipment such as life-rafts and the rest, we have come up with a solution where the pilothouse is attached with explosive bolts to be fired for release in an emergency. It could be fitted with a small diesel and a stern drive, the perfect lifeboat if the ship should sink underneath you.

We looked at all the options for propulsion because power is the key to high speed. Gas turbines are almost essential to get the right power/weight ratio, but they have a higher fuel consumption than diesels, so you have to find a careful balance. There is also the need to reduce weight as much as possible, so that the maximum amount of fuel can be carried. The sums are quite difficult, but gradually you narrow down the options, and the best solution we reckon is a single gas turbine coupled to a pair of water jets. The single turbine would produce about 20,000 hp, adequate for a speed of 65 to 70 knots with the vessel empty of fuel, and 50 knots when full. By splitting the drive through two water jets, it is possible to keep the installation more compact and mounted lower in the hull. The water jets would not have any steering or reverse as is normal with these units. These just add weight, and we would only want the high thrust for going ahead. Steering would be by interceptors, vertical plates that extend just slightly below the transom, technology that is already being used for fast ferries. For slow speed manoeuvring, there would be a pair of wing diesels connected to retractable drives. The diesels could also provide electrical power at sea, saving more weight.

The plan would be to leave harbour in New York with the two diesels running for propulsion. Out in open water, the diesels would be stopped. From this point, it would be a case of just lighting the blue touch paper of the turbine, and taking off. Next stop would be England, and I reckon we could make the crossing in a shade over two days. Not quite the airline timetable but getting close. Imagine crossing the Atlantic in two days! It might sound like Mission Impossible but I fully believe that it can be done. All we need now is around $20 million to fund the project, and I can die a happy man. The same craft could also be used to set a proper Round the World record, something I have not achieved and would dearly love to do.

Then there is the project to restore VIRGIN ATLANTIC CHALLENGER II. Two years ago this wonderful boat lay rotting on the quay at Beaulieu, in the South of France, The Arab owner had not used it for 10 years. Because he was not paying his boatyard bills, the boat was put up for auction. It was bought by a British guy, Marshall Rice who had plans to restore it and bring it back to this country. He asked me to supervise the restoration, because I knew the boat intimately. I got the original engineer, Eckie Rastig, over to look at the engines and he pronounced them perfect. We launched the boat, and after 10 years they started on the second crank of the starter. There is still a lot of work to do on the fuel and the steering systems, but it was a very emotional moment for me to take the boat to sea again after all that time. Just like yesterday with every memory flooding back.

We coaxed the boat as far as Palma in Majorca, where the refit work could be done, planning to make an attempt on the Monte Carlo-to-London record when she is ready. At the time of writing everything is on hold because the owner has serious cancer, but it would be wonderful to get it back for the twentieth anniversary of the record in 2006. By the time you read this, it may even have happened. That boat was just such an important part of my life, and part of Britain's maritime heritage too. It ought to come back and at least be on public view, but it all costs money.

So where does retirement go? Well I do not have too many plans for that, there are so many things left to do. The trouble is, as you get old in this all too-regulated world, people want to stop you simply because of your age. I cannot renew my Master's Certificate because I am too old, so all that hard-won experience cannot be used, at least in theory. I remember having to tell highly experienced life-boatmen that they were

WINNIE
No engines, no computers, no knobs and dials. Falmouth working boats are simple, the spirit of real seamanship with only the sails to set and a few ropes to pull.

too old for the job and would have to retire at 50. Now I know how they felt. Fortunately in my case there are ways around these restrictions.

Nobody has yet decreed that I cannot drive a fast-boat, so I

Racing a Falmouth working boat
These heavy gaff-rigged sailboats are a tremendous contrast to power, but I love them.
Especially racing at Fowey in the Annual Regatta week, where the annual working boat races
mark the start of the oyster dredging season. Mmm!

continue. Maybe I am too old for racing and record-breaking. Maybe I should grow old gracefully and watch from the shore. But that is not my style. I want to be out there and hands-on, fully involved.

I have discovered a new sport in racing Falmouth working boats. These are sailboats that were used in the oyster fisheries off Falmouth, and they make for exciting sailing, everything having to be done by hand. There is no engine, no electronics and no power. They are heavy gaff rigged sailboats around 30-feet in length and WINNIE, the boat I sail, is 107 years old. It is a tremendous contrast to fast powerboats, but I love it.

In place of the thrill of hot competition, I can get excitement from adventurous cruising, going off the beaten track and reaching those parts the others cannot reach. That is certainly one of my continuing ambitions, and I am sure that the consultancy and expert witness work will bring their own excitements in the future. As you have probably gathered from this book, I am not risk-averse and have probably pushed my luck too far on many occasions. However, I am not a great believer in luck. As I have already said, once you believe in luck, you begin to rely on it. That is something that I have never done. I have tried to look at the risks, tried to evaluate them. If they cannot be eliminated, it is the time to decide whether they are acceptable or not. In most cases, risks can be minimised by careful preparation. But always when you go into the unknown, to areas where there is only limited experience to draw on, you never fully know how far you can take it. You never know the limits until you find them, and then it could be too late. I consider myself lucky in having the chance to get very close to the limits on several occasions, then having the resources to cope. In this modern world, people are so protected from risk and danger, they have no idea how to cope when disaster strikes.

My love affair with the sea continues. I read of people who feel that they have to battle with the sea, who have to fight to survive in what they consider to be a hostile environment. My approach is much more gentle. You have to negotiate with the sea. It is not going to change, whatever you do. But it will always offer escape routes or an easier passage, if only you know where to look. It offers the bliss of balmy summer days and the challenge of winter storms. Above all it offers excitement, and that is what I love. It can be just so elemental out there, uncomplicated by human behaviour, and I am sure a lot of people who fear the sea and feel the need to battle with it, do so through a lack of understanding. I am still learning about the sea after 65 years of experience. It is a great voyage of discovery.

On a final note, you may think that my long career at sea has been mainly for self-indulgence, that I have taken risks and pushed the limits largely for my own misguided pleasure. Well I think otherwise, and would like to suggest that exploring the limits has long-term benefits for boat design in general. Look at those fast-boats we were racing back in the 1980s, with long thin hulls and two steps in the planing surfaces. These are now the standard design for virtually all the fast leisure craft and fast patrol boats built today. That big deep-vee hull concept, tested close to the limits in VIRGIN ATLANTIC CHALLENGER II, is now the standard for a number of modern large fast motor yachts. And what about the development of the RIB? Nobody can argue that they have not had a major influence in boat design across nearly every sector, from rescue to long-range cruising.

Finally, my personal experience of pushing the human body to the limits in fast-boats has been useful in developing seating and the layout of rescue and patrol boats that may have to operate in extreme

EARTHRACE from Craig Loomes Design Group - a 24-metre wavepiercer trimaran built for a Round the World record attempt. Circumnavigating the globe represents the pinnacle of powerboat challenges, and at 24,000 nautical miles, is also the world's longest record distance to break. The current record of 75 days was set by the British boat CABLE & WIRELESS ADVENTURER in 1998. EARTHRACE aims to smash this record by completing the voyage in less than 65 days, and will mark the first time in history that an official UIM Powerboat record will be attempted using renewable fuel. The entire boat is intended to wave pierce, minimising pitching motions and preventing slamming or pounding of the bottom shell.

Existing Round the World record holder CABLE & WIRELESS ADVENTURER

conditions. No, there has been a big payback in much of what I have done. I am proud to have done it, and hope I can continue to do it for a long time. As I get older there is still a great deal left to do, books to write, records to break and cruises to undertake. The challenges are still out there if you know where to look, and I hope I can continue to meet them for many years to come.

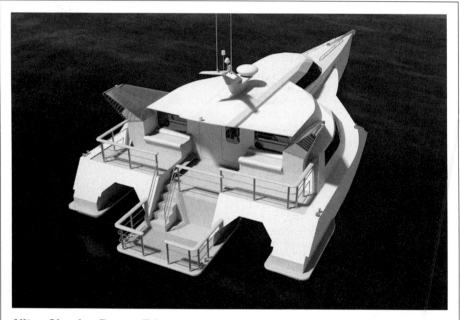

Ultra Slender Power Trimaran
This project has thrown me right into the new wave-piercing technology, as significant to the development of fast boats today as the RIB was forty years ago. I am the consultant in a three-way undertaking with the Craig Loomes Design Group in New Zealand and builders Diogene Marine in Mauritius. Described by Diogene as an Ultra Slender Power Trimaran, the 75 foot C-REX was developed from the test craft for an even more ambitious project, Craig Loomes' wave piercer attempt on the round the world record with EARTHRACER, scheduled for March 2007, when they will go for a new record of 65 days. As this book goes to press I am leaving for another record attempt: Reunion to Mauritius. Though a private yacht, C-REX will be used by owners Diego Cruise as a research base for a revolutionary fast ferry service for the open sea crossing between Mauritius and Reunion.

INDEX

UNITED STATES, SS, 111, 129,
163
Uphelya, 69

V

Vee hulls, 79
Versen, Rolf, 169
VHF, 199, 212
Vitelli Paolo, 150, **151,** 153,
154
Venice-Monte Carlo, **101,** 174
Virgin Atlantic Challenge, 100,
121
VIRGIN ATLANTIC CHALLENGER,
105, **112,** 155, 190, 198,
199, **202,** 247
VIRGIN ATLANTIC CHALLENGER II,
24, 129, 141, 151, 160,
163, 177, 249, 252
Virgin Atlantic Trophy, **162**
Viking longboat, 69
Vosper Thorneycroft, 234
Volvo, 87
Very Slender Vessel, **234**

W

Watt B, 37
Wally Power, 236
Weather, 168
WIG boat, 235
WINNIE, **250**
Wrecks, 43, 45
World Champion, 89, 92, 101
World Powerboat
Championships, 174
WHITE IVECO, **96**
Witty Chris, 121, 122

Y

Yachting World, 74
Yachting Journalists
Association, 82

ACKNOWLEDGMENTS

Bosun Publications would like to thank those friends of the author who have kindly supplied photographs and information. In a personal work much of the visual material comes from the author's own records. Where there are contact details, many are out of date. In these cases every effort has been made to trace copyright owners of photographs and illustrations in this book. Please contact the publisher to identify any images we have used without provenance.

Bosun Publications
The Ferry Point
Ferry Lane
Shepperton on Thames
TW17 9LQ

CERTIFICATE O

MAS

OF A HOME TRAD

To *Roderick*

WHEREAS you have been fou
Master of a Home Trade Passenger Ship in t
and Civil Aviation, in exercise of his powers un
powers enabling him in that behalf, hereby gran

SIGNED BY AUTHORITY OF THE MINISTE

dated this *21st* day of *Mar*

Countersigned

Registrar General

REGISTERED AT THE OFFICE OF THE REGI